Scouts and Spies of the Civil War

William Gilmore Beymer

INTRODUCTION TO THE BISON BOOKS EDITION BY
William B. Feis

ILLUSTRATED BY HOWARD PYLE AND OTHERS

University of Nebraska Press
Lincoln and London

Introduction © 2003 by the University of Nebraska Press
Manufactured in the United States of America
∞
First Nebraska paperback printing: 2003

Library of Congress Cataloging-in-Publication Data
Beymer, William Gilmore.
[On hazardous service]
Scouts and spies of the Civil War / William Gilmore Beymer; with an introduction by
William B. Feis.
p. cm.
Originally published as: On hazardous service: scouts and spies of the North and South.
New York: Harper and Brothers, 1912.
ISBN 0-8032-6206-X (pbk.: alk. paper)
1. United States—History—Civil War, 1861–1865—Secret service. 2. United
States—History—Civil War, 1861–1865—Scouts and scouting. 3. Spies—United
States—History—19th century. 4. Scouts and scouting—United States—History—19th
century. I. Title.
E608.B57 2003
973.7'85—dc21 2002040934

To
MY MOTHER
first guide of my pen
and to
MY WIFE
by whose help this book has
been bettered in every line

Contents

List of Illustrations, ix

Preface, xi

Introduction, xv

Rowand, 1

"Williams, C.S.A.", 28

Miss Van Lew, 54

Young, 81

Bowie, 107

The Phillipses—Father and Son, 121

Mrs. Greenhow, 140

Landegon, 164

John Beall, Privateersman, 185

Timothy Webster: Spy, 200

Illustrations

Following page 118

Rowand in his Confederate uniform

Miss Van Lew

Harry Young

John Y. Phillips

Mrs. Greenhow and her daughter

Timothy Webster

Miss Van Lew's cipher code, 71

Preface

In undertaking the preparation of the following chapters, which were first published in *Harper's Magazine* and in *Harper's Weekly*, it was not expected that serious difficulty would be met with to obtain the data. Nevertheless, the articles were written only at the cost of the most unforeseen effort and nearly three years' time. Hundreds of letters were written to persons in almost every State in the Union, and in the Philippine Islands, Canada, France, England, Gibraltar. Frequent trips became necessary to Washington and Richmond, also to Chicago, Boston, Pittsburgh, etc. A bibliography of the books, newspapers, and pamphlets consulted would show a list of hundreds of volumes. No expenditure of time, effort, or money has been spared, not only in collecting *all* the data obtainable for each of the subjects, but also in verifying it—where not absolutely impossible—to the smallest detail. The following chapters are in every sense historical.

The original plan for obtaining data was to secure permission to examine the original records in the War Department, of the Bureau of National Police and the Secret Service. To this request President Wm. H. Taft, who was then Secretary of War, replied, through the Adjutant-General of the Army, that "all such documents that are of any historical interest or value, and which are in the possession of the War Department, have been published in the *Official Records of the Union and Confederate Armies*." But though the *Official Records* approximate 139,000 pages, very little is to be found regarding the work of individual members of the Secret Service. The very nature of the work made the keeping of written records an additional and unnecessary hazard to the men. In an effort to discover the whereabouts of some of the men and women who served the North and the South as scouts and spies I went to Washington. Few members of the Secret Service were alive when these chapters were begun. Of the ten stories that follow only three are personal narratives—"Rowand," "Phillips," and "Landegon"—and John Landegon died last year.

Every assistance possible was given me in Washington by Col. Gilbert C. Kniffen, of the Bureau of Pensions; W. H. Crook, of the White House police ever since President Lincoln's time; Maj. Albert E. H. Johnson, for years the private secretary to Secretary of War Stanton; Major Sylvester, of the Metropolitan Police; Chief John E. Wilkie, of the present Secret Service (not organized till 1869), and Gen. Michael V. Sheridan. Only by the guidance, assistance, and advice of Maj.-Gen. F. C. Ainsworth (retired), then Adjutant-General of the Army and one of the compilers of the *Official Records,* have several of these chapters been made possible.

For the "Bowie" chapter I am indebted to Col. John S. Mosby, who, when he had told me all he could of "Wat" Bowie, gave me introductions to two members of his old band of partisans, Dr. Jas. G. Wiltshire and Mr. Chas. Vest, who were with Lieutenant Bowie on his last raid.

But the actual starting-point of the series was the second chapter, "Rowand." The late Judge Julius J. C. Langbein, Commander-in-chief of the Medal of Honor Legion in 1905, referred me to Gen. St. Clair A. Mulholland's *The Military Order of the Congress Medal of Honor Legion of the United States,* which contained a brief record of Mr. Rowand's services. Interviews with Mr. Rowand in Pittsburgh, Pennsylvania, resulted from this discovery, and from the publication of his story two other chapters grew. Mrs. Eleanor Vinton Blake, having read "Rowand," offered me the letters, papers, and portraits of her brother, Col. H. H. Young. Mr. John J. Stanton, editor of the Sussex (New Jersey) *Independent,* obtained for me Capt. Theodore F. Northrop's invitation to visit at his home, that I might write of the services of his guest and fellow-scout, John Landegon.

To Capt. Luis F. Emilio I am indebted for much information, especially in the "Williams" and the "Greenhow" chapters; no less for his courtesy in placing his fine Civil War library at my disposal.

In connection with the "Williams" matter I am under obligation to Capt. Robert B. Lee not alone for information, but for delightful hospitality at his home in Virginia, and for the introduction to Mr. Custis P. Upshur, from whom I obtained letters and papers of Colonel Williams's.

Former Secretary of the Interior Jas. R. Garfield and Maj.-Gen. William H. Carter supplied links in the chain of evidence.

Miss Susie Gentry, of Franklin, Tennessee, aided me greatly not only in the "Williams" case, but also in the story of Captain Beall.

Likewise, for assistance, I must thank Mr. R. A. Brock, editor of the *Southern Historical Society Papers;* Mr. S. A. Cunningham, editor of the *Confederate Veteran;* Miss Mary Hilliard Hinton, editor of the *North Carolina Booklet,* and Mr. F. H. Smith, secretary of the Maury County [Tennessee] Historical Society.

Much of the data for the chapter on "Mrs. Greenhow" came from her daughter, the late Mrs. Rose Greenhow Duvall, and her granddaughter, Mrs. Louis Marié. Assistance also of great value was given by Mrs. Richard Price, Secretary of the United Daughters of the Confederacy, Cape Fear Chapter No. 3, at Wilmington, North Carolina; Mrs. Caroline Phillips Myers, of Savannah, Georgia; Mrs. Constance Cary Harrison (whose husband was private secretary to Jefferson Davis); Hon. Geo. B. McClellan of Princeton, N. J., and Mr. Worthington C. Ford, editor of the Massachusetts Historical Society.

Miss Van Lew's executor, Mr. John Phillips Reynolds, of Boston, turned over to me all of her diaries, manuscripts, and letters, without which the chapter never could have been written, and assisted me in every manner in his power. To Miss Van Lew's neighbor, Mr. J. Staunton Moore, I am grateful for kindly hospitality, information, and much helpful criticism of my manuscript. Also from Dr. Wm. H. Parker, her physician, and when I met him occupant of the old Van Lew mansion, have I had much help.

Except for Mr. Peter N. Johnston, of the old Astor Library, I would never have met "Charlie" Phillips.

Mr. Isaac Markens generously turned over to me the results of his long-continued researches into John Beall's life and history.

From Mr. William A. Pinkerton, whose father, Allan Pinkerton, established the Federal Secret Service, there came the data which made possible the writing of "Timothy Webster: Spy."

This preface would be incomplete without a word of appreciation for the courtesy and indispensable aid from the librarians and their assistants at the Carnegie Institute, Pittsburgh, Pennsylvania; the Library of Congress, Washington, D. C., and in New York City the New York Historical Society, the library of Columbia University, the Mercantile Library Association, the Society, and the New York Public Libraries. My thanks are especially due to the late A. Noël Blakeman, Recorder of the New York Commandery of the Military Order of the Loyal Legion, by whose advice and help I was enabled to make the best use of the Legion's unsurpassed collection of reference works. Through Mr. F. A. Nast I owe to Mr. A. T. Gurlitz the privilege of admission to the Legion's library.

To the many whose names I have already mentioned, and to the many more for whom individual mention is impossible, in General Sheridan's words, "I tender my gratitude."

WILLIAM B. FEIS

Introduction

A scan of the bibliographies of books written about Civil War scouts and spies confirms that, though published nearly a century ago, William Gilmore Beymer's *Scouts and Spies of the Civil War* (formerly titled *On Hazardous Service: Scouts and Spies of the North and South*) continues to be an important resource on intelligence and espionage in the Civil War. Originally serialized in *Harper's Magazine* and *Harper's Weekly* between 1910 and 1912, the chapters included here chronicle the harrowing wartime experiences of scouts and spies for both the Blue and the Gray. Though there were numerous exceptions, scouts were typically volunteers on "detached service" from the ranks, who served as guides, undertook reconnaissance patrols, or went on special missions in enemy territory. Spies were most often civilians who lived behind enemy lines and reported via secret messenger or traveled through hostile territory on assignment and then returned to their own lines. Beymer examines both to provide a diverse picture of secret operations during a war in which neither side possessed formal army- or government-wide intelligence establishments, which in turn made intelligence operations very much an ad hoc enterprise. The informal and extemporized nature of this undertaking produced a fascinating array of individual experiences. These highly secretive, often chaotic, and mostly improvised endeavors, however, also make the historian's task of uncovering them that much more difficult, especially in comprehending the actual impact these operations had upon the conflict. It was into this confused and complex underworld of the war that William Beymer ventured in order to provide a historical account of some of these operations and to show the human drama that makes them such fascinating reading. The fact that the book remains a much-consulted source for the study of Civil War intelligence reveals how successful he was in achieving his goal. Perhaps a reviewer in 1912 summed up Beymer's contribution best when he wrote that he provided "true stories obtained from original sources, so that it may be said his book is an important addition to the literature of the war, and also that it is a valuable contribution to the history of American bravery and patriotism."[1]

The Civil War most likely attracted William G. Beymer during his early childhood. Born in Chambersburg, Pennsylvania, in 1881, the young Beymer probably heard numerous war stories at the knees of old Union veterans—maybe even relatives—and perhaps even visited nearby Gettysburg less than thirty miles away. Undoubtedly, Chambersburg's own brush with the war also fired Beymer's interest. In 1863, just eighteen years before the author's birth, Gen. Robert E. Lee used the town as a concentration point for his armies during the Gettysburg campaign. The following year Confederate cavalry under the leadership of Brig. Gen. John McCausland entered Chambersburg and demanded five hundred thousand dollars in retribution for recent acts of destruction by Union troops in the Shenandoah Valley. When the town leaders refused their demands, McCausland's men destroyed more than five hundred structures and caused more than one million dollars in damage. The searing memory of this act probably still burned in Chambersburg during Beymer's youth and may have spurred his desire to write about the war.[2]

Before embarking upon a literary career, however, William Beymer headed to California to attend Stanford University and then returned East to try his hand as an artist. Between 1903 and 1907 he studied at the New York School of Art and exhibited his work at the National Academy of Design in New York and at London's Kensington Garden. He turned away from painting when *Harper's Magazine*, a nationally renowned periodical, hired him as a staff writer in 1909. For the next two years he wrote both period fiction and published articles about Civil War scouts and spies, pieces that were combined in 1912 to form this book.[3]

After publication of *Scouts and Spies of the Civil War*, Beymer held a variety of interesting occupations. Between 1920 and the outbreak of World War II he lectured on short story and scenario writing at the University of California, and then became city editor of the Los Angeles bureau of the Associated Press. Perhaps most interesting, from 1933 to 1942 Beymer parlayed his writing skill and historical knowledge to become a technical adviser for some major motion picture studios working on films dealing with American history. In 1941 he served as an advisor on the film *Lady for a Night*, the fictional story of a gambling boat owner and her quest for acceptance into New Orleans society, starring Jenny Blake and John Wayne.[4] For a brief time during World War II Beymer served as an instructor at the Army Air Force Technical Training College and worked on an aircraft assembly line at Lockheed. In 1944 he returned to writing, this time focusing specifically on fictional stories set in the World War II era. His novel *12:20 P.M.*, first serialized in the *Saturday Evening Post*, was published in 1944; a short story entitled "Strange Welcome" appeared in the same magazine in 1947. His second novel, *The Middle of Midnight*, came out that same year.

The most enduring of his writings, however, has been *Scouts and Spies of the Civil War*. The importance of Beymer's detailed depiction of "secret service," a catch-all phrase used at the time to describe a wide variety of clandestine activities, is threefold.[5] First, though he chronicles the careers of some well-known spies, a number of his chapters deal with the accounts of lesser-known—but no less important—operatives. In some cases Beymer's work was probably the first place their stories had come before a wider reading audience. For historians these pages offer a glimpse into the careers of a variety of secret operatives that might otherwise have been lost. In addition, as a writer of fiction Beymer knew how to breathe life into the stories and engage the reader.

Second, he obtained much valuable information from personal interviews of former scouts and spies. He patiently listened to the stories of Archibald Rowand, Charlie Phillips, and John Landegon. If his interview with Landegon is any indication, Beymer worked hard to keep his interviewee focused on the subject and pushed the storyteller to dig deeper to find hidden-away memories. For stories of those no longer living, Beymer tirelessly tracked down relatives and contemporaries to help bring their stories into sharper focus. Some of these other sources included the famous partisan ranger Col. John S. Mosby and William A. Pinkerton, the son of Allan Pinkerton who served as Maj. Gen. George B. McClellan's intelligence chief and who later founded the Pinkerton Detective Agency.

Finally, and perhaps most important, Beymer attempted to substantiate these accounts by going beyond oral testimony. "No expenditure of time, effort, or money has been spared," he proclaimed, "not only in collecting *all* the data obtainable for each of the subjects, but also in verifying it—where not absolutely impossible—to the smallest detail" (xi). This was no doubt a difficult task, especially since relevant documentation was either already destroyed, buried deep in War Department files, scattered in personal papers, or possibly never existed. In fact, then–Secretary of War William H. Taft denied Beymer's request for access to War Department records and other documents relating to "secret service" activities, stating that the author could find all he needed in the pages of *The War of the Rebellion: The Official Records of Union and Confederate Armies,* a massive collection of wartime reports and correspondence compiled and published by the War Department between 1880 and 1901. As modern researchers know, and as Beymer discovered, however, the *Official Records* offer only scattered glimpses into secret service operations and contain little substantive detail to help bring the secret intelligence picture into focus. Only by digging deeper into unpublished War Department records can a researcher begin to unearth some answers. Yet given the nature of the intelligence "business," even these sources may not shed much light. The success and survival of scouts and spies depended upon secrecy; the fewer people who knew about or witnessed their business the better. One tiny mistake could mean incarceration or, even worse, a date with a firing squad. As a result, most operatives carefully avoided leaving paper trails that could reveal their true identities and occupations. Moreover, since the life and success of a scout or spy depended upon false identities, subterfuge, and isolation, finding corroborating witnesses or documentation was problematic. Together these make verification a tremendously difficult enterprise, and not just for researchers. After the war former scouts and spies were often frustrated in their quest for postwar pensions by the lack of evidence to authenticate their service.[6]

Nevertheless, Beymer painstakingly pursued leads in personal correspondence, pension records, newspaper articles, the *Southern Historical Society Papers*, and the *Confederate Veteran*, as well as in other publications. He mined the collections at the Carnegie Institute, the Library of Congress, the New York Historical Society, the New York Public Library, and the library of the New York Commandery of the Military Order of the Loyal Legion of the United States. In short, this writer of fiction sought the truth with the zeal of a historian.

Beymer's pursuit of independent corroboration for the claims of his subjects marked a distinct departure from earlier books and articles on Civil War espionage. Imbued with the Victorian romanticism that permeated the literature between 1863 and 1900, books and articles about spies often dripped with "moonlight and magnolia" sentimentality and were replete with cloak-and-dagger intrigue, mysterious strangers, secret meetings, death-defying exploits, and narrow escapes. "Most of the memoirists," wrote historian Curtis Carroll Davis, "indulged in one or another of the stylistic devices that are the traditional property right of the romancer."[7] Though their stories are exciting reading, few authors offered any documentation to buttress their claims and even fewer attempted to show the true impact the information they acquired had upon the course of military campaigns—and those who did often embellished the importance of their contributions. For most writers the main story was the daring pursuit of information, not its impact. When it came to the intelligence war, therefore, it was far easier to take dramatic liberties and showcase the romantic ideal rather than pursue documented fact.

Moreover, these stories, especially if written by an actual participant, possessed an authoritative air that even the lack of supporting evidence failed to undermine. Some crossed the line into fiction in order to make money for causes, for personal gain, to prove a point, or for prestige. Allan Pinkerton penned his memoirs to cover mistakes he made during the war (and there were many) in order to safeguard his postwar reputation and that of his burgeoning detective agency. To most readers, therefore, the espionage that took place during the Civil War conjured images of dainty damsels dashing though enemy lines with a dispatch sewn into their hems, arriving just in time to provide crucial information at a critical time.[8] "[T]heir accounts," wrote one historian, "are strangled by episode." Spy biographies and autobiographies "are such a merry-go-round of raids, surprise attacks, pursuits, and group and/or individual encounters that a grey whirl results which transmutes the business of warfare into a game of cops-and-robbers."[9] As a result, much of what passed as intelligence history had but a nodding acquaintance with reality. At times Beymer's narrative falls prey to these same tendencies and the wise reader must exercise caution. But his efforts to make the chapters "in every sense historical" separates his work from those of earlier writers and explains why even today the book remains a much-consulted source on the secret side of the Civil War (xi).

Beymer's selection of scouts and spies offers the reader an interesting array of personalities and adventures. For example, the first chapter retraces the exploits of Archibald H. Rowand, a Pennsylvanian who served with the First West Virginia Cavalry and who later received a Medal of Honor for his bravery in getting a dispatch through enemy lines to Maj. Gen. Ulysses S. Grant in 1865. Beymer recounts not only that episode but others recalled by Rowand in the interview. Aside from the official Medal of Honor citation, Rowand's account as told to Beymer was likely the first time a wider reading public learned about his amazing and dangerous service to the Union. Moreover, Beymer included copies of Rowand's personal wartime correspondences (which still exist in the hands of his grandson) and a rare picture of the young scout in a Confederate uniform.[10]

Beymer also included the stories of two of the more famous women spies of the war, Rose O'Neal Greenhow (Confederate) and Elizabeth Van Lew (Union). Beymer relies heavily upon Greenhow's diary and other correspondence to show that, after an early success in alerting the Confederates to the movement of federal troops out of Washington before First Bull Run in 1861, the value of the most well-connected Southern spy in Washington diminished markedly. He also shows that before Greenhow drowned running the blockade in 1864, her final contribution to "the Cause" was as an ardent Confederate promoter and fundraiser in Europe. Though his treatment of Greenhow remains sympathetic in the main, Beymer attempts evenhandedness. For example, he does not allow Greenhow's memoir, *My Imprisonment, or the First Year of Abolition Rule in Washington* (1863), to pass as the unchallenged truth. The book, he notes, was "a brilliant veneer of personal wartime experiences laid alluringly over a solid backing of Confederate States propaganda" (161).[11]

As for Elizabeth Van Lew, Beymer reveals that though she certainly lacked the flash and high society glamour of Greenhow, she contributed more to the Union cause from her home in Richmond than her counterpart did living in the federal capital. Unlike Greenhow, Van Lew remained active for almost the entire war but never sought accolades or fame for her service. In fact, she feared those things lest her fellow Richmonders use it to put her in jail during the war or shun her after it. To protect herself she destroyed some of her papers—both personal and official correspondence—that would have shed more light on her service to the Union. She also kept a diary but excised some entries that might have incriminated her. Her efforts ultimately failed. After the war her neighbors uncovered her secret and ostracized her. Destitute and unable to find work, Van Lew then used her wartime loyalty to the Union to gain a patronage position in the federal government. Beymer treats the Union spy sympathetically, and uses her diary and official correspondence, including testimony of key Union commanders, to demonstrate that she was indeed a valuable intelligence asset within the Confederate capital. Perhaps her most important contribution, however, was the aid and comfort she provided Union soldiers languishing in Richmond's infamous prisons. Not only did she bring them food, she also risked all by hiding escapees within her house and helping them find passage out of the city. Beymer recounts these and other episodes in gripping detail.[12]

The remaining chapters in *Scouts and Spies of the Civil War* provide more examples of the diverse, complex, and ad hoc—not to mention exciting—nature of Civil War intelligence operations. Beymer recounts the discovery and execution of two Confederate spies in Tennessee; the exploits of Maj. Gen. Philip Sheridan's favorite scout, Maj. Henry H. Young; the services of Marylander "Wat" Bowie; the dangerous intrigues of the father-and-son spying duo of John and Charles Phillips;

the little-known but fascinating deeds of federal scout John Landegon of the Second New York Cavalry; the intrigues of John Yates Beall as part of the ill-fated "Northwest Conspiracy"; and, finally, the woeful tale of the detection and execution of Allan Pinkerton's favorite spy, Timothy Webster.[13] Though somewhat sympathetic to his subjects and burdened by the fact that, as one later historian noted, all too often his "pioneer exercise in oral history seemed to defy documentation in less self-serving, independent sources," Beymer provided a valuable look at a topic too often shrouded in the mists of romanticism and cloak-and-dagger fantasies. Though he sheds a more critical light on these fascinating individuals and their deeds, perhaps what he wrote about the difficulty of getting at the truth of Rose Greenhow's spying career best describes the challenges that he—and anyone attempting to penetrate the secret side of the Civil War—faced: "It is improbable that the story ever will be told," he confessed. "Months of effort to learn details have resulted in but vague glimpses . . . [just] as one sees an ever-receding figure at the turns of a winding road" (161).

NOTES

The author would like to thank Ms. Ann Klavano, reference librarian at Buena Vista University Library, for her invaluable help in tracking down information on Beymer.

1. Review of *On Hazardous Service: Scouts and Spies of the North and South, New York Times*, 24 November 1912.

2. David S. Heidler and Jeanne T. Heidler, eds., *Encyclopedia of the American Civil War: A Political, Social, and Military History* (Santa Barbara: ABC-CLIO, 2000), 1:390–91.

3. Entry for "William Gilmore Beymer" in *Eminent Californians, 1953* (Palo Alto CA: C. W. Taylor, 1953), 557.

4. *Lady for a Night*. The Internet Movie Database, *http://us.imdb.com/Plot?0033806*. (17 July 2002).

5. The North had no agency officially called the "Secret Service." The Confederate government did create a Signal and Secret Service Bureau in 1862, but it was not government- or army-wide, had little involvement

in military operations, and focused primarily on covert activities in the North.

6. For an example of the difficulty in verifying "secret service" activities see William B. Feis, "Charles S. Bell, Union Scout," *North & South* 4 (September 2001): 34.

7. Curtis Carroll Davis, "Companions of Crisis: The Spy Memoir as a Social Document," *Civil War History* 10 (December 1964): 398.

8. Davis, "Companions of Crisis," 386–87. For more on Pinkerton's motives see Patrick Bass's introduction to the Bison Book reprint of Allan Pinkerton's 1883 thriller *The Spy of the Rebellion* (Lincoln: University of Nebraska Press, 1989), 20.

9. Davis, "Companions of Crisis," 391–92.

10. See Mark Roth, "Secrets of a Union Spy," *Pittsburgh Post-Gazette*, 3 May 1998.

11. For more on Greenhow see Edwin C. Fishel, *The Secret War for the Union: The Untold Story of Military Intelligence in the Civil War* (Boston: Houghton-Mifflin, 1996), 58–70, 575–78. Fishel has done more than any other historian to scrutinize and challenge the claims made by famous scouts and spies.

12. For more on Van Lew see Meriwether Stuart, "Colonel Ulric Dahlgren and Richmond's Union Underground," *Virginia Magazine of History and Biography* 72 (April 1964): 152–204. For a transcript of Van Lew's diary see David D. Ryan, ed., *A Yankee Spy in Richmond: The Civil War Diary of "Crazy Bet" Van Lew* (Mechanicsburg PA: Stackpole Books, 1996). See also William B. Feis, *Grant's Secret Service: The Intelligence War from Belmont to Appomattox* (Lincoln: University of Nebraska Press, 2002), 237–58.

13. For more recent historical accounts of some of these figures see Fishel, *The Secret War for the Union*; Richard P. Weinert, "The South Had Mosby: The Union Had Maj. Henry Young," *Civil War Times Illustrated* (April 1964): 38–42; and Meriwether Stuart, "Of Spies and Borrowed Names: The Identity of Union Operatives in Richmond Known as 'The Phillipses' Discovered," *Virginia Magazine of History and Biography* 89 (July 1981): 308–27.

S COUTS AND S PIES OF THE C IVIL W AR

Rowand

To Major M. H. Young, of my staff, chief of scouts, and the thirty or forty men of his command, who took their lives in their hands, cheerfully going wherever ordered, to obtain that great essential of success, information, I tender my gratitude. Ten of these men were lost.—*From Gen. Philip H. Sheridan's report of the expedition from Winchester to Petersburg, Virginia. February 27—March 28, 1865. Official Records, Vol. 46: 1: 481.*

"Thirty or forty men, of whom ten were lost." It was not chance which worded that phrase. Sheridan has chosen his words well. Of the ten, no one of them died as do men in battles; two were found by their comrades hanging by their own halter-straps; several more died like trapped animals, fighting desperately, at bay. And the others—never returned. Until the Great Book opens it will never be known where, or how, they died; they never returned, that is all. Of the ten, not a man was wearing the uniform of the country for which he died.

How many more went down in the remaining twelve days of the war I do not know; those twelve savage days that saw Five Forks and Sailor's Creek, Dinwiddie Court House, Deep Creek, Farmville, and Appomattox Station and the Court House; those days when the scouts worked night and day, and were in their own lines only long enough to give "information."

To-day, of all that brave band to whom Philip Henry Sheridan tendered his gratitude, there remain but four—Sergeant McCabe, "Sonny"

Chrisman, Jack Riley, and Rowand. This is the story, in part, of Archie Rowand—"Barefoot" Rowand of "the Valley," one of the two scouts for whom Sheridan himself asked that greatest distinction the nation can give a soldier—the little bronze star on whose reverse is read:

"The Congress—to—Archibald H. Rowand, Jr.—FOR VALOR."

When the dusk of the winter day had fallen, and we had thrown away our cigars, when the story—such a small part of which I may retell here—was done, I asked two questions:

"Should war come now, would there be found men who could do as you have done?"

"Yes," he said, and the answer came grimly, "if they begin as young as I began, and have no better sense."

And, "Why did you ever begin?"

"It was as I told you—Company K had been on detached service—scout duty—for some time. When the company was drawn up in line, and the captain called for volunteers for 'extra dangerous duty,' I looked at Ike Harris and Ike looked at me, and then we both stepped forward. They took us to headquarters and gave us two rebel uniforms—and we wished we had not come."

"But why did you volunteer?"

He peered at me over his glasses. "*I* don't know! We were boys—wanted to know what was the 'extra dangerous duty,' and"—chuckling to himself at a hidden recollection—"when we found out we hadn't the face to back down." And that's how it all began.

This, you must know, is not the story of a spy, but, gray clothes and all, of a *scout!* The point was rather insisted upon.

"This," he said, "is what I would say is the difference between a scout and a spy: The regular spy was a man who generally remained inside the enemy's lines, and was not supposed to fight except in self-defense. [And, let me add, was usually a civilian.] We scouts were men who dressed in the enemy's uniform in order to deceive their pickets and capture them so that the main body could be surprised. Or, we would ride up to a Southern citizen, man or woman, for information, and since we were dressed in the Confederate uniform they would tell us everything they knew. Of course, under strict military law, we were subject to the penalty of spies if taken within the enemy's lines."

It was in the fall of '62 that Rowand and Ike Harris had looked into one another's eyes, discovered that they were of one mind, and had stepped forward—into the gray uniform. Since July 17th of that year Rowand had been with Company K of the First West Virginia Cavalry, under General Milroy. He had come to the cavalry from a Pennsylvania infantry regiment, which—he all but whispered it, lest Disgrace should find him out— was "not much better than a home guard," and where "the musket was too heavy to tote." But the cavalry just suited him, and in the rough scouting through rugged West Virginia he grew from the stoop-shouldered, cough-racked railroad clerk into the tireless young daredevil who would volunteer for extra dangerous duty just to see what was extra dangerous about it.

"It was exciting," he said.

It must have been! With each day of service in the ranks of the scouts danger became more imminent; the chances increased of meeting again some party of Confederates with whom previous lies and explanations would not tally with present movements. Also, in the Federal army there were sure to be Southern spies whose business it was to report descriptions of the scouts, and, if possible, their movements; within the Confederate lines recognition because of these descriptions might take place at any moment. That meant death by the noose, or, at best, to be shot down in a last-stand fight. Rowand tells how a man rode into their lines at Salem and claimed to be one of Averell's scouts. He was recognized as being a particularly dangerous Confederate spy, and they shot him where he stood, without even the formality of a drumhead court martial.

And then there was the danger of meeting death at the hands of their own men. It happened not once, but many times, that, discovered and hard pressed by the enemy, the scouts in their gray uniforms rode for their lives for the safety of the Union lines, only to be met by the murderous volley of their own mistaken pickets. But it was exciting!

As compensation they had freedom and privileges beyond those of any men in the army. For them there were no camp drudgeries, no guard or picket duty; their courage and their duties bought them immunity from camp discipline; and their quarters, where they all lived together, were the best that could be obtained in the field. Each man was entitled to keep four horses—the pick of the command. In their scoutings through the countryside they lived on the best that the land afforded; in those parts nothing was too good for the "boys in gray," and the gulled Confederate sympathizers fed them like wedding-guests. Then there was the money, good gold—no less. They were paid in proportion to the value of the information they brought in and the services they performed; expense money was portioned out with a prodigal hand from the Secret Service chest. They were the Aristocracy of the Army! But most of all they risked their necks because it was exciting.

Training came chiefly from dear-bought experience, except that given them by "Old Clayton," one of the scouts who had come with General Frémont from the West. He conceived a great fancy for "the boys," and gave them a deal of advice and instruction. There was one thing that even old Clayton could not give Rowand—Rowand's command of the Southern manner of speech. The years spent at Greenville, South Carolina, as a child of from two to seven, stuck the speech to his tongue—so that not even the next ten years in Pittsburgh could entirely efface the mark of the South, and now, with the need, he slipped easily back into the tongue that seemed to identify him with the gray; it was too obviously unassumed not to deceive. To this Ruwand attributes his great success as a scout.

Courage, too, must have had something to do with it! It was Rowand and Ike Harris who carried General Milroy's despatches to Halltown, West Virginia. They were discovered and recognized as couriers the moment they left the Union lines, and a rebel battery turned its entire fire on them in an effort to check the message known to be for help; theirs was a wild ride under the bursting shells.

It was Rowand who, in the Winchester battle the next week, rode General Milroy's wounded and hobbling horse across the battle-field, and brought back the great white charger of the General. In that same fierce fight the man on either side of him was killed, and Ike, poor Ike Harris—that was his last battle. He was killed soon afterward. The Confederates, Lee's advance, brushed aside and scattered Milroy's little command, and swept on unchecked till rolled back from the high-water mark of the northern field of Gettysburg. Rowand was back in his regiment, but Custer needed scouts, and Rowand was chosen. And there he proved that he possessed the great qualification of the born scout—the illusive seventh sense. He had been in the locality but once before, and at that in the confusion of a fight at Piedmont Station, yet he established a "V" of couriers through nineteen miles of a country cross-hatched by innumerable byways, and reported them placed that same dark night. That was no small achievement.

But it was in "the Valley" (the Shenandoah) that he felt at home, and he was glad when he was ordered back there to report to General Averell in the fall.

"Nothing much happened to me that winter," he said. (I wonder what really did!) "So I'm going to tell you about the second Salem raid in the next spring.

"To begin with, I hanged a man. It was this way: On the first Salem raid a citizen named Creigh had, with an ax, killed a Union soldier and thrown his body into a well. The scouts now discovered this; Creigh was captured, tried by a drumhead court martial, and sentenced to be hanged.

"As I was going up to headquarters the next morning I met Captain Jack Crawford, of Averell's staff, who said to me, 'Rowand, you hang the prisoner.' I indignantly told him I would do nothing of the sort—I hadn't enlisted for an executioner. It was the General's order, he told me angrily; and of course that settled it. I sent a couple of the boys for some rope from a bed (have you ever seen the beds of that day?—with an interlacing of rope in lieu of bed-springs), and put the rope around the prisoner's neck, tied the other end to the limb of a tree, mounted him on the scout's wagon, and drove the wagon from under him." He paused; then, more slowly, "I have seen civil executions since, but then I didn't know enough to tie the hands and feet of the condemned."

I hastened to break the silence. "After all, it was the General's order—you could only obey." I spoke in sympathy—if I could see, how much more clear would the sight be to the eyes that had really seen!

He only said: "That was the joke of it! Averell had never mentioned me; it was Crawford's job, and he foisted it off on me.

"Well," he went on, "I was captured that raid—for the first and last time. Four of us were started in the late afternoon, about dark, to get through Breckinridge's lines and bring back General Duffié, whose brigade had been sent to go around Lynchburg. We did not know then that Hunter's scouts had tried to get through and had been driven back. We rode for some hours, and then, about half past ten, spied a light in a house; we rode up and asked for something to eat—offering to pay. There was a woman sitting up with a sick child; she looked at our gray uniforms; then, her eyes shining, 'Pay?' she said. 'I do not charge our boys anything!' The other two were left outside to watch; Townsend and I went in. The woman gave us bread and cold meat, and milk to drink; we thanked her and went out to take our turn at watching while the others ate. The men were gone. There was a fence about twelve feet from the house, and from behind the fence came the order to surrender; it was very dark, but we could see a dozen heads above the top of the fence and the gleam of the leveled carbines.

" 'Are you Yanks?' I called.

" 'No!'

" '*Oh*'—as though relieved. 'That's all right, then; we surrender!' They came in and took away our revolvers. Then I remembered that in my pocket there was a pass, naming me as scout and passing me through the Union lines at all times; I managed to get the small pocketbook and by a flip of my fingers shoot it up my sleeve and hold it in the hollow of my arm. Then they took us into the house and the inquisition began."

As he talked, the memory of that night seemed to grow and brighten till he lived it in the present—yes, and made me live it, too.

"See," he said, getting to his feet and moving swiftly about the room. "Here is the fireplace, a big one, and there is a window—there where that one is; and there is another one, and here is the door into the hall—open, and there is one into the next room that is closed. And here am I with the light strong on my face, so that they could see the flicker of an eyelid or the twitch of a muscle, and the captain, with his back to the light, sits facing me, with our chairs close together. Townsend and a scout, close facing too, are over there more in the shadow."

See? Of course I saw: the guards at the windows, dim seen in the night outside; the guards at the door into the big bare hall; behind them, peeping in, the frightened, white-faced woman with the sick child in her arms; and, strong in the glare of the unshaded lamp, the slender boy of eighteen, lounging easily in his chair, fighting coolly and shrewdly for his life—a half-smile on his face, and the damning pass held in the hollow of his arm.

"Townsend and I never even glanced at one another, but each strained his ears for the other's answers. If we had been examined separately, we would have contradicted each other in something, and—been hanged. But we kept our stories straight. Townsend was in grave danger, because he was a deserter from the Confederate General Jenkin's command, and the man who was questioning him was one of Jenkin's scouts; but that very fact saved him, for he was so well posted that he quickly allayed suspicion.

"We were couriers from McCausland—I told the captain—with verbal messages. Why were they not written?—ask McCausland that! As to what the messages were, that was different; they were for General Breckinridge at the Rockfish Gap, and could not be told to any captain met in the road who asked for them. Describe General McCausland? Certainly; and the number of his regiments and the number of guns—(that was easy; I had been in his camp two nights before!)

"The scout examining Townsend called over, 'This man is all right, Captain.' But the captain shook his head over me—he was troubled; something did not ring quite true. 'Where are you from?' he sharply asked. 'Lewis County—West Virginia,' I told him. In Weston? Yes, I know Lawyer Jackson, and old Doc Hoffman, and—Describe them? Sure! (You see, we had been camped there in August and September, '62.)

" 'My name is Hoffman,' the captain said. 'Lee Hoffman, of Hampton's Legion.' He was still looking at me with a frown of perplexity, and I laughed in his face. 'You think I am a deserter?' I asked. 'No, I don't. I don't understand you—you puzzle me. You are a Southerner—you are no Yankee, I am sure of that.' 'Then to make sure what we are, you had better send us under guard to Breckinridge's headquarters.' It was that that shook down his last doubts. 'I have a letter,' he said, abruptly, 'for General Breckinridge. Take it and get through as quick as you can. Hurry.'

" 'Hurry!' I sneered. 'We'll need to!—you've kept us here an hour and a half now.' We took the letter. It is the one found on page 759, vol. xxxvii, of the Official Records; it begins: 'New Fairfield, Va., June 12, '64.—II P.M. Major-Gen. J. C. Breckinridge. General:—The enemy are now at Lexington, camped; not moving to-day. . . .' "

Rowand gleefully gave this letter to General Averell next morning, but not before he and his companion had again come near to being hanged. They gave up the attempt to reach Duffié, and trusted that their comrades had got through. All the rest of that night they rode by a circuitous route over the mountains to the Lexington and Staunton Pike, and so toward Lexington. At dawn they struck the Union pickets—an Ohio volunteer infantry regiment, by whom they were arrested, haled before the colonel, who would believe nothing except that they were in gray uniforms, and who cursed them for spies, and vowed to hang them both within the hour. Rowand demanded to be sent to headquarters; the colonel said he was insolent, and cursed him again. But finally they were sent to Averell—footing it, while their captors rode their horses; and then "somebody else caught—."

He told how Jubal Early had defeated them at Lynchburg, and of how, in that awful retreat through a world of mountains to Charleston, he had seen men and horses in the very midst of the army fall down in the road and die of fatigue and starvation.

He told of lying in a clump of bushes on a little hill in Pennsylvania at the edge of ill-starred Chambersburg—he and his partner, John Lamis—momentarily expecting Averell at the head of his cavalry to come and save the town. They had sent their companion to tell him to hurry, but still he did not come. Nor did he come all the long, hot July morning, and they lay in the bushes and watched the Confederate cavalrymen of McCausland and Bradley Johnson burn and pillage the town.

He told of the nine-day pursuit back into West Virginia, and of how, near Moorefield, the scouts had captured the picket without firing a shot; and of the surprise of the camps at dawn, and the scattering of the commands of Bradley Johnson and McCausland to the four winds.

His face wreathed in smiles and he shook with laughter as he told of the snake and the frog. How he and four other scouts had reconnoitered the enemy near Bunker Hill, and were riding leisurely back to Averell in Maryland; how, as they rode through Hedgesville, he had stopped to chat with a young girl who was an old friend; and then had rejoined his men in a great wood near the Potomac, and there they had found a big black-snake which had half swallowed a large bullfrog that was fighting stoutly against taking the road that lay before it. And instantly there was no war, and they were not scouts in an enemy's country in peril of their lives, but they were boys again and it was summer, and here in the cool woods was one of nature's fierce battles—to be wagered on! In a moment they were off their horses, and now they cheered the snake, and now for the frog; Mike Smith held the stakes. He told how there had suddenly flamed a volley from out the wood, and they had flung themselves on their horses and made a dash out of the ambush—all but Smith; Smith the stakeholder! His horse was down, shot through the side, struggling and thrashing on the ground; Smith ran in silence for the river. And how as he passed he caught Smith by the collar and dragged him across his own big gray horse; then, firing as they rode, they all had dashed for the ford. The disappointed enemy maliciously told the girl in Hedgesville that they had killed the Yank on the big gray horse, and she grieved for many a day.

He told of a lonely duel in the middle of a great, sunny field. There was neither sight nor sound of armies nor of war: only summer sights and sounds—wind in the long grass, and bees; and the great white clouds overhead. And he was going toward the rebel lines, and that other boy was headed for the lines of the Blue. Each knew that the other must not go on; they fired. Of all the memories of those harsh, savage days, the one of most bitter regret is that of the lonely, sunlit field where lay the huddled body of the other boy.

"And now this," said Rowand, "is the last scouting I did for Averell; it came near being the last that I ever did."

He told how he and John Lamis had been sent to go around Martinsburg, get in the Confederate rear, and find what cavalry were there. And how as they rode through a wood, believing themselves to be in the rear of the rebel army, there sounded the rebel yell behind them, and the cavalry came charging through. They were swept into the charge against their own men. They yelled as loud as any one, but kept edging out to the flank so as to drop out at the first chance. But they had to keep right on into the town, and as they went charging through he was next the sidewalk, and a young lady whom he knew—her name was Miss Sue Grimm—stood with her mother at their doorway. She was so surprised to see him in such a place that she called, "Why, Archie Rowand, what are you doing with—"

"Shut up your mouth!" he yelled—he was frightened half to death; had she finished—"with the rebels"—he would not have been with the rebels long; he would have been with the angels! But she was too astonished and too angry to say another word, and so he and Lamis got through and joined the Federals a mile and a half north of the town. It took him three months to make peace with that young lady.

Of such stories a score, and I reluctantly pass them by. All that he had done up to this time was but the novitiate of his service.

Then Sheridan came to the Valley. His coming meant much to the nation; it meant much to Rowand, too. It meant the opportunity to do work that was of great value to his flag; it meant such an increase of the dangers and the excitement he loved as to make most of what had gone before seem but playing. For him it meant friendship—almost intimacy—with this greatest of cavalry generals; and a hero-worship begun as a boy has continued to this day.

From their first interview Sheridan seemed to take to the boy, perhaps for his very boyishness, perhaps for his audacity and independence of speech, as much as for his cool daring in his work. "I'd like to report to you personally, General, or not at all; if not, please send me to my regiment," he said at that interview. This was because under Averell the scouts reported to Major Howe, who repeated the reports to the general. He got one of Rowand's mixed; as a consequence Averell lost a number of men, and angrily ordered Rowand to his regiment in disgrace. Rowand was able to prove he had reported correctly, and that he *had* reached a certain point (he proved it by the dead body of his comrade who fell at that place). After that he refused to report except to Averell, and his demand was acceded to. He meant to start right with Sheridan.

"I wanted to stay with Averell; begged to stay. He said he was sorry to lose me, but that I would have to go. I went accordingly. I had never seen General Sheridan, never had him described. Averell and Milroy were big men—somehow I expected to find another big man; he was

big only in fight. (Sheridan was but five feet five.) He was pointed out
to me in front of headquarters, and I went up and saluted. He looked
me up and down.

" 'I asked General Averell for his oldest scout,' was all he said.

" 'I am his oldest in point of service—in knowledge of the Valley,' I
answered.

" 'How old are you? How long have you served?' he inquired. I was
nineteen, I told him, and had scouted for over two years in the Valley.
He took me into headquarters and pumped me for an hour and a half;
then sent me for four or five good men as 'quick at you can get them.'
I got Jack Riley, Dominic Fannin, Jim White, Alvin Stearns, and John
Dunn. A scout named James Campbell came to Sheridan from the
Army of the Potomac."

These men, and two or three others, seem to have been the nucleus
of Sheridan's scouts in the Valley of the Shenandoah—the Secret Service
organization which a little later, having been recruited up to forty, under
command of Major H. H. Young, became the most efficient, the most
noted, in the Federal army.

"Months afterward General Sheridan asked me what I supposed he
saw when I first reported to him: 'Two big brown eyes and a mouth,
Rowand; that was all!' I weighed less than a hundred and forty then—
you mightn't believe it now—and I was six feet tall. He had that way
with us, that easy friendliness; we would have done anything for him.
He was a fine man!"

Silence fell; he stared unseeing out the window, musing; the office,
and me, and the stenographer with poised pen, I saw he had quite
forgot. And I envied him that inner sight of the great dead leader—the
chance to live over again in memory his close service with Philip H.
Sheridan, the beau-ideal of the war.

Presently he began again, slowly: "General Sheridan was the best
officer by all odds that I have served under. He stood by his scouts in
everything, and they one and all would have gone to any ends to get
for him the information that he desired. He himself gave his orders
to us—his 'old' scouts, that is, those of us who were with him before
Major Young took command—and he personally received our reports.
He was impulsive, but not in the least the rough bully that some writers

have tried to make him out. I saw him very angry only once—and that was at me. [The chuckle left no doubt as to how it had come out.] It was on the James River Canal Raid, one very dark night just after a storm—it did nothing but storm those days (early March, '65)—that a party of us scouts found, unguarded, a great warehouse containing about three hundred thousand dollars of supplies. We galloped back, and I was sent in to Sheridan to report.

" 'Did you burn them?' he asked, sternly.

" 'Why, General,' I said, 'we did not have orders—' He was getting madder all the time; and at that he roared: 'Orders hell! Why didn't you burn those things—why didn't you think!'

"It was only a couple of days afterward that we ran across more stores. Of course we burned them. When I came to that part of my report about finding the stores he gripped the arms of his chair and, leaning forward, asked, 'You didn't burn *those?*'

" 'Yes,' I said, proudly, 'I set them on fire.'

"He leaped from his chair and shunted: 'What in hell did you burn those for! I'm going up that way tomorrow.' He kind of glared at me for a minute, and then he remembered the last time I had reported to him, and he burst into a big laugh.

"After General Sheridan came to the Valley I made several uneventful trips into the enemy's lines. [Unless he escaped by a hair's-breadth any trip was "uneventful," and he could not be got to say much about it.] The night before Cedar Creek I had got in from a hard trip to Moorefield and Romney; Sheridan was away, and I came back to scouts' headquarters and went to sleep. About 2 A.M. or later I was wakened by Dominic Fannin and Alvin Stearns getting in, and damning Crook right and left. They had been sent up the Valley to New Market and Woodstock at the same time I was sent to Romney, and when coming back they fell in with some of Early's stragglers at Fisher's Hill, where the enemy was camped, and with them, under cover of night, they had worked their way into the Confederate lines, and discovered that the Federals were about to be flanked in their camp on the banks of Cedar Creek. With all speed they withdrew from the enemy's lines and made for the Union camp. Sheridan was in conference with Halleck in Washington, and so they reported to General Crook, who commanded the Eighth Corps—known as the Army of West Virginia. 'The enemy will attack at dawn!' said they. Crook pooh-poohed the idea; treated the news very lightly; made them feel like a five-cent shinplaster, as Fannin said to us at the scouts' headquarters.

" 'We'll be attacked at daylight—you see!' they grumbled, and then they fell to swearing at Crook again, and wishing Sheridan had received their report. They made such a fuss that I said, finally: 'Lie down, you two fools, and let me sleep. If Crook can stand it, we ought to!' And I fell asleep."

In the light of what followed it is not surprising that General Crook has made no report of the information brought him by the scouts that night before Cedar Creek. That he should have treated their report so lightly is because he had, as he believed, good reason to think such an attack impossible. At eight o'clock that very evening he had reported to General Wright that a brigade reconnoissance sent out by him that day had returned to camp, and reported nothing was to be found of the enemy in their camp, and that they had doubtless retreated up the Valley. This seemed sound, General Wright goes on to say in his official report, because the enemy was known to be without supplies. Yet the mistake was not easy to explain. Probably the reconnoitering party had not advanced so far as it supposed—had not really reached the enemy's lines, which were some miles in advance of the Federal.

This reconnoitering party from the Army of West Virginia returned to camp through its own lines (where the first blow fell next day), and undoubtedly, as they passed the pickets, confided their belief that the Confederates were in retreat up the Valley. How else, except for this fancied security and lulled suspicion, could the enemy next morning have swept over their entire picket-line without firing a single shot?

This is the new story of what might have been, what should have been, at Cedar Creek, October 19, 1864. General Crook was given by these two scouts the chance to redeem the incomprehensible blunder of his reconnoitering brigade, but he refused to credit their report, and the battle of Cedar Creek was fought and lost, and fought again and won, between day-dawn and dark. Had Crook heeded the scouts, there would have been no surprised army in the cold fog of an autumn morning, no routed and panic-shaken army to peer down the Valley to

Winchester twenty miles away, no chance for General Phil Sheridan to make his famous ride on Rienzi and turn the tide of fugitives, and with them at his back change defeat into victory. . . .

That night there came down through the deep, wooded ravines of Fisher's Hill an army as gray and as silent as the river fog that rolled to meet it and envelop it with a cold, sheltering veil. The march was a march of gray shadows; canteens and the very swords of the officers had been left behind lest their jangle sound a warning; the fog muffled into a low patter the rush of thousands of footfalls. In the half-light of coming dawn they struck—in flank, in front, in rear. Solid battle-lines, without skirmishers, swept up and over every picket-post, swallowing picket, patrol, and reserve, whose scattered firing was as pebbles flung into the sea. So swift and certain was the attack, so sure the surprise, that they were in the camp and upon those regiments of the Army of West Virginia, where reveille had been sounded, ere the unarmed men at roll-call had time to arm and form. It was but a matter of minutes before all were swept together into a panic-stricken mob, on whom the Confederates turned their own cannon and mowed them down as they ran. In other regiments men heavy with sleep, their arms laden with their clothing—having been wakened only by the attack—plunged out of their tents into a twilight of fog and low-rolling, ever-densening smoke, in which they ran here and there in bewilderment. Officers, no less confused, raged about, desperately trying to rally the fleeing men; here and there groups held for a moment and turned to fight, but, overwhelmed by numbers and attacked on two sides, they scattered, and, like the rest, fled once more for the support of the Nineteenth Corps. The wreck of the Army of West Virginia, like driftwood on the crest of a wave, shattered and demoralized the Nineteenth; surprised and already attacked in flank, they too crumbled and ran; and the unchecked Confederates swept victorious over the camps of plenty. Pillage began.

To the sleeping scouts the attack, expected though it was, came in its suddenness with equally bewildering surprise. Rowand tells how a bullet that cut through a blanket over the window was their first warning that the enemy was so near. There was no time to change to blue uniforms; capture for them meant certain death; they made a rush for the door and flung themselves on their horses and galloped away. Once across the creek, they rode more slowly, often looking back.

And he tells of General Wright, harassed though he was with the anxiety of command, yet recognizing them as they passed, and shouting, "You scouts had better fall back—this will be no place for those uniforms in a few minutes!"

The roads were filled now with struggling teams fighting for a passage to the rear; long lines of wounded staggered and lurched along the roadsides, desperately afraid of the plunging teams, and of the enemy behind, and of their own bleeding wounds. On either side, and far out into the fields that bordered the roads, there hurried hundreds of uninjured stragglers in groups of twos and threes and tens—groups of hundreds. Now and again the cry would go up "They're coming!" and the panic would spread, and in a moment every man would be running again, flat-footed, furious, in a blind haste to escape from the terrified comrades who pressed hard on his heels; in the roads, teamsters stood up on the seats of the lurching wagons and lashed their horses and screamed at drivers of wagons ahead who blocked the way; from where the wounded, frantic at being left behind, struggled to keep up, there rose one long wail of pain and terror. From behind there came ever the roar of battle where the Confederates who would not pillage fought the Federals who would not run.

And then Sheridan came up the Valley. Rowand and Campbell, who had stuck together all the morning, were already north of Newtown when they met him.

"I looked across a large clear field and saw a black horse at full speed coming out of the woods, and I said to Campbell, 'There comes the "Old Man" '—we always called General Sheridan the 'Old Man'; and he said, 'Can't be; he's in Washington.' I looked again for a moment, and then said, 'It's him; there come a couple of his staff officers a hundred yards behind.' We stopped, and General Sheridan came up, pulled in his horse, and said, 'Boys, how is it?' Campbell replied, 'General, it's a rout!' He threw his eyes quick at me and said, 'Not quite that bad! The Eighth and Nineteenth are scattered, but the Sixth is solid!'

"A young lieutenant, with a Nineteenth Corps badge on his cap, was hurrying by; Sheridan wheeled around to him. 'Lieutenant, where is your command?' 'I don't know,' the lieutenant shouted, and was hurrying on again. 'Damn you, turn back and find it!' Sheridan yelled, and passed on. The lieutenant stopped. 'Who was that, scout?' 'That was General Sheridan,' I said. 'I'll turn back!' he cried.

"It was the same all along the road; the men were coming back up the Valley faster than they had run down it; ahead of us they were running toward the road, and lining up on either side, and as we rode along there was just one great roar of cheers."

He told of the ride back to the front, where the Sixth Corps and remnants of the Nineteenth had been sullenly battling—holding off the Confederate army all the day; of how the ebb-tide that had turned came roaring back to the fight in a flood of men who could scarce be held back from the attack until the lines were sufficiently reinforced and reformed. And when he told of Sheridan, bareheaded, riding along in front of his battle-line where it waited the command to advance, he rose from his chair, and his eyes alight with the old battle-fire, he pounded the desk with his fist. "There has been a lot told and a lot written of what Sheridan said that day, but here is what he did say—the very words; *I* was there, *I* heard, and these are his very words. A man, out of the ranks, called, 'General, where will we sleep to-night?' General Sheridan stopped his horse and turned; he didn't speak loud, but in the hush that fell his words seemed to ring: 'We'll sleep in our old camps to-night, or we'll sleep in hell!' And a moment or two after that he gave the signal to advance, and the whole line moved out, cheering like mad. History tells the rest."

What a different story history would tell of the battle of Cedar Creek if General Crook had heeded the message of the two long-since-forgotten men of the Secret Service!

There was little enough for the army to do for a time, but for the scouts there was no rest. For as many times as they left the Federal lines so are there stories—nearly all untold. Untold, because familiarity breeds contempt—they were just scoutin', like the day they shot Captain Stump. They had been in the mountains—"Oh, just some little scout, I don't remember why!"—and at a house where they had stopped they had "gathered in" a Confederate captain—Stump. It was bitterly cold that day, the roads heavy with snow; to have bound his hands would have meant that he would freeze; they put him in their midst and rode swiftly away. He was an oddly genial soul—he kept up a continual gay chatting with the men. An angry shout went up from one of the scouts; the prisoner had been caught in the act of stealing a revolver from a drowsy member of the band. He was defiant, yet laughing as he talked: he had a right—he had not surrendered, only been overpowered, and they would never get him into the Federal lines, he said.

"I'll have you killed if you try that again," Major Young told him.

It was savagely cold; the worn men, drowsy with the frost, nodded in their saddles; only the prisoner was wide awake; he rode now at Major Young's side, talking gayly, laughing at his own jests. Rowand, close behind, woke from a doze in time to see the prisoner straighten in his saddle and snatch his hand from behind Major Young's back.

"He's trying to get *your* gun," Rowand called, sharply.

Young reined in his horse with a jerk. "I told you!" he calmly said. "Ride aside, boys—plug him, Rowand!"

Half a dozen men fired on the instant. They left him lying in the snow where he fell.

This is a good place to tell the story of Sergeant Richards. Major Harry Gilmor had just been captured within his own lines—that story will be told further on. Prisoner Gilmor was being brought along by the Federal cavalry several miles behind Major Young and Rowand and the other gray-clad scouts. Rowand spied a Confederate soldier on the door-step of a house in the fields back from the road. "I'm going to get that fellow!" Rowand said. The scouts rained in their horses and watched with amused interest; they foresaw a fight. Rowand, in his gray uniform, rode over to the unsuspecting Confederate. Of all Confederate soldiers who should it be but Sergeant Richards, the man whom Rowand had captured two years before at Cheat Mountain near Monterey! The recognition was not mutual. Comedy was too scarce those days to overlook such an opportunity.

"Sergeant Richards," Rowand saluted—"Major Gilmore wants to see you." The name of Harry Gilmor was a potent one in that county.

"Wait till I get my horse," said Sergeant Richards. Rowand, chuckling, waited. Presently they rode over to the group of scouts, and Rowand, with a wink, introduced Sergeant Richards to Young: "This is the man Major Gilmor wants to see!" Young and the scouts rode on, laughing boisterously. Then suddenly from around the bend came the Federal cavalry, in their midst prisoner Gilmor. Too late, Sergeant Richards saw the trap.

"You've got me," he said, sullenly. "But what I want to know is, how did you know my name? 'twas that that fooled me so!" Rowand told him. "It's tough," said Sergeant Richards. "For two years I've been in the prison where you sent me; now, less'n a month after I'm freed, along *you* come again and send me back!"

Rowand thoughtfully rode ahead to his place with the scouts. "I don't want to send that fellow back again," he finished, when he told Major Young the story. "All right," Young said, good-naturedly.

Rowand galloped back to the cavalry: "I want this fellow. Ride aside, Richards!" No mere cavalrymen were permitted to question the doings of a scout; they turned Richards over to him. When the cavalry was out of sight he paroled his astonished prisoner—set him free on his promise to fight no more until properly exchanged.

As he told me the story Rowand laughed delightedly: "*I* hadn't the authority, by any manner o' means, to parole any one. I just did it anyhow!"

Night after night the "Jessie Scouts" rode out. The odd name they bore was an inheritance handed down to them since the days of Frémont in the Valley; in the command of this general of pomp and panoply there had been a company dear to his heart because of their rich uniforms faced with velvet, and to them, in honor of his wife, he gave the name "Jessie Scouts." Long after Frémont and his Jessie Scouts had left the Valley the name lingered in the minds of citizens and soldiery, and at last it came to be attached to those Federal scouts who wore the gray uniform. Where they rode and what they did no man now remembers— few men but themselves ever knew—and they left no written record of their service; the vague memories of those many nights are held in dusty, inner chambers of the mind, to which, long since, the tongue has lost the key.

But one night—the 21st of January—is in no danger of being forgot. It is not because they captured the enemy's picket-reserve at Woodstock that I tell it here; nor because of the desperate fight that followed in the cold winter dawn, when two hundred Confederate cavalry swooped down on them before they had left Woodstock a mile behind. Some one had blundered; the fifty "picked cavalrymen" sent for the scouts' support were but the rawest of raw recruits, who stampeded at the first fire. The twenty scouts covered their panic-stricken flight, fighting like madmen when overtaken, breaking away and pushing their jaded mounts to topmost speed until overtaken again. For ten miles the fight lasted, until at Fisher's Hill the pursuit was given up and those that were left were safe. Those that were left! The prisoners were all gone; among the cavalry there galloped wildly many riderless horses; and of the scouts one was dead, two mortally wounded, one seriously hurt, and in the hands of the enemy were four, of whom one was Cassidy, the only one dressed in full Southern gray. And it is because of Cassidy, and because of a keen-eyed Southern girl who nearly ended Rowand's story here, that I tell what follows.

He would be hanged!—Cassidy, one of the best of them all. Sheridan, in an effort to save him, sent a staff officer, Major Baird, under a flag of truce with an offer of exchange. And Rowand, wearing again his blue uniform, was sent as part of the escort, to pick up any information that might come to his trained hand; among the escort he would never be recognized—nor would he have been by men.

At Woodstock Major Baird was met by Major Grandstaff of the Seventeenth Virginia Cavalry, who received his offer of exchange.

"Cassidy was taken in our uniform inside our lines; we will hang him," he said.

"He was not in your lines, for we captured your pickets," Major Baird argued.

Grandstaff laughed. "We will hang Cassidy," he jeered.

"Then, by God! there'll be a rebel officer swing in Winchester to-night," shouted Baird.

They had met in the street of Woodstock; as they talked, a group of town-folk gathered close about them, listening in eager curiosity; there were men and many women, even some children too. Suddenly a young girl ran forward and pointed her finger almost in Rowand's face.

"Hang this one, too," she cried. "He is one of their 'Jessie Scouts.' I saw him here yesterday in gray. He is a spy—spying now!" She stood, still pointing; her shawl had fallen back and the wind was whipping her hair across her angry eyes; she, too, would serve her South—let this be "one" for her. It was a shocking surprise; it seemed long before any one moved or spoke. A Confederate cavalryman pushed his way through Grandstaff's escort; a sullen, vindictive fellow he was, with murder in his eyes.

'I'll kill him *now*; he is one of them that killed my brother yesterday," he snarled.

Rowand, glad of any distraction, drew his revolver and sprang to meet him half-way. "Step out to one side and we'll settle it, then," he challenged.

Major Grandstaff rode between them and drove them to their respective commands, then he turned angrily to Major Baird. "Is this one of your scouts—one of your spies?" he asked. It was Rowand himself who answered; the place was a bit too tight to trust any one else's wit than his own.

"You know, or ought to know, that I belong to the First West Virginia Cavalry. I was one of the thirteen men under Lieutenant Smith that charged through your command on the top of Fisher's Hill!" And this story was true, and it was one the Confederates much preferred to forget.

Grandstaff curtly closed the interview, and the Federals rode slowly back. Rowand was safe in their midst, but Tom Cassidy they had to leave behind.

Rowand was fumbling among a bundle of old letters, and I sat silent and watched eagerly; such worn, yellow letters they were—broken at all the creases, frayed along the edges; the faded words had been written in a vigorous boyish hand.

"Letters home—from the front!" he said. He picked one up and cleared his throat to read, then sat silent, staring at it in his hand. . . . The boy of nearly fifty years ago is to come back and speak again of deeds that were done but yesterday—not of what happened in the Civil War, but what he did yesterday. What weight have words written to-day to compare with those faded letters on that yellow page? "At the front!"—that front to which we cannot follow even could he lead

the way; that front where for four years—*Four Years*, you reader—
letters home were written by men with weapons in their hands, by
men with throbbing, unhealed wounds. By some this letter will be
read aright, as I and you may not read it. Old grayheads will read
and nod: the Grand Army of the Republic, they will know—they
know! . . .

MY DEAR FATHER,—I received a letter from you some days since.
As I had just written to you the same day, I thought I would wait
a few days before answering it. I have just returned from a three
days' trip to Wardensville, Moorefield, and Romney.

Our trip was a perfect success. Succeeded in capturing the
notorious Major Harry Gilmore and fifteen men of different
commands. On Tuesday I was ordered with one man to go to
Moorefield. By order of Gen. Sheridan, went to Moorefield and
returned on Thursday, reported to the General the whereabouts
of Harry Gilmore and command. The General requested me to
send in a written report to be filed. On Saturday morning a force
of cavalry (300) and twenty scouts left this place for Moorefield,
distant fifty-eight miles. Traveling all Saturday night, we arrived
at Moorefield Sunday morning just before day. Leaving the town
surrounded by a strong picket, we struck the South Fork river
road. I advanced with five scouts. Two miles from town we came
in sight of two large, fine houses: William's and Randolph's, where
Major Gilmor was supposed to be.

On coming in sight of them we started on a gallop for Randolph's house, when an order came from Major Young to go
to William's house. Dashing across the fields, we surrounded
William's house and caught one of Rosser's men. Major Young
went on to Randolph's and there caught Harry in bed. He was a
little astonished, but took things coolly. You may be sure that we
gave him no chance to escape. He is now under strong guard in
our quarters. To-morrow three of us will take him to Baltimore,
so I will have a pleasant trip. I spoke to you of going to Edenburg
and capturing the picket-post and of being followed and whipped
by a superior rebel force.

The following Sunday we again surprised them and captured the lieutenant and twenty-two men. So we more than got even with them, as they got only sixteen of our [first] party. So, you see, for the last three Sundays I have had some doing in the fighting line. On the last trip I captured two fast horses; I have now three number one horses. . . .

Your son,
ARCHIE H. ROWAND.

Not as we would have written it? Years of fighting, of marches, and of hardships make details seem trivial and commonplace; the result is the thing. His "to Moorefield, distant fifty-eight miles," sounds like a railroad journey. It was a forced march of hardship and exhaustion, in bitter cold, and over mountain roads that were alternately sheeted with ice and deep in snow-drifts. It would have been good reading for us had he described the imminent, constant peril he was in during all the lonely trip when gathering "that great essential of success— information"; the letter was not written to us; it was to the father and mother at home, and it is kinder and braver as it stands. My quarrel with his letter is in not telling how well he did his work; it was great work to have done.

Sheridan in his *Memoirs* says: "Harry Gilmor(e) was the most noted of these [West Virginia guerrillas] since the death of McNeill. . . . Thus the last link between Maryland and the Confederacy was carried a prisoner to Winchester, whence he was sent to Fort Warren. The capture of Gilmor(e) caused the disbandment of the party he had organized at the 'camp-meeting'; most of the men he had recruited returned to their homes, discouraged. . . ."

This "camp meeting," Rowand had learned, was nothing less than the rendezvous of Gilmor's band, who were reorganizing and preparing for the spring campaign. A party of about twenty young Marylanders were expected soon; the Federal scouts in their gray uniforms, by their own story, became these expected Marylanders; their desperate haste was caused by the pursuit of Yankee cavalry—no other than Colonel Whitaker's support of three hundred cavalrymen, who followed the scouts at a distance of fifteen miles. The whole country-side gave the gray-clad scouts Godspeed and much help on their way; coming back, they shot at them from the dark!

Nor does the letter tell of the quarrel between the scouts and the cavalry as to the custody of the prisoner; it ended by Major Young and his scouts angrily riding away from the cavalry with whom they had been obliged to leave him. But by the time they had reached Big Capon Springs, Rowand and Young were so fearful for the safe keeping of the prisoner that Rowand, in spite of his exhaustion from having been almost constantly in the saddle for a week, went back with three men to take charge of Gilmor; they arrived in the very nick of time. It was years afterward before they knew how critical had been the moment.

In his book, *Four Years in the Saddle*, Gilmnr says: "We were then some distance ahead of the main column . . . none in sight except the colonel and his orderly, the surgeon, H—— [Gilmor's cousin, who had been captured with him], and myself. We halted, and the orderly was sent back to hurry up a fresh guard for me. The doctor and H—— were on their horses, while the colonel and I were standing in the road in advance of them. The place, too, was a good one, on the side of a small mountain, and I made up my mind to seize the colonel before he could draw his pistol, throw him down, and make my escape. I was about three paces from him when I formed this plan, and I moved up close to carry it into effect. . . . I put my hands on H——'s horse, when suddenly up dashed four scouts."

It was the end of Maj. Harry Gilmor's military career.

"It is growing late," Rowand said. "Just time for one more letter—my big letter—and then that must be all. It is dated 'City Point, Virginia, March 13, 1865,' and it begins:

MY DEAR MOTHER,—I suppose you will be surprised to receive a letter from me from this place.

I arrived here yesterday afternoon from Gen. Sheridan's raiding forces with despatches for Gen. Grant. There were two of us. We left Gen. Sheridan at Columbia on the James River Canal, one hundred miles west of Richmond. At the time we left he had destroyed the Virginia Central Railroad between Charlottesville and Staunton; blew up both bridges of the Rivanna River near

Charlottesville. It will be impossible for the Rebels to rebuild their bridges during the war. We were forced to stay in Charlottesville two days on account of the heavy rain. Leaving there, we struck out for Lynchburg, destroying the Railroad as we went; burned the large bridge over the Tye River, eighteen miles from Lynchburg. By this time the Rebels had collected a large force of infantry and cavalry at Lynchburg. When Gen. Sheridan got all of the Rebels at Lynchburg he turned around and came north, destroying the Canal beyond repair during the war. He burned and blew up every lock, culvert, and aqueduct to Columbia—a distance of forty miles.

We left at one o'clock Saturday morning and came into our pickets near Harrison's Landing on Sunday morning at eleven o'clock. Came from there here in a special boat under charge of Gen. Sharp of Gen. Grant's staff. On arrival at Headquarters, after delivering our despatches, the Acting Adjutant-General took us around and introduced us to Mrs. Gen. Grant and several other ladies whose names I have forgotten. They had expressed a wish to see the two men that came through the Rebel lines in open day. Gen. Grant was well pleased with our success in getting through. The staff was surprised at our getting through at all. They quite lionized us last night. Several of them invited us to drink with them. We took supper with them. Then the Sanitary Commission took charge of us. We had a nice bath, good underclothes given us, and a bed that felt better than all, considering we had no sleep for forty-eight hours. We rode one hundred and forty-five miles in thirty-six hours, and walked ten miles, and came north of Richmond. Of course we came a roundabout way, or rather a zigzag way. Several times we were within ten miles of Richmond and talked to some fifty Rebels; gained valuable information. We had quite a confab with four of Gen. Lee's scouts; passed ourselves off for Gen. Reese's scouts. Being dressed in gray, they never suspected us. They, in fact, never expected to see two Yankees right in the midst of their lines in broad daylight. We were never suspected until we were within two miles of the Long Bridges, where suspicion was raised, and we were forced to leave our horses at the Bridges and paddle across in a small boat to the south side. When we came to the river there was a small boat floating down the river. I swam with my horse to the boat, got off my horse into the boat, and went back for my partner. We left our horses and made quick time across these swamps. We get into the woods before the Rebels got to the river. They, of course, got our horses—the two best in the Sixth Cavalry. The fleetness of our horses alone saved us, as we had time to get across the river before the Rebels got to the bank. Although we could see them coming down the road, they did not follow us any further than the bank of the river, as there is no boat, and they could not swim their horses across. Then we got from there to our pickets, most of the time being in the woods; the compass father gave me had done me great service, as I have a military map of Virginia. With both, it is not difficult to go the nearest way to any point. When I swam my horse I got my clothes wet and boots full of water. When I got to our pickets I was perfectly dry, but was so crippled in my feet I could scarce walk. I am all right to-day.

We are to-day quartered with Gen. Grant's scouts. They think it is the biggest and boldest scout trip of the war.

We will start back in a couple of days. We are to be sent to the White House [Landing] on the York River gunboat, and with good fast horses start for our command again.

Love to all. Hoping that these few lines will find you in good health, I remain,

Your Affectionate Son,
ARCHIE H. ROWAND."

It was as though I had heard read a crisp, succinct scenario of one act of a brilliant drama. I wanted to take the letter in my own hands and read it over and over in order to bring back such pictures—the boy on the horse in the river, struggling in pursuit of a drifting boat— a boat which only a great God could have placed in reach at such a moment. . . . The man on the shore, pistols drawn, grimly waiting, his eyes on the road, and his ears strained for the sound of galloping hoofs. . . .

I have read it again, a score of times, have planned where to amplify and detail; it is not for me to meddle with; the story is told, the pictures already painted for those who care to see.

He was talking again, and I but half heard.

"Of the wind-up of the war, when we were around Petersburg, I could tell as many stories as I've told already, but—not to-night. Every proper story should have a climax, and this it the climax of mine. I missed the Grand Review! I had to leave Washington the very day before. General Sheridan had sent for a few of us 'old' scouts—he needed us along the Rio Grande. But I didn't stay long, for I was tired of war, tired of fighting, and half sick besides. August 17, 1865, I got myself mustered out at New Orleans, and came home.

"And now," he said, good-humoredly, "I am tired again. My tongue has made a long march to-day. Look at this, if you want to, and then we must say good night." It was a copy of a letter of Sheridan's, and I give it here, because its terse, soldierly words form a greater and finer appreciation than could any words of mine:

> To the Adjutant-General of the Army, Washington, D. C.:
>
> Sir,—I respectfully recommend that a Medal of Honor be given to private Archibald H. Rowand, Jr., First W. Va. Cavalry, for gallant and meritorious service during the War.
>
> During the James River Raid, in the winter of '64–5, private Rowand was one of the two men who went from Columbia, Va., to General Grant, who was encamped at City Point.
>
> He also gave information as to the whereabouts of the Confederate scout Harry Gilmor(e) and assisted in his capture, besides making several other daring scouts through the enemy's lines. His address is L. B. 224. Pittsburg, Penna.
>
> I am, sir, very respectfully, your obedient servant,
>
> (Signed) P. H. Sheridan,
> Lieut.-Gen. U.S.A.

When I had done he handed me in silence a small morocco case. Its contents stood for so much of work, and of achievement, and of honor, that I took it almost with reverence; presently I closed the case softly and said good night.

I looked back when I had reached the door. All the room was vague in shadows except where, from the shaded lamp, there fell on the desk before him a circle of brilliant light in which he was slowly reopening the little leather case, and with him I seemed to read, graved in the dark bronze, the shining words, "FOR VALOR."

"Williams, C.S.A."

"Who had done his work, and held his peace, and had no fear to
die."

Two men come riding out of the dusk of the June day.

Why?

For nearly fifty years the reason has been sought— and never found.
They came from out the dusk, tarried for a little in the twilight, then
passed on into the great night, bearing with them the answer to a
question that will never die as long as history tells their story.

If it might have been that they had lived, and that their completed
work had been an answer to that ride up Figuer Hill, what might not the
history of the Confederacy be to-day?—that Confederacy, passionate,
hot-blooded, all-loving, all-sacrificing Confederacy, struggling to slay a
nation, travailing to bear a nation, and who died, her nation yet unborn.
They, too, died, and with them passed the answer.

The 8th of June, 1863, was nearly done. Within the earthen bastions
of Fort Granger, perched on the crest of Figuer Hill, the camp-fires
which had cooked the evening meal were dying to dull red heaps
of embers; to the west, at the foot of the bluff, a hundred and fifty
feet beneath the muzzles of Fort Granger's guns, lay the little town of
Franklin, the gray thread of the Harpeth River between. The Tennessee
hills ringed the town; the enemy were somewhere beyond the hills,
for the war had come the winter before to Tennessee. "Stone's River"
had been fought at the coming of the new year, and the Confederate

army had sullenly withdrawn to the south, to Tullahoma, thirty-six miles away. Winter had passed, spring was passing into early summer; Rosecrans sulked at Murfreesborough; Bragg, at Tullahoma, lay in wait for him. But the cavalry of the South waited for no man. They menaced everywhere, but most of all at Franklin, the Federal right—an outpost—weakened now by the withdrawal of all but two regiments and a small force of cavalry. Forrest's Cavalry ranged the country somewhere just beyond the hills; Wheeler was circling, no man of the North knew where, yet very sure were they that he would strike—somewhere.

That part of Tennessee dominated by Federal troops, the Army of the Cumberland, was in shape a fan, a partially spread fan upside down. Nashville, the base of supplies, was the pivot; from Nashville there radiated roads—pikes they call them in Tennessee—the sticks of the fan: to the southeast, to Murfreesborough—and Rosecrans with the main body of his troops; to Triune, more nearly south—the vertex of the fan; to Franklin, a little southwest—the outpost of the army. Of dark blue was this half-open fan, dark blue, dusty and worn; not jeweled, but aglitter with points of steel.

Franklin had been attacked on the 4th, and Colonel Baird had beaten off the attacking force. Since then they had waited, watchful and oppressed; expecting Forrest, dreading Wheeler, all but certain of the return of the Confederates from Spring Hill, but six miles to the south.

It was hot that night, they say—"a hot, murky night." At headquarters, up at Fort Granger, Colonel John P. Baird—of the Eighty-fifth Indiana—commandant of the post, sat at his tent door, talking with Colonel Van Vleck—that same Carter Van Vleck from whose time-yellowed letters have been plucked so many of the intimate details of this story.

Two men rode out of the dusk; two stranger officers, unattended, unescorted. Colonel Baird, in surprise, rose to greet them. They were superbly mounted; their uniforms and equipments showed them to be officers of rank and distinction. At their new merino havelocks Colonels Baird and Van Vleck must have stared; havelocks were known to officers and men, North or South, only as something "foreign," something to be looked on askance. They dismounted and strode forward, tall, straight, dignified. The elder and taller of the two introduced himself as Colonel Auton of the Army of the Potomac; his companion as Major Dunlop, assistant in the inspection of the Western troops, for which business they had been sent from Washington. They had just come from General Rosecrans at Murfreesborough. Oh yes, they had of course come through Triune, and had seen General Gordon Granger too. As this Colonel Auton talked he made more and more of an impression on Colonel Baird; it was with positive regret that he heard they must push on to Nashville that very night. There was something very engaging about this handsome, dignified young officer, with his easy grace of bearing; a note of brilliance to his conversation, which was withal frank and quiet; an indefinable air of distinction and individuality in all he said and did. Colonel Baird seems to have grown more and more interested and attracted. He urged them to stay the night with him.

It was impossible. Would Colonel Baird kindly have their passes made out? And so the order to make out the passes was given, and while they waited Colonel Auton told of their misfortune. They had lost their way from Murfreesborough, and had got down as far as Eagleville; the rebels had attacked them, had captured their servant, his (Colonel Auton's) coat and all his money; they had been pursued for a long distance and had finally escaped with difficulty. It was all very unfortunate. The distressful situation of the two officers appealed to Colonel Baird.

The passes to Nashville were brought out just then, but ware sent back for correction; they had been made out to Colonel "Orton." Auton led Colonel Baird adds; it was most unfortunate, but—they were quite without money. Could Colonel Baird oblige them with the loan of one hundred dollars apiece—any sum, then—for their immediate expenses?

Colonel Baird did not have the money, but went at once to Colonel Van Vleck, who had bean sitting smoking in incredulous silence; of him he asked the money—when they were out of earshot, that the strangers might not be embarrassed! Colonel Van Vleck's letter of October 28, 1863, gives his own reply:

I told him that I thought the men were not what they represented themselves to be; for, said I, the Government would not send two officers of their rank from the Potomac to inspect the Army of the Cumberland, when we already have more inspectors of our own than we know what to do with. Neither would Rosecrans send them from Murfreesborough through the enemy's country without an escort, and if he had done so foolish a thing, and they are what they pretend to be, why should they insist upon going to Nashville to-night without any offer to inspect the troops here, and this after such peril to get here? Again, I added, is it not strange, if true, that the rebels should be able to capture the Colonel's servant and coat and all his money and yet he get off so safely himself and with his lieutenant?

I declined to let the money go, immediately arose, and went to my own tent, saying to my surgeon, whom I found there, that the two men who were attracting so much attention by their havelocks were certainly spies.

Colonel Baird, disquieted, asked awkwardly for their orders; Colonel Auton, who seemed to have taken no offense at the request coming at such a time, readily handed them to him, and with returning composure he read—written on the long envelop:

HEADQUARTERS DEPARTMENT OF THE CUMBERLAND.
MURFREESBOROUGH, *May 30, 1863.*
All guards and outposts will immediately pass without delay Col. Auton and his assistant, Major Dunlop.
By command of Major-General Rosencrans: J. A. GARFIELD
Vol. Chief of Staff and Asst. Adjutant-Gen.

There were many papers in the envelop, and Colonel Baird gravely read them all:

Special orders ⎫   WAR DEPARTMENT,
No. 140 ⎬   ADJT. GEN'S OFFICE.
IV. . . . ⎭   WASHINGTON, *May 25, 1863.*

Col. Lawrence W. Auton, cavalry, United States Army, and acting special inspector-general, is hereby relieved from duty along the "Line of the Potomac." He will immediately proceed to the West, and minutely inspect the Department of the Ohio and the Department of the Cumberland, in accordance with special instructions Nos. 140–162 and 185, furnished him from this office and that of the Paymaster-General.

V. Major George Dunlop, assistant quartermaster, is hereby relieved from duty in this city. He will report immediately to Col. Auton for duty. By order of the Secretary of War:

E. D. Towsend,
Assistant Adjutant-General.

Col. Lawrence W. Auton, U. S. A., Special Inspector-General.

| Special orders No. 140. V. . . . } | War Department, Adjt. Gen's Dept. Washington, *May 25, 1863.* |

Major Geo. Dunlop, Assistant Quartermaster, is hereby relieved from duty in this city. He will report immediately to Colonel Auton, special inspector-general, for duty.

By order of the Secretary of War:

E. D. Townsend,
Assistant Adjutant-General.

Maj. George Dunlop, assistant quartermaster, Special Duty.

Headquarters Department of the Cumberland.
Murfreesborough, Tenn., *May 30, 1863.*

Col. L. W. Auton, Cavalry Special Inspector-General.

Colonel:—

The major-general commanding desires me to say to you that he desires that, if you can spare the time at present, that you will inspect his outposts before drawing up your report for the War Department at Washington City.

All commanding officers of outposts will aid you in this matter to the best of their ability.

The Gen. Desires me to give his respects to you.

I remain, very respectfully, your obedient servant,

J. A. Garfield,
Brig. Gen. of Vols., Chief of Staff, and Asst. Adjt. Gen.

HEADQUARTERS UNITED STATES FORCES,

NASHVILLE, TENN., *June 5, 1863.*

All officers in command of troops belonging to these forces will give every assistance in their power to Col. L. W. Auton, special inspector-general, under direct orders from the Secretary of War.

By Command of General Morgan:

JNO. PRATT,

Assistant Adjutant-General.

John P. Baird, Colonel of Volunteers, was more than satisfied; he handed the written papers back, and, it is presumed, apologized handsomely for demanding the papers of officers acting under the direct orders of the Secretary of War. He procured for them money—fifty dollars—gave them the corrected pass to Nashville, gave them the countersign, heartily wished them God-speed on their journey, and watched them ride away into the night. It was quite dark now—a hint in the air already of the mist that was later to envelop Franklin in its dank gray mantle; they were swallowed up in the darkness almost instantly; it seemed that the darkness blotted out the very sound of the hoof-falls of the horses. And then Colonel Baird thought for the first time of forgery! He was alone there in front of his tent—no one can ever know, only guess at—the shock of the thought that, in spite of the convincing papers, the men might be the destructive wedge of the Confederate army. Imagine his position—the anguish of indecision as vital second followed second and still he could not decide. The men, if Federal officers, were officers of importance who could not be lightly ordered back, virtually under arrest; he had seen the papers once—he had no grounds for calling them back to see them again. He must have grown more confused—there in the dark with no one to see. Perhaps he was an imaginative man; perhaps he saw the men at that very moment presenting *his* past to the advance pickets out there at Spencer's Creek on the Nashville pike; saw the pickets salute, and the men ride on—where? There must have been always that subconscious thought, "How far have they got by now?" And still he had not decided what to do.

Col. Louis D. Watkins, colonel of the Sixth Kentucky Cavalry, must have been surprised at the greeting from his superior officer, as he approached headquarters just then. Colonel Watkins was an officer of the "old" army—a regular; Colonel Baird tensely told him the story, his own suspicions, Van Vleck's outspoken charge, then thrust upon him the question. Colonel Watkins was very grave; some things looked very wrong, he said. Colonel Baird's indecision passed: the men must be brought back, their paper re-examined. "Tell them there are despatches to be sent to Nashville, tell them anything—bring them back, Watkins," he cried. Colonel Watkins was already mounting; with his orderly he galloped away. Colonel Van Vleck's letter tells that Colonel Baird "came immediately to see me, and was much excited, and asked me again if I thought they were spies. I replied that I did, and he jumped on his horse and followed Colonel Watkins."

Many of the newspapers of that day—very brown and fragile they are, in texture and in truth!—tell lurid tales of the pursuers and the pursued riding "with lightning speed" through the black night; of the "plan that was laid for the orderly to unsling his carbine, and if, when he (the Colonel) halted them, they showed any suspicious motions to fire on them without waiting for an order." How Colonel Auton, when overtaken, "like Major André, for an instant lost his presence of mind. He laid his hand on his pistol!"

Colonel Watkins overtook the two riding leisurely along, before they had reached the outpost at Spencer's Creek. They readily consented to return; if they were surprised that an officer of Colonel Watkins's rank had been sent posting after them to carry such a message, they did not show their surprise. The cavalry camp was of course outside that of the infantry. At Colonel Watkins's quarters he suggested that they wait until the despatches were brought to them—they had twenty miles to ride to Nashville, no use to ride clear to headquarters for the despatches— more excuses, probably equally poor. They thanked Colonel Watkins and entered his tent. Colonel Watkins rode on to consult with Colonel Baird. After a time, becoming impatient and restless, Colonel Auton went to the door of the tent and found that he and Major Dunlop were prisoners; the tent was surrounded by sentries who would not let him pass. Presently they were taken under guard to Headquarters and brought before Colonel Baird. It must have been a strange, unhappy meeting for them all, a meeting of which there is no record, one which can be pictured only in the mind. Colonel Auton and Major Dunlop, insulted, humiliated, flushed with anger at the indignity placed upon them; perhaps voluble and eloquent, threatening; more likely, dignified and coldly distant to the uneasy officers who faced them, challenging their word.

The papers were examined again, minutely. The form and phraseology of the papers were beyond cavil: there was shown to be a reason for new inspectors in the West; they had but just been relieved of duty in the East; the department commander apparently had accepted the detail, and had assigned them to duties which accorded with the spirit of the instructions from army headquarters. It was all very regular so far as logic and circumstance went.

The newspapers make much of the fact that the papers were not written on the regular form-paper used by the War Department; that point made little impression on Colonels Baird and Watkins, who were as much in doubt as before; Colonel Baird doggedly held them as prisoners still. In his impatience and anxiety he himself climbed to the signal station back of Fort Granger, in order to receive at the first reading the reply to his message which he was about to send to Triune. The mist was fast thickening to fog; they stood in a blur of pale, dead, unwavering light; the signalman with his torch wig-wagged the question, and then they waited in the heavy silence of the fog. The man at the telescope stared into a gray void, but presently he flung up his hand for silence and jerkily read off the message: Triune could not understand, but would send Lieutenant Wharton to investigate. Colonel Baird dictated another message; the signal officer looked anxiously at the fog; if Triune saw and answered, it could not be seen there on the fog-shrouded hilltop at Franklin. Colonel Baird went down to the fort again. Triune was nearly fifteen miles away, and Lieutenant Wharton could not arrive for several hours. There was nothing to do now but lay the matter before General Rosecrans at Murfreesborough; perhaps he had hoped that it would be unnecessary to report such an occurrence to his commanding officer; there was nothing else for it now. He sent the following telegram, the first of that singular series of messages sent and received that night:

FRANKLIN, *June 8, 1863.*

Brigadier-General Garfield, Chief of Staff:

Is there any such inspector-general as Lawrence Orton, colonel
U. S. Army, and assistant, Major Dunlop? If so, please describe
their personal appearance, and answer immediately.

J. P. BAIRD,
Colonel, Commanding Post.

There is no time given on this message—probably it was by then nine
or nine-thirty. Ten o'clock, half past ten, eleven, and no answer to the
question. It seems to have aroused little interest at Murfreesborough; it
was grudgingly answered, and was delayed in getting on the wire.

Lieutenant Wharton of Triune had not yet arrived. It was an anxious
interval. What took place during the wait? It is most likely that Colonel
Auton or Orton—already there seems to have arisen a doubt as to
which name was correct—and his assistant remained under guard at
headquarters; it is probable that they were shown every courtesy except
that of liberty during the long and anxious wait. When Colonel Baird
could stand the suspense no longer he wired a detailed account of
the case:

FRANKLIN, *June 8, 1863*—11:30 P.M.

[Brigadier-General Garfield:]

Two men came in camp about dark, dressed in our uniform,
with horses and equipments to correspond, saying that they were
Colonel Orton, inspector-general, and Major Dunlop, assistant,
having an order from Adjutant-General Townsend and your order
to inspect all posts, but their conduct was so singular that we
have arrested them, and they insisted that it was important to go
to Nashville to-night. The one representing himself as Colonel
Orton is probably a regular officer of old army, but Colonel
Watkins, commanding cavalry here, in whom I have the utmost
confidence, is of opinion that they are spies, who have either
forged or captured their orders. They can give no consistent
account of their conduct.

I want you to answer immediately my last despatch. It takes so
long to get an answer from General (Gordon) Granger, at Triune,

by signal, that I telegraphed General (R. S.) Granger, at Nashville, for information. I also signaled General Gordon Granger. If these men are spies, it seems to me that it is important that I should know it, because Forrest must be awaiting their progress.

I am, General, your obedient servant,

J. P. BAIRD,

Colonel, Commanding Post.

Within fifteen minutes there came the answer to the first despatch, and either just preceding it or just following it, Lieutenant Wharton of Triune. It must have been a dramatic moment when the prisoners rose to face him. He looked at them steadily; no one spoke or moved for a very long time. They had not been at Triune that afternoon, nor ever, he said. He examined the papers one by one, and one by one pronounced them beyond all doubt forgeries. Why he could do so so positively I do not know. This telegram was scarce needed, but it, too, dragged them down:

HEADQUARTERS DEPARTMENT OF THE CUMBERLAND.

MURFREESBOROUGH, *June* 8—10:15 P.M.

Colonel J. P. Baird, Franklin:

These are no such men as Insp. Gen. Lawrence Orton, Colonel U. S. Army, and Assistant Major Dunlop, is this army, nor in any army, so far as we know. Why do you ask?

J. A. GARFIELD,

Brigadier-General & Chief of Staff.

There is a note of irritation, a phrase of ridicule in the message, as of a man who answers the inconsequential questionings of a child; "nor in any army"!—a very different message from the terse, sharp—almost savage— military order which was to follow it.

There *is* something almost boyish about Colonel Baird, particularly in the message which he rushed to send. It is a voluble, jubilant composition, a little triumphant at his vindication (perhaps he had felt the sting in the tone of the despatch from Murfreesborough). Perhaps it is just the effect of the reaction that came when he found that he had not made a serious mistake, but instead had made an important capture. He had not yet begun to consider the men, nor what he would be called upon to do. Unless the date is in error, the message must have been sent before midnight—showing that events had moved swiftly there at Headquarters tent.

FRANKLIN, *June 8, 1863.*

Gen. Garfield, Chief of Staff:

I had just sent you an explanation of my first dispatch when I received your dispatch. When your dispatch came, they owned up as being a rebel colonel and lieutenant in rebel army. Colonel Orton, by name, but in fact Williams, first on General Scott's staff, of Second Cavalry, Regular Army. Their ruse was nearly successful on me, as I did not know the handwriting of my commanding officer, and am much indebted to Colonel Watkins, Sixth Kentucky Cavalry, for their detention, and Lieut. Whartan, of Granger's staff, for the detection of forgery of papers. As these men don't deny their guilt, what shall I do with them? My bile is stirred, and some hanging would do me good.

I communicate with you, because I can get an answer so much sooner than by signal, but I will keep General Granger posted. I will telegraph you again in a short time, as we are trying to find out, and believe there is an attack contemplated in the morning. If Watkins gets anything out of Orton I will let you know.

I am, General, your obedient servant,

J. P. BAIRD,
Colonel, Commanding.

The telegram (in answer to his second message) that was handed him almost immediately after he had penned this remarkable despatch must have come like a dash of icy water in the face—so stern and harsh it is, so insistent upon such brutal haste:

HEADQUARTERS DEPARTMENT OF THE CUMBERLAND.
MURFREESBOROUGH, *June 8*—12:00 P.M.

Colonel J. P. Baird, Franklin:

The two men are no doubt spies. Call a drumhead court martial to-night and if they are found to be spies, hang them before morning, without fail. No such men have been accredited from these headquarters.

J. A. GARFIELD,

Brigadier-General & Chief of Staff.

It must have been after the sending of Colonel Baird's last despatch that the search of the persons of the two Confederate officers was made—else the evidence discovered would have been contained in the message. There was found on their hatbands, concealed by the havelocks, their names and their rank in the Confederate army. On one sword was etched, "Lieutenant Walter G. Peter, C.S.A." Of the other, Williams's, Colonel Van Vleck writes: "He had a fine sword with a presentation inscription on it, which gave his name, if I remember rightly, as 'Colonel L. O. Williams.' It was from some Confederate general, but I forget who. He had also $1,500, Confederate money, or thereabouts, a silver cup, and quite a number of small trinkets. Whether there was a watch I cannot now remember." Were men ever so overwhelmed by the weight of evidence?

Of the hours that passed from midnight to three o'clock there is nowhere an account. It was the twilight that preceded the fall of utter darkness; a period to the excitement that had just passed; harder even than the short hours which were to follow, when uncertainty was at an end.

They were cousins, these two—playmates as children, comrades in their young manhood; Colonel Williams would be twenty-five within the month, Lieutenant Peter was but twenty-one. The one had led always, the other had gladly always followed, followed with boyish admiration that was scare less than hero-worship. Those who knew them all their short young lives tell to-day of the devotion of Lieutenant Peter to his brilliant, accomplished, fearless cousin, Orton. It is true beyond all doubt that Lieutenant Peter had not known the purpose, the real mission, on which he and Colonel Williams had entered the Federal lines; it is probable that he never knew. Orton had led, and he had followed.

This is no time for imaginative writing—of what their thoughts must have been; of what they may have said or done. They were left alone, undisturbed by the Federal officers; they are to be left alone now.

Orderlies hurried through the sleeping camp, stopping here and there to rouse some listed officer: "The Colonel orders, sir, that you assemble at once at Headquarters for drumhead court." . . . "The Colonel orders, sir, that you assemble at once at Headquarters for drumhead court," the order was monotonously repeated here and there. The swiftest and most terrible of all courts of law, the midnight drumhead court martial, convened. Officers greeted one another with voices unconsciously lowered; the chairs as they were drawn up to the table made a great scraping on the bare board floor. One of the lamps went out, and an orderly placed a row of lighted candles along the edge of the long table; the row of tiny flames threw bizarre, wavering shadows on faces and walls, threw garish shimmers of light on side-arms and brass buttons; burned with the solemnity of waxen tapers on an altar of sacrifice; then flickered and danced again.

The prisoners were brought in. The trial began; the trial of spies who had made no attempt to gain information, who had no drawings of fortifications, who had naught to condemn them but an intention that was never known.

In the Official Records of the the Union and Confederate Armies, volume XXIII, Part II, pages 424, 425, thus stands the record of their trial:

RECORD OF THE MILITARY COMMISSION.

HEADQUARTERS POST, FRANKLIN, JUNE 9, 1863.

Before a court of commission assembled by virtue of the following order:

HEADQUARTERS POST OF FRANKLIN,
June 9—3:00 A.M.

A court of commission is hereby called, in pursuance of orders from Major-General Rosecrans, to try Colonel Williams and Lieutenant Peter, of rebel forces, on charge of being spies, the court to sit immediately, at headquarters of the post.

Detail for Court:—Colonel Jordan, Ninth Pennsylvania Cavalry, President; Lieutenant-Colonel Van Vleck, Seventy-eighth

Infantry; Lieutenant-Colonel Hoblitzel, Fifth Kentucky Cavalry; Captain Crawford, Eighty-fifth Indiana Infantry, and Lieutenant Wharton, Judge Advocate.

By order of J. P. Baird, colonel commanding post.

The court and judge advocate having been duly sworn according to military law, the prisoners were arraigned upon the following charges:

Charges and specifications against Col. Lawrence Auton, alias Williams, and Lieut. Walter G. Peter, officers in rebel forces.

Charges:—being spies.

Specifications:—In this, that said Col. Lawrence Auton, alias Williams, and Lieut. Walter G. Peter, officers in the so-called Confederate States of America, did, on the 8th day of June, 1863, come inside the lines of the Army of the United States at Franklin, Tennessee, wearing the uniform of Federal officers, with a pass purporting to be signed by Major-General Rosecrans, commanding department of the Cumberland, and represented to Col. J. P. Baird, commanding post of Franklin, that they were in the service of the United States; all this for the purpose of getting information of the strength of the United States forces and conveying it to the enemies of the United States now in arms against the United States Government.

E. C. DAVIS,

Captain Company G, Eighty-fifth Indiana Infantry.

Some evidence having been heard in support of the charge and specifications, the prisoners made the following statement:

That they came inside the lines of the United States Army, at Franklin, Tenn., about dark on the 8th day of June, 1863, wearing the uniform they then had on their persons, which was that of Federal officers; that they went to the headquarters of Col. J. P. Baird, commanding forces at Franklin, and represented to him that they were Colonel Auton, Inspector, just sent from Washington City to overlook the inspection of the several departments of the West, and Major Dunlop, his assistant, and exhibited to him an order from Adjutant-General Townsend assigning him to that duty, an order from Major-General Rosecrans, countersigned by Brigadier-General Garfield, chief of staff, asking him to inspect his outposts, and a pass through all lines from General Rosecrans; that he told Colonel Baird he had missed the road from Murfreesborough to this point, got too near Eagleville and ran into rebel pickets, had his orderly shot, and lost his coat containing his money; that he wanted some money and a pass to Nashville; that when arrested by Colonel Watkins, Sixth Kentucky Cavalry, after examination they admitted they were in the rebel army, and that his (the colonel's) true name was Lawrence Orton Williams; that he had been in the Second Regular Cavalry, Army of the United States once, on General Scott's staff in Mexico, and was now a colonel in the rebel army, and Lieutenant Peter was his adjutant; that he came into our lines knowing his fate, if taken, but asking mercy for his adjutant.

The court having maturely considered the case, after hearing all the evidence, together with the statements of the prisoners, do find them, viz., Col. Lawrence Auton Williams and Lieut. Walter G. Peter, officers of the Confederate Army, guilty of the charge of being spies, found within the lines of the United States Army at Franklin, Tennessee, on the 8th day of June, 1863.

THOS. J. JORDAN,
Colonel Ninth Pennsylvania Cavalry, President of the Commission.

HENRY C. WHARTON,
Lieutenant of Engineers, Judge-Advocate.

The trial ended. Thus it stands on the record.

In the oft-quoted letter to Colonel Williams's sister, Col. Carter Van Vleck, member of the court, writes:

The court was called together and your brother freely confessed all except as to the object of his mission, which to this day is a most mysterious secret to us all. In course of a conversation with Colonel Watkins your brother said to him, "Why, Watkins, you know me. We served in the same regiment of the United States

Army. I am he that was Lieutenant Williams." Watkins at once recognized him.

In his remarks to the court your brother said that he had undertaken the enterprise with his eyes open and knew what his fate must be if he was discovered, but said that the value of the prize at which he grasped fully justified the fearful hazard he had made to gain it, and acknowledged the entire justice of his sentence, and said that he had no complaint whatever to make. He at no time denied being a spy, but only denied that he had designs against Franklin. I believe that he said the truth; he had a greater prize in view. He asked for mercy for Lieut. Peter on account of his youth and because he was ignorant of the objects or dangers of the mission, but said that he had no right to ask for mercy for himself, as he knew what his fate must be if convicted, before he entered upon his mission. . . . Your brother did say that he intended to have gone to Europe immediately if he had been successful in his undertaking.

The trial had lasted scarce an hour; when it was at an end Colonel Baird sent another telegram to his commanding officer—a very different message from the thoughtless, exultant one, with its flippant, "a little hanging would do me good"—which had just preceded it:

FRANKLIN, *June 9, 1863.*

Gen. Garfield, Chief of Staff:

Colonel Watkins says Colonel Williams is a first cousin of General Robert E. Lee, and he says so. He has been chief of artillery on Bragg's staff.

We are consulting. Must I hang him? If you can direct me to send him somewhere else, I would like it; but, if not, or I do not hear from you, they will be executed. This dispatch is written at the request of Colonel Watkins, who detained the prisoners. We are prepared for a fight.

J. P. BAIRD,
Colonel, Commanding.

Within the hour there came back the relentless decree:

HEADQUARTERS DEPARTMENT OF THE CUMBERLAND.
MURFRESSBOROUGH, *June 9, 1863*—4:40 A.M.

Col. J. P. Baird, Franklin:

The general commanding directs that the two spies, if found guilty, be hung at once, thus placing it beyond the possibility of Forrest's profiting by the information they have gained.

FRANK S. BOND,
Major and Aide-de-camp.

In the face of such an order Colonel Baird could only bow his head. Day was dawning. Loud, clear bugles shrilled the reveille from all quarters of the camp; thin blue spirals rose above rekindled embers; men, fresh from their night's rest, streamed out of tent and hut, and stretched and shook themselves and began the old life anew under the brightening sky. They made the camp hum and buzz with shouted jests and greetings and the rough, loud banterings of soldiers. Then grim Rumor rose like a carrion bird and flapped heavily from group to group, and where Rumor had paused in its passing, men's voices grew less loud, and they turned and stared often at headquarters with curiousness and vague trouble in their eyes. Colonel Baird sat haggard and listless at his table, waiting. Presently an orderly, followed by the chaplain, appeared. He was the Rev. Robert Taylor, chaplain of the Seventy-eighth Illinois, and he too has written to the sister of Colonel Williams—kindly, gentle letters they are, full of whatever grains of comfort there might be. He tells how he was awakened at dawn and ordered to report immediately to headquarters, and how he learned there for the first time what had happened while he slept. The prisoners had asked for him, Colonel Baird said.

It must have been that Colonel Williams and Lieutenant Peter had been taken away when their examination was at an end, and had not been brought in again after the deliberations of the court, for Chaplain Taylor in a letter writes:

Colonel Baird went with me, introduced me, and announced to them their sentence. They received the announcement with sadness, but with great dignity and composure. When the sentence had been announced to them your brother asked Colonel

B. whether or not this sentence would be read to them in due form as the sentence of a court martial, and I think he added, "The charge of being spies we deny."

They asked if they might write a few letters, and when paper and pens were brought Chaplain Taylor and Colonel Baird withdrew for a short time.

To his sister, Colonel Williams began his letter: "Do not believe that I am a spy; with my dying breath I deny the charge."

The rest of the letter is made up of hurried messages to family and friends—concise statements of minor business matters; no sighings, no complaints against Fate.

It is but a note, written on one side of a small sheet, inscribed in a firm, unfaltering hand. There was a letter to General Bragg, of which I have not seen even a copy, but it, too, could have been but a note of farewell; all the letters, of necessity, had to be carefully read before sending through the lines. The last letter, of which the copy is in a woman's hand, was written to the lady who had promised to be his wife. History has the right only to these words:

When this reaches you I will be no more. Had I succeeded I would have been able to marry you in Europe in a month. The fate of war has decided against us. I have been condemned as a spy—you know I am not.

When the brief letters were finished they asked for Colonel Baird again, and when he had come Colonel Williams asked if he might send a telegram to General Rosecrans, who had long ago known his father. Baird eagerly clutched at the straw of hope, and together they wrote the message:

FRANKLIN, *June 9, 1863.*

General Garfield, Chief of Staff:

Will you not have any clemency for the son of Captain Williams, who fell at Monterey, Mexico? As my dying speech, I protest our innocence as spies. Save also my friend,

LAWRENCE W. ORTON (formerly W. Orton Williams).

I send this as a dying request. The men are condemned, and
we are preparing for execution. They also prefer to be shot. If you
can answer before I get ready, do.

                                                    J. P. BAIRD.

No answer ever came.

In the *United Service Magazine* of twenty years ago Col. William
F. Prosser writes of General Rosecrans in relation to this unanswered
telegram:

> Being a man of tender and sympathetic feeling, he was somewhat
> apprehensive that his judgment might be overcome by appeals
> for mercy; therefore when he retired to his sleeping apartment,
> between three and four o'clock in the morning, he gave positive
> instructions to General Garfield to have his former orders carried
> out promptly, with directions at the same time not to bring him
> any more telegrams, dispatches, or appeals of any kind whatever
> on the subject.

Pilate had washed his hands.

Hours passed, restless, anxious hours for Colonel Baird; hoping
against hope, he yet waited for an answer to his message. When at
last he gave up, he already risked a severe reprimand; his mercy and
pity could do no more. He gave the order for the execution, and the
order was obeyed.

In the forty-nine years that have passed since that June morning
there have appeared a score of times in newspaper columns the letters
of officers and men who that day were formed in hollow square down
by the Harpeth River, and who stood stern and silent till the work was
done. In all these accounts there is not one but has (crudely expressed
at times) its note of respect and admiration and pity. But of them all, I
turn once again to the yellowed leaves of Col. Carter Van Vleck's letter,
and copy his words:

> Your brother died with the courage of a true hero. He stepped
> upon the scaffold with as much composure as though he had
> gone there to address the multitude. There was no faltering in his

step, no tremor in his nerves. He thanked the officers for his kind treatment, and said that he had no complaint to make; that one of the cruel fates of war had befallen him, and he would submit to it like a man. On the scaffold the unfortunate men embraced each other and Lieutenant Peter sobbed and said: "Oh, Colonel, have we come to this!" Your brother at once checked him by saying, "Let us die like men." And they did die like men, with the heartfelt sympathy of every man who saw them die.

FRANKLIN, *June 9, 1863.*

General Garfield, Chief of Staff:

The men have been tried, found guilty and executed, in compliance with your order. There is no appearance of enemy yet.

I am, ever your obedient servant,

J. P. BAIRD, Colonel, Commanding Post.

In the afternoon, when he had somewhat regained his composure, Colonel Baird sent the last despatch of this strange series; a message which, had it been sent before, and which, had it been heeded, might have given time for the solving of a mystery which will now never be solved:

FRANKLIN, *June 9, 1863.*

Brigadier-General Garfield:

Dispatch received of rebel account of fight. No truth in it. The officers I executed this morning, in my opinion, were not ordinary spies, and had some mission more important than finding out my situation.

They came near dark, asked no questions about forces, and did not attempt to inspect works, and, after they confessed, insisted they were not spies, in the ordinary sense, and that they wanted no information about this place. Said they were going to Canada and something about Europe; not clear. We found on them memorandum of commanding officers and their assistant adjutant-generals in Northern States. Though they admitted the justice of the sentence and died like soldiers, they would not

disclose their true object. Their conduct was very singular indeed;
I can make nothing of it.

> I am, General,
> J. P. BAIRD,
> Colonel, Commanding.

There seems to have been no one who ever believed these young
officers to have been common spies. In his weekly letters to the New
York *Herald,* Mr. W. F. G. Shanks, war correspondent in the field with
the Army of the Cumberland, writes:

> They did not explain upon what grounds they made the plea of
> not being spies under these circumstances. It is to be regretted that
> they did not, as it might have explained their reason for coming
> into our lines. No such unimportant matter as a proposed attack
> on Franklin could have induced two officers of their rank and
> character to undertake so hazardous an enterprise.
>
> No plausible reasons have been given explaining the expedition
> upon which these men were engaged; probably will never be
> explained. Were not anxious in regard to works and troops at
> Franklin. . . . Some have imagined that their mission was one
> to the copperheads of the North. . . . These are the first rebel
> officers hung during the war. The case will form a precedent.
> Col. Baird regrets that the trial was not more deliberate, but
> the Government has approved and sustained the action. The
> President has telegraphed to General Rosecrans his approval of
> the prompt action.

This same correspondent tells of the sending from Murfreesborough
of the effects of Colonel Williams and Lieutenant Peter to the Confederate lines. The flag of truce was halted eight miles out by the vedettes of
the Fifty-first Alabama Mounted Infantry, Lieutenant-Colonel Webb
commanding.

In the course of informal conversation one of the Confederate officers said that he was sorry for Orton, but he had played the spy, and
had been hung according to military law.

Colonel Webb curtly corrected him, and said that nothing of the sort
was admitted. He abruptly closed the conversation. It seems useless to

consider Franklin as aught but a stepping-stone on which they tripped and fell.

There are three statements in this article which must be corrected here. Lawrence Orton Williams was not his name; why he changed it from William Orton Williams is another mystery which will never be revealed; it was a change which has puzzled and distressed relatives and friends to this day. Only four of the many letters he wrote his sister during the war ever got through the lines. In one of them, the letter of December 19, 1862, he makes this single unexplained allusion to the change. He closes: . . . "your affectionate brother (I have changed my name), Lawrence Williams Orton."

Above all, that he should have taken the given name of his elder brother, serving as major in the Federal army, caused endless confusion in newspapers, North and South. An incident which may have been the cause of this change of name occurred while Colonel Williams was serving under Bishop-General Polk, shortly before Shiloh. Colonel Williams with his strict ideas of military discipline—new and distasteful to volunteer soldiers—became involved with a private, and the result was the death of the soldier.

Colonel Williams's report of the affair concluded with the words: "For his ignorance, I pitied him; for his insolence, I forgave him; for his insubordination, I slew him."[1] An investigation was commenced, but in the confusion resulting from the sudden evacuation of Columbus, Kentucky, it was dropped; Colonel (then Captain) Williams was merely transferred to another command. But the affair had made him so unpopular with the soldiers that, in spite of his gallantry soon after at Shiloh, for which he was twice mentioned in general orders, when he was assigned to the colonelcy of a cavalry regiment under General Van Dorn, the officers and men of this new command refused to serve under him, and he was again transferred.

Perhaps it was then that he changed his name. That it had not been changed until then is evidenced by his sword. In the Confederate correspondence published in the Official Records is the report of Col. J. J. Neely, of Forrest's Cavalry—June 29, 1864: "A sabre was captured

---

[1] From Colonel (now Major-General) Wm. H. Carter's *From Yorktown to Santiago with the Sixth United States Cavalry.*

[La Fayette, Georgia] by Captain Deberry . . . bearing the inscription: 'W. Orton Williams, C.S.A., Chief of Artillery, Shiloh, April 6, 1862.' "

How came this sword with the Federals? It was not the sword that he wore at Franklin, and which he is said to have presented to Colonel Watkins—Colonel Van Vleck would never have forgotten such an inscription as that. His very sword had its mystery.

Colonel Williams was not a first cousin of General Robert E. Lee, but of General Lee's wife, who was of the Custis family—a direct descendant of Martha Washington.

Nor was Colonel Williams on General Scott's staff in Mexico. His father fell at the head of his column at Monterey; the son was on the staff of General Scott, commander-in-chief of the army, in Washington in 1861. Because of his continued visits to Arlington—where his sister made her home—after General Robert E. Lee had joined the Confederacy, he was sent to Governors Island, New York, and kept there until any information he might have had to aid the Confederacy was rendered useless by time. June 10, 1861, he resigned, to swing his sword for the South, and to die at Franklin, Tennessee, as a spy.

What was his mission? He had failed; why did he not dignify his act by giving it the importance it deserved? Orton Williams's bravery was more than physical—he was willing to do more than die for his Cause; he was willing to live through the pages that men call History as a spy rather than block the pathway of the man, and the man, and the man after that one, if need be, who he knew would follow him. Who knew his mission? Not his companion; not General Joe Wheeler, on whose staff he had been but two months; not even General Bragg, to whom he wrote farewell—not if the press of that day may be believed. The daily Richmond *Examiner* of July 3, 1863, in commenting bitterly on the case, says:

> None of our commanders in Tennessee are aware of any such mission being undertaken by these officers, which could only have been at the suggestion of a superior officer, or certainly with some knowledge on his part of the object of such an enterprise within the enemy's lines.

The Chattanooga *Rebel* of June 17, 1863:

> Lawrence Orton Williams was one of the most honorable officers in this service. . . . The expedition that ended so tragically was undertaken on his own account and was unknown to his brother officers.

To judge by the following letter, Colonel Williams was known to Judah P. Benjamin, then Secretary of War of the Confederacy, of whose letter, found among the Confederate Correspondence, this is a part:

> Sir: I have received your several communications from Capt. Williams, and he has been detained a day or two to enable us to obtain such information of the late engagement at Fort Donelson and the movement of our troops as would authorize a definite decision as to our future movements. (To General Polk at Columbus, Ky. Feb. 20, '62.)

Thirty-four years later there came to light, among a dead man's private letters, another letter of Secretary Benjamin's (at that time Secretary of State), a letter written but three weeks after Colonel Williams died at Franklin, of which this is a part and substance (published in the Richmond *Times* of July 16, 1896, republished in the Papers of the Southern Historical Society, Vol. XXIV):

> DEPARTMENT OF STATE, RICHMOND, *July 3, 1863.*
> [To Lieutenant J. L. Capston.]
> Sir:
> You have, in accordance with your proposal made to this department, been detailed by the Secretary of War for special service under my orders. The duty which is proposed to entrust to you is that of a private and confidential agent of this government, for the purpose of proceeding to Ireland, and there using all legitimate means to enlighten the population as to the true nature and character of the contest now waged in this continent, with the view of defeating the attempts made by the agents of the United States to obtain in Ireland recruits for their army.

It is understood that under the guise of assisting needy persons to emigrate, a regular organization has been formed of agents in Ireland who leave untried no methods of deceiving the laboring population into emigrating for the ostensible purpose of seeking employment in the United States, but really for recruiting in the Federal armies. . . .

Throw yourself as much as possible into close communication with the people where the agents of our enemies are at work. Inform them, by every means you can devise, of the true purpose of those who seek to induce them to emigrate. Explain to them the nature of the warfare which is carried on here. Picture to them the fate of their unhappy countrymen, who have already fallen victims to the arts of the Federals. Relate to them the story of Meagher's Brigade, its formation and its fate. Explain to them that they will be called on to meet Irishmen in battle, and thus to imbrue their hands in the blood of their own friends, and perhaps kinsmen, in a quarrel which does not concern them, and in which all the feelings of a common humanity should induce them to refuse taking part against us. Contrast the policy of the Federal and Confederate states. . . .

In this war such has been the hatred of the New England Puritans to Irishmen and Catholics, that in several instances the chapels and places of worship of the Irish Catholics have been burnt or shamefully desecrated by the regiments of volunteers from New England. These facts have been published in Northern papers, take the New York *Freeman's Journal,* and you will see shocking details, not coming from Confederate sources, but from the officers of the United States themselves.

Lay all these matters fully before the people who are now called on to join these ferocious persecuters in the destruction of this nation. . . .

I am, sir, respectfully,
Your obedient servant,
(Signed) J. P. BENJAMIN,
Secretary of State.

Colonel Williams may not have been Lieutenant Capston's predecessor, but who knows but that he too had had a personal letter—which was not a War Department order—from Judah P. Benjamin, Secretary of State of the Confederacy?

Colonel Williams went to Franklin, Tennessee, where he was hanged. I believe that that is all which we shall ever know.

Miss Van Lew

On a bronze tablet set in the face of a great gray stone in the Shockhoe Hill Cemetery of Richmond, Virginia, there is carved the inscription:

Elizabeth L. Van Lew.

1818.   *1900.*

She risked everything that is dear to man—friends, fortune, comfort, health, life itself, all for the one absorbing desire of her heart—that slavery might be abolished and the Union preserved.

---

*This Boulder
from the Capitol Hill in Boston is a tribute from Massachusetts friends.*

Miss Van Lew, a Richmond woman, was a spy for the Federal government—the most important spy of the Rebellion, inasmuch as her work merited General Grant's tribute, "You have sent me the most valuable information received from Richmond during the war." For four long years, without respite, she faced death to obtain that information; day after day suspected, spied upon, threatened, persecuted, she worked with a courage far higher than the excitement-mad valor of battle-fields.

The greater part of the military information received from Richmond by the Army of the Potomac was collected and transmitted by Miss Van Lew. She established five secret stations for forwarding her cipher despatches—a chain of relay points whose farther end was the headquarters of General George H. Sharpe (the authority for these statements), Chief of the Bureau of Military Information, but the Richmond end of the chain was the old Van Lew mansion. There she received and harbored the secret agents who stole in from the Federal army; when no Federal agents could reach her she sent her own servants as messengers through the Confederate armies. There, in the Van Lew house in the heart of Richmond, she concealed many of the escaped Union prisoners from Castle Thunder, the Libby, and Belle Isle; there she planned aid for those who remained in the prisons, to whom she sent or carried food and books and clothing; for their relief she poured out her money—thousands of dollars—until all her convertible property was gone. Clerks in the Confederate War and Navy departments were in her confidence; counsel for Union sympathizers on trial by the Confederacy were employed by her money; for a long, long time she represented all that was left of the power of the United States government in the city of Richmond.

These statements of General Sharpe's were made in a letter which was written to recommend that Miss Van Lew be reimbursed by the government to the amount of $15,000; the money was never collected; she had given no thought to recompense, but only "that slavery might be abolished and the Union preserved"—for that she had risked "all that is dear to man"; and all that she risked—"friends, fortune, comfort, all but life itself"—she lost.

This is her story. It is written from the remains of her diary, which, because of its menace, lay for months buried in the ground, and which lost many pages expurgated by its author as being unsafe even there; other manuscript of hers there is—more than a thousand pages, an unpublished volume, part history, part treatise, here and there personal memoir; it is written from old letters; from newspapers—Northern and Southern; from the Official Records of the Union and Confederate Armies; and from the statements of men and women who knew Miss Van Lew long ago.

There are faded pages which tell of her childhood, how she was sent North to school—to Philadelphia, her mother's early home. There, a school-girl, she accepted those principles which were to determine the course of her whole life; she went back at last to Virginia an unwavering abolitionist. She gave freedom to nine of the Van Lew slaves; others were bought, that they might be reunited with a husband or a wife already in the Van Lew possession.

There are tales of the state and splendor in which the family lived, in the now famous Van Lew mansion (which still stands on Church Hill, the highest of the seven hills of Richmond). There were balls and receptions in the great house, garden-parties in the wonderful gardens, journeyings in the coach drawn by six snowy horses to the White Sulphur Springs and other resorts of the day. Great men and distinguished families were their guests and intimates—Bishop Moore and Chief Justice Marshall, the Lees, the Robinsons, Wickhams, Adamses, Cabels, Marshalls, Carringtons; Fredrika Bremer, the Swedish novelist, visited at the Van Lew house and wrote of it and its household in her *Homes in the New World;* Jenny Lind at the height of her career sang in the great parlor; Edgar Allan Poe there read aloud "The Raven"; and, after an interval of years, there came the last great guest, General Ulysses S. Grant.

And so the time is passed over in a great sweep of years; Betty Van Lew has become a woman of forty, a woman of delicate physique and a small but commanding figure; brilliant, accomplished, resolute, a woman of great personality and of infinite charm. For her the years of quiet ended when Colonel Robert E. Lee, then of the United States army, stormed Harper's Ferry engine-house and captured John Brown. "From that time on," she says "our people were in a palpable state of war." "We"— "our"—in all her writings the South is ever in the first person; it is the token that her love for Virginia never was forgotten.

It was at this time that she began her work for the Federal government; she wrote letter after letter to Washington describing conditions in the South—letters of warning, of advice; these letters she sent through the mails.

A year passed; winter came, and the South, State by State, began to secede. Sumter was fired upon; the first flush of fever—the John Brown Raid—had become the delirium of civil war.

A greater decision than slavery or abolition was demanded of Betty Van Lew, openly and fearlessly she made her choice—the Union! On the streets she would impulsively enter into argument with strangers,

"speaking impassionedly"; for years she had been known as an abolitionist, now all Richmond knew her for a Unionist, audaciously outspoken. Then, three days after the little garrison marched out of charred
and smoking Sumter, Virginia passed the Ordinance of Secession, and
Richmond went war mad.

"Such flag-making—such flag-presentations!" (Miss Van Lew has
written). "The drum, the fife, and *Dixie;* for my life I would not have
dared to play *Yankee Doodle, Hail, Columbia,* and the *Star-Spangled
Banner,* our hallowed national airs. The blood-stained *Marseillaise* re-
sounded through our streets. . . . My country, oh, my country! God
help us, those were sorry days."

Troops began to pour in from other States, and Virginia became one
great military camp. "Help us make shirts for our soldiers," the ladies
of Richmond cried to the Van Lews; mother and daughter resolutely
refused, and their lifelong persecution began. Surprise, sneers, then
threats, till at last they carried to Camp Lee books and flowers—
"innocent 'aid and comfort' " that for the time being added greatly
to their own.

The ladies of Richmond sewed and knitted for the Confederacy,
and shot with pistols at a mark; Miss Van Lew wrote despatches for
the Union—specific information of Confederate troops, their numbers
and their movements. She had ceased to use the mails; the despatches
now went North by special messenger. So the hot tumultuous days of
summer passed; Bull Run was fought, and Richmond for the first time
filled with wounded Southern men and wretched Northern prisoners.
Here at last was work to do; from one official to another she hurried,
begging that she might nurse the wounded Union soldiers; until at
last, from General Winder, Provost-Marshal-General of Richmond, she
obtained "permission to visit the prisoners and to send them books,
luxuries, delicacies, and what she may wish." Thus her four years' service
began.

The Libby Prison was her special care; it stood at the base of Church
Hill, almost beneath her very door. There, in command, she found
Lieutenant Todd, brother of Mrs. Lincoln, and won his "kind feelings"
for herself by gifts of buttermilk and gingerbread. Castle Thunder—
"Particular Hell"—with Caphart, "Anti-Christ Caphart," in control;

Belle Isle in its stockade lying like a bleached bone in the midst of the turbulent river—for four bitter years she was known at them all.

From the moment that she gained access to the prisoners her despatches to the government increased a hundred-fold in accuracy and value; for, though her hospital and prison ministrations were sincere and genuine for humanity's sake, they were also a cloak to cover her real mission: Mis Van Lew above all else was a spy.

The Federal prisoners furnished her with much more information than might be supposed possible; from the many-windowed prisons in the heart of the city, and from within the stockade of Belle Isle, much that went on could be observed; they accurately estimated the strength of the passing troops and supply-trains, whose probable destination they shrewdly conjectured from the roads by which the Confederates left the town; then, too, there were snatches of conversations to be overheard between surgeons in the hospital or between the prison guards. Mere scraps of information all, but of infinite value to Miss Van Lew when combined with other scraps from here and there— some confirming, some setting an error right, some opening inquiry into fresh lines.

Her ministrations were indeed genuine. Clothes, food, books, money, all dealt out with a lavish, self-forgetting hand, were but part of her great kindliness; letters that had no part in war—home letters—she secretly carried past the censor; what this benefaction meant no one but him who has been a prisoner can understand. Among her effects there are many little mementoes, trifles, toys, but all that they had to give— napkin-rings, cuff-links, buttons, patiently and laboriously carved from bones that had been gnawed for the last morsel of food.

One deed of kindness at this time bore golden fruit twenty years after the war. Thirteen men accused of piracy had been tried in New York City, convicted, and sentenced to be hanged. They saved themselves by their claim that they were Confederate privateersmen and must be treated as prisoners of war; the Confederate government, to which they appealed, at once espoused their cause; thirteen Federal officers were thrown into a dungeon of Libby Prison to await the execution of these men; the thirteen officers were then to be hanged in reprisal. Miss Van Lew secretly communicated with them and with their families; she smuggled in to the hostages letters and money from home, gave them money of her own, and at last sent North the glad news that they had been restored to the footing of prisoners of war.

Colonel Paul Revere of the Twentieth Massachusetts Regiment was one of these officers, and it was his relatives in Boston, the friends which he had made for Miss Van Lew, who long years later were to come to her aid in her greatest hour of need.

And so throughout the war there passed between Miss Van Lew and the prisoners an almost uninterrupted exchange of question and answer, by which was derived much of the information that Miss Van Lew furnished to the Federal armies. In the prisons the information was conveyed in a score of ways—whispered words, friendly little notes with hidden meanings in words harmless to a censor's eye, books which were loaned or returned with here and there a word or a page number faintly underscored, questions and answers that were concealed in baskets of food. There was one curious old French contrivance, a metal platter with a double bottom, originally intended to hold hot water beneath the plate to keep the contents warm. Its frequent use and clumsy appearance aroused a keen-eyed guard's suspicions; Miss Van Lew, turning away with the empty plate one day, heard the threat he muttered to a fellow-guard. Within a day or two the platter was again presented at the prison door.

"I'll have to examine that," the sentry said.

"Take it, then," Miss Van Lew replied, and deftly slipping the shawl from around it she placed the plate suddenly in his hands; that day the double bottom contained no secret messages, but was filled with water blistering hot, and he dropped it with a roar of pain.

Yet for the most part she had little trouble with the soldiery; "Crazy Bet" they called her, and let her wander about within the prisons almost at will; they laughed as she passed singing softly to herself or muttering meaningless words.

For this gentlewoman had utterly submerged self in a passionate love of country; she was as one inspired by a mighty ideal; there was nothing which she would not herself endure that "slavery might be abolished and the Union preserved." Little by little she reared and fostered the belief that she was harmlessly insane; "Crazy Bet" she became, and the bitter rôle was unflinchingly borne and cunningly sustained. In another the part would have been unconvincing, suspicious, but for her the way had been already paved; her abolition sentiments—her love and labors for the negro race—had long marked her as "eccentric," "queer"; it was but a step further to brand her "crazed."

Now and then, indeed, the authorities, for one reason or another, revoked her permit to visit the prisons; then she would go to General Winder or to the office of the Secretary of War, and sooner or later win it back again.

And so, by flattery and cajolery, by strategy or by the charm of personality, she succeeded most of the time in remaining in the good graces of the authorities; to the minor officials and the soldiery she was only harmless "Crazy Bet," and they gave her little heed; but to the people of Richmond she was still Miss Van Lew, a Southern woman who had turned against her neighbors and against the South; and as the war lengthened and bore more heavily upon them, their resentment turned to implacable hatred.

"The threats, the scowls, the frowns of an infuriated community—who can write of them?" she wrote. "I have had brave men shake their fingers in my face and say terrible things. We had threats of being driven away, threats of fire, and threats of death. . . . 'You dare to show sympathy for any of those prisoners!' said a gentleman. 'I would shoot them down as I would blackbirds—and there is something on foot up against *you* now!' About the last week in July [1861] the press and people became so violent that no one was permitted to visit the prisons or do anything for their relief." The "violence of the press" is manifested in clippings of editorials found among her papers:

"RAPPED OVER THE KNUCKS"

One of the city papers contained, Monday, a word of exhortation to certain females of Southern residence (and perhaps birth) but of decidedly Northern and Abolition proclivities. The creatures though specially alluded to were not named . . . . If such people do not wish to be exposed and dealt with as alien enemies to the country, they would do well to cut stick while they can do so with safety to their worthless carcasses.

On the margin, in faded ink, there is written: "These ladies were my mother and myself—God knows it was but little we could do." After a while the visits were quietly resumed, and except to let some spasm of the people's rage die down her work for the captives continued throughout the war.

Spring came, and, with its coming, McClellan at the head of the Army of the Potomac swept up the Peninsula to Richmond's very doors. The houses shook with the cannonading, and from their roofs the people could see the bursting of the shells.

There are pages of description in the diary of Miss Van Lew telling of the battle she witnessed as she rode in the rear of the Confederate army—"the bright rush of Life, the hurry of Death on the battle-field"; there are pages of exultation at the sight of deliverance so near; and of how, "with new matting and pretty curtains we prepared a chamber to be General McClellan's room." Then came the Seven Days, and the onrushing Federal tide slowly turned, and ebbed, and drew away over the hills; and bitter disappointment and dead hope were locked in "McClellan's room," which Miss Van Lew had prepared for him, and which was not to be opened again for many and many a day.

Richmond gave a great gasp of relief and joy—that turned to sighing, that ended in a sob; for night and day, for many days and many nights, the streets re-echoed with the ceaseless roll of wheels as Richmond's sons came home; "the air was fetid with the presence of the wounded and the dead."

Then the city drearily settled itself back between the millstones—upper and nether—powerful North and impoverished South; and the stones slowly turned in the pitiless grind of war.

Miss Van Lew tirelessly worked on. Through the stifling summer nights she schemed and planned and conferred secretly with the handful of Richmond's Unionists. Disguised as a common farm-hand (the buckskin leggings, one-piece skirt and waist of cotton, and the huge calico sunbonnet were found among her effects and are in existence to this day), a little, lonely, unnoticed figure, she stole about in the night on her secret missions. Through the blazing days of summer she worked; in the ill-stocked markets she bargained for the food that sick men need—paying for it with money, that, after a time, she could so ill afford to give; in the reeking prisons and the fever-ridden wards, in the unfriendly crowds of the city streets, she sought and found the recompense of her toil—the "information" that was inestimably to aid in saving the Union.

Information came from another source—from the Confederate officers and officials themselves, many of whom, notwithstanding the animosities and suspicions which the townspeople, the non-combatants, felt for the Van Lews—continued to call there and were entertained by them throughout the war. In the after-dinner conversation directed by a clever woman, many a young officer unwittingly revealed much, the importance of which he never realized, much that in itself was without value, but which was of the greatest value when combined with what Miss Van Lew already knew or later learned.

Her method of reaching President Davis in his least-guarded moments is evidence of her genius as a spy and a leader of spies. The Van Lews had owned a negro girl of unusual intelligence; several years before the war she had been given her freedom, sent North, and educated at Miss Van Lew's expense. This young woman, whose name was Mary Elizabeth Bowser, was now sent for; she came, and for a time was coached and trained for her mission; then, in consummation of Miss Van Lew's scheming, she was installed as a waitress in the White House of the Confederacy. What she was able to learn, how long she remained behind Jefferson Davis's dining-chair, and what became of the girl ere the war ended are questions to which Time has effaced the answers.

For many months Miss Van Lew was dependent solely on her own resources for sending her despatches to the Federal generals and receiving their replies; but it was accomplished in countless different ways by her cunning and ingenuity. It was seldom difficult for her to procure passes for her servants to make the trip between the town house and the Van Lew farm below Richmond, which was the second of the stations that she established for relaying the despatches between her house in Richmond and the Federal armies.

Large baskets of eggs were brought in often; of each lot one egg was but a shell which contained a tiny scroll of paper—a message from some Union general. An old negro, shuffling in his clumsy thick-soled shoes, pressed with each step on a cipher despatch in a slit in his shoe sole.

A little seamstress carried the implements of her trade to and fro from house to farm; the dress-goods and bewildering patterns were returned to her after but a cursory examination by the patrols and guards, who unwittingly had held a Federal despatch in their hands. Countryman, slave, and sewing-girl—humble agents whose very names will never be known—they bore time after time evidence that, if found, would have hanged them to the nearest tree.

As for Miss Van Lew, the likelihood of detection seemed inevitable. "From the commencement of the war until its close my life was in continual jeopardy," she wrote. "I was an enthusiast [who] never counted it dear if I could have served the Union—not that I wished to die." Morning after morning she awoke to a new day of suspense and threatening danger such as few men and fewer women can be made to understand. Night after night—and what must the nights have been! And for four years this lasted without respite. No soldier but had his days and weeks of absolute safety—for her there was not one hour; betrayal, friends' blunders, the carelessness of others and their reckless disregard of prudence—all these she had to dread; but worst of all she was forced to intrust her life to men and women whom she herself had not chosen.

There came one day a stranger, a countrywoman of the lowest class. She bore openly a sheet of letter-paper, folded, addressed to "Miss Van Lew"; inside was scrawled a request for immediate information as to the provender and stores in Richmond and where the sick of the hospitals were being taken; the note was signed by a Federal general. So ignorant was his carelessly selected messenger that when Miss Van Lew expressed surprise and horror at her having such an incriminating paper, the woman indignantly replied, "I'd like to see any one try to put their hand in my pocket!"—as though the loss of the paper had been all!

There came a letter from General Butler to be delivered to X——, of ——, one of General Winder's officers. (His name and residence and position are given in Miss Van Lew's manuscript.) In the letter General Butler asked this man to come through the lines and communicate with him—in short, to "tell what he knew"; also it contained promises of reward; had it fallen into Confederate hands the letter would have been the death-warrant of him whom it was to tempt and of her who

bore the temptation. Miss Van Lew carried that letter straight to X——
at his post in the office of General Winder, commander of the city of
Richmond; she coolly took it from the bosom of her dress, gave X——
the letter, and watched him as he read. Had she judged him aright?
She had sounded him, had found him dissatisfied, approachable, and
she had marked him for an Arnold to his cause. Against her estimate
of character she had staked her life; was she to win or lose? In the
next room were the detectives and armed guards, the machinery of the
Confederate capital's secret police; X—— had but to raise his voice. . . .
She saw his face blanch and his lips quiver; as he followed her out
he begged her to be prudent—if she would never come there again
he promised to go to her. She had added one more to the weapons
with which she was striking at the very heart of the Confederacy.
Long years after the war X—— brought some of his friends to her that
she might corroborate his story of what one woman had dared and
risked.

There came a day when no messenger was at hand by whom to send
a despatch to Grant—a message of supreme importance: he had asked
of her that by a certain date she make a report of the number and
disposition of the forces in and about Richmond. The cipher despatch
was written, and, if it were to reach Grant in time, not one hour was
to be lost in finding a messenger. Apparently no Federal agent was able
to enter the city; she knew that just then no servant of hers might leave
it. In desperation she took the great market-basket that had become so
familiar a sight to the people of Richmond, and started in her customary
manner for the market.

As she walked she childishly swung the basket and softly sang and
hummed her little songs and smiled her vacant smile into the faces of
those who, as she passed, mocked at "Crazy Bet"—this woman who
dared walk Richmond's streets while in her hand she held—for the
Federal army—a key to Richmond's defenses.

A man overtook her and whispered as he passed: "I'm going through
to-night!" She gave no start of surprise, no look of curiosity; the man
walked just ahead and she followed. Was the Federal agent come at
last?—or was this another of the countless traps of the secret police? The
man was an utter stranger to her, but the need was urgent, imperative—

should she take the chance? She quickened her pace, and, as she in turn passed him, again came the whisper: "I'm going through the lines to-night!" In her hand she held the cipher despatch, torn into strips and each strip rolled into a tiny ball; should she commence to drop them one by one? In great perplexity and fear she quickly glanced back for a look at his face. And instantly some instinct, some woman's instinct, said "No," and on that inner prompting she impulsively turned into a side street and hurried home. Next day she saw that man, a junior officer, marching past her house for the front with his Confederate regiment. By such hairs as these did the sword hang over her day after day, day after day.

What was the outcome? Was she able to contrive a means of sending the despatch to Grant by the appointed time? It is not known. Miss Van Lew's story is difficult to tell; it is similar to a mosaic in fragments; here and there pieces may be put together to reconstruct a part of the picture, a figure, a group, an incident of the story. Though there is a great quantity of material, it seems to have been spread upon a wide-meshed sieve, through which there has sifted—and dropped into oblivion—most of the detail, the "when and where and how" of the story, leaving behind only great blocks of background—cold fact and vague and generalized statement.

The wide-meshed sieve was Fear; for forty years Miss Van Lew's every written and spoken word was sifted through it. Long after the war was ended a Northern friend wrote of her and her mother: "Neither talks about themselves or ever answers a direct question."

Miss Van Lew herself has written:

"Among the Union people of the city I was the recognized head—the leader—my word was law. . . . Earnestly in service from that time [the John Brown Raid] I did anything and everything I could until the close of the war, but when, and where, and how 'It boots not to remember' or write now; for the story will not 'Quicken love's pale embers' in this locality; I cannot say of our people that they have 'Loved me for the dangers I had passed.' . . . Of those perilous days and perilous times I cannot even now write—it agitates me."

In her mutilated war diary, or "Occasional Journal," as she called it, there is written, by way of preface:

The keeping of a complete journal was a risk too fearful to run. Written only to be burnt was the fate of almost everything which would now be of value; keeping one's house in order for government inspection, with Salisbury prison in perspective, necessitated this. I always went to bed at night with anything dangerous on paper beside me, so as to be able to destroy it in a moment. The following occasional journal . . . was long buried for safety.

Was such extreme caution necessary? It was imperative. Confederate spies were everywhere.

"If you spoke in your parlor or chamber to your next of heart, you whispered—you looked under the lounges and beds. Detectives were put upon their[1] tracks by citizens and the government. Visitors apparently friendly were treacherous. They were brought to the attention of the Grand Jury, by those they regarded as true friends, for trafficking in greenbacks, when they had none of them. They were publicly denounced, and walked the streets for four years shunned as lepers. . . . I shall ever remember the pale face of this dear lady [her mother]— her feeble health and occasional illness from anxiety; her dread of Castle Thunder and Salisbury—for her arrest was constantly spoken of, and frequently reported on the street, and some never hesitated to say she should be hanged. . . . Unionists lived ever in a reign of terror—I was afraid even to pass the prison; I have had occasion to stop near it when I *dared* not look up at the windows. I have turned to speak to a friend and found a detective at my elbow. Strange faces could sometimes be seen peeping around the columns and pillars of the back portico. . . . Once a lady and a dear friend staying with this family was sent for to General Winder's office, and requested to state if she could learn aught against them, but she replied that she was 'not with them as a spy.' " (The note demanding her guest's presence is to be found among Miss Van Lew's papers. "You need not see Mrs. Van Lew, nor will your name be mentioned to her," the note concluded, affably.) . . . "Once I went to Jefferson Davis himself to see if we could

---

1 In these excerpts from the manuscript of her unpublished book, Miss Van Lew frequently refers thus indirectly to her family or herself, but within a few lines slips back into the first person.

not obtain some protection. He was in Cabinet session, but I saw Mr. Jocelyn, his private secretary; he told me I had better apply to the Mayor. . . . Captain George Gibbs had succeeded Todd as keeper of the prisoners; so perilous had our situation become that we took him and his family to board with us. They were certainly a great protection. . . . Such was our life—such was freedom in the Confederacy. I speak what I know."

Summer came and passed and came and passed again; the third year of the war was drawing to its close in the terrible winter of '63–4. In February Miss Van Lew's only brother, John, was conscripted and, in spite of having been pronounced unfit for military duty because of ill health, was ordered to report immediately to Camp Lee. No previous mention in this story has been made of John Van Lew; in all his sister's and his mother's activities he remained but the silent partner, quietly conducting his hardware business, and from its dwindling proceeds supplying much of the money used for the aid of the Federal prisoners and for his sister's secret operations. Now, when conscripted into the Confederate army, he immediately deserted and for a time was concealed by Unionists in the outskirts of the city. While he still awaited an opportunity to escape to the Federal lines his sister (wearing her disguise, she says) visited him, on the evening of February 9th—the most unfortunate date, events proved, which she could have chosen. Her story of that night and of the next succeeding day is found among her manuscript.

"I went to the kind family where my brother was secreted; they were poor; and I passed the night with them. In the morning our driver came out with a basket of supplies. As soon as he entered he said that there was great trouble and excitement, and that brother was in great danger—that many prisoners had escaped during the night, and some had come to the outer door—the servants' room door on Twenty-fourth Street—and knocked and asked for Colonel Streight and begged to come in, but that he was afraid they were not prisoners— only our people [Confederates] in disguise to entrap us, and [he] would not let them in; that some had stood off by the churchyard wall and watched, and he was afraid." (Unfortunately these were indeed Federal officers; it was not until roll-call next morning that it was discovered that

109 officers had escaped through Colonel Rose's tunnel out of Libby Prison.) "Brother then had to give up all hopes of escape, because we knew vigilance would be redoubled, and we were in great trouble for the family he was with; for it was to be expected that their house would be searched, and it would have gone very hard with them had a deserter been found secreted there. We were greatly distressed, too, on account of the prisoners; we knew there was to be an exit—had been told to prepare—and had one of our parlors—an off, or rather end room; had had dark blankets nailed up at the windows, and gas kept burning in it, very low, night and day for about three weeks—so we were ready for them—beds prepared in there.

"I went home as quickly as I could, in despair. As desperate situations sometimes require desperate remedies, I determined to go to General Winder." And so the story goes on at considerable length to tell how General Winder personally made great efforts to induce the medical commission again to declare John Van Lew unfit for service; the General failed in that, but he did succeed in getting him into his own regiment, and there he was able to give such effectual protection that John Van Lew never wore a Confederate uniform, and only once shouldered a Confederate musket, to stand, on a great "panic day," a figurehead guard at the door of a government department. But at last, during the summer of '64, when even General Winder's protection could no longer save him from active service at the front, John Van Lew deserted again, and this time reached the Federal army, where he remained until after Richmond had fallen—and so passed from this story.

As for the fugitives from the Libby, it has been told in Richmond and is told to this day, that Colonel Streight and a number of his comrades lay hidden for days in the secret room of the Van Lew mansion. The story that they were in the secret room is forever set at rest by the diary for Monday, February 15, 1864:

"I shall ever remember this day because of the great alarm I had for others. Colonel Streight and three of the prisoners . . . were secreted near Howard's Grove. After passing through the tunnel they were led by a Mrs. G—— to a humble home on the outskirts of the city; there Mrs. R——received them. By request of some of their number she came . . . for me, and I went with her to see them. . . . We had a little laughing and talking, and then I said good-by, with the most fervent God bless you in my heart toward all of them."

The parlor—that "off, or rather end, room" with its blanket-curtained windows and its extravagant waste of gas is used by Miss Van Lew as dust to throw in our eyes for some unfathomed reason of her own; in none of her writings does she mention the true secret room; yet it was there then, and it is there—no longer a secret—to this present day.

It extends in a long, low, narrow cell just back of where the main roof slopes up from its juncture with the flat roof of the great rear veranda; the garret is squared, and between its west wall and the sloping roof lies the hidden room. When it was built and by whose hand, whether it was designed for the purpose to which it was put, and how many men it may have sheltered during the war, may now never be known. Its existence was always suspected, and though the house was searched time after time for that very room it was discovered just once, and then by a little child; save for her it might have remained a secret till the old house should come to be torn down; for Miss Van Lew never told of the spring door in the wall behind the antique chest of drawers.

Long years after the war—after Miss Van Lew had died—she who had been the little girl visited the old house, and rediscovered the secret room; after more than forty years her fingers searched out and again pressed the hidden spring. And then she told of that other time when she had opened the door: how with childish curiosity she had stealthily followed Aunt Betty up through the dark, silent house to see where the plate of food was being carried in the night. She has never forgotten what she saw as she peeped fearfully into the attic from the head of the stairs—the shadows and the ghostly shapes of the old furniture around the walls; her aunt, shading the candle with her hand, standing before a black hole in the wall, from which peered a haggard soldier with shaggy hair and beard, his thin hand outstretched for the food. When she saw him looking at her, before he could speak she laid her finger on her lips and fled. But after her aunt had gone she stole up to the attic again, and called softly to the soldier; he told her how to open the door, and when she had done so he talked to her; she remembers that he laughed as he said, "My! what a spanking you would have got if your aunt had turned around!"

Presently she shut him into the secret room again and crept off to bed; she never dared go to the attic after that, nor tell her aunt what she had seen.

There was at least one other secret recess in the house—the hiding-place for despatches. In the library there was—and still remains unchanged—an ornamented iron fireplace; on either side of the grate are two pilasters, each capped by a small sculptured figure of a couchant lion. Accident or design had loosened one of these so that it could be raised like a box-cover; it was in the shallow cavity beneath that Miss Van Lew placed her despatches. There was no whispered conference between mistress and messenger—to be overheard by spies within the house, to be watched by those without. Miss Van Lew, perhaps with her back to the mantel, would deftly slip the cipher letter under the couchant lion; later the old negro servant, while alone in the room, dusting the furniture, would draw the message out, and presently go plodding down the dusty road to the farm, bearing some such tidings as that Lee was being reinforced by fifteen thousand men.

Of all the many despatches which Miss Van Lew sent through the Confederate lines there to-day exists but one. Inquiry addressed to the War Department shows that "all papers in this department relating to Miss Van Lew were taken from the files December 12, 1866, and given to her." These papers—cipher despatches from Miss Van Lew and all reports in which she was mentioned—must have been immediately destroyed by her, for there is no trace of them. The one despatch must have been in some way overlooked when her letters were returned to her by the War Department, and so escaped being destroyed. It is a strange chance that it should have been the one to be thus preserved, for it is this despatch—so closely connected by time and circumstance with the Kilpatrick-Dahlgren Raid—which seems to establish the real motive which inspired Miss Van Lew and some of her fellow-Unionists to take the desperate risk of stealing Colonel Dahlgren's body. The despatch, like most of those sent by Miss Van Lew, was in cipher, but, though only its jumbled letters had been published, it nevertheless might now be translated and understood; for when Miss Van Lew died there was found in the back of her watch—where it had been constantly carried for nearly forty years—a worn, yellowed bit of paper on which was written the faded letters of the cipher code, here published for the first time.

Miss Van Lew's cipher code

Many years after the war the following translation of her despatch was published in the Official Records of the Union and Confederate Armies. [Series I; Volume XXXIII, Part I, page 520.]

HEADQUARTERS EIGHTEENTH ARMY CORPS,
FORTRESS MONROE, *February 5, 1864.*
HONORABLE E. M. STANTON,
Secretary of War.
SIR,—I send enclosed for your perusal the information I have

acquired of the enemy's forces and disposition about Richmond. The letter commencing "Dear Sir," on the first page, is a cipher letter to me from a lady in Richmond with whom I am in correspondence. The bearer of the letter brought me a private token showing that he was to be trusted. . . . You will see that the prisoners are to be sent away to Georgia. Now or never is the time to strike. . . . I have marked this "Private and immediate," so that it shall at once come into your hands.

Respectfully your obedient servant,

BENJ. F. BUTLER,

Maj.-Gen. Commanding.

January 30, 1864.

DEAR SIR,—It is intended to remove to Georgia all the Federal prisoners; butchers and bakers to go at once. They are already notified and selected. Quaker [a Union man whom I know—B. F. B.] knows this to be true. Are building batteries on the Danville road. This from Quaker: Beware of new and rash council! Beware! This I send you by direction of all your friends. No attempt should be made with less than 30,000 cavalry, from 10,000 to 15,000 to support them, amounting in all to 40,000 or 45,000 troops. Do not underrate their strength and desperation. Forces could probably be called into action in from five to ten days; 25,000, mostly artillery. Hoke's and Kemper's brigades gone to North Carolina: Pickett's in or about Petersburg. Three regiments of cavalry disbanded by General Lee for want of horses. Morgan is applying for 1,000 choice men for a raid.

Then, under date of February 4th, there follows—in the form of question and answer—the account of the circumstances under which this letter was received. The messenger, in his answers to General Butler's questions, told how Miss Van Lew had asked him to take the letter, promising that General Butler would take care of him; how a man had been paid $1,000 (Confederate money) to guide him, but had "fooled" him, deserted him at the banks of the Chickahominy River, how nevertheless he had got a boat, crossed, and kept on. He repeated his verbal messages: "They are sending the prisoners to Georgia. Richmond could be taken easier now than at any other time since the war began. 'Quaker' (that is not his name, but he says he does not want any one to know his name) said his plan to take Richmond would be to make a feint on Petersburg; let Meade engage Lee on the Rappahannock; send two or three hundred men and land them at the White House [Landing] on the other side of Richmond, so as to attract attention, then have ten thousand cavalry to go up in the evening, and then rush into Richmond the next morning."

Did Miss Van Lew and "Quaker" and the other Unionists of Richmond hold themselves responsible for the ill-fated raid to release the Federal prisoners? Was it indeed the information in Miss Van Lew's despatch which inspired the raid? Thus, when the body of the crippled boy-leader, Colonel Ulric Dahlgren—he was not yet twenty-two—lay in secret among the ten thousand grassless graves below Oakwood Cemetery in Richmond, what was it which moved Miss Van Lew and the Unionists to risk their very lives to steal his body and send it through the Confederate pickets to a "friendly grave"—was it pity only, or was it that they felt that they had brought him there?

The Kilpatrick-Dahlgren Raid was primarily to release the Federal prisoners in Richmond. On February 28, 1864, General Judson Kilpatrick and Colonel Ulric Dahlgren at the head of four thousand picked troopers left Stevensburg and made direct for Richmond. There was the feint—the simultaneous demonstration by Meade upon Lee's left; there was the plan for Dahlgren to engage Richmond on the south with a small force while the main body was to enter on the north; there was to be the release of the prisoners who were so "soon to be removed to Georgia"—is there doubt that Miss Van Lew and "Quaker" saw in it all a responsibility that rested in a measure on themselves?

The raid—though it penetrated to within five miles of Richmond—failed. By a series of accidents—chief of which was the treachery of Dahlgren's negro guide—the two forces, after separating for the attack, lost each other and were never able to unite. Tuesday, March 1st, found both Kilpatrick and Dahlgren—widely separated—in retreat, and riding hard for the Peninsula. But that night, in the storm that raged, Dahlgren and his advance (about one hundred men) with whom he rode became lost from the remainder of his little command. In all the history of the war there is no more pathetic figure—with crutches strapped to the saddle, and in the stirrup an artificial limb to take the place of the leg lost but a few months before—none more dramatic than young Ulric Dahlgren as he led his handful of exhausted men through the roused country. In King and Queen County there came the end; the little band rode into an ambush, and at the first volley from out the thicket Colonel Dahlgren, who was in advance, was shot dead; some of his men managed to escape, but the remainder were taken.

In her manuscript Miss Van Lew tells of the turmoil into which Richmond was thrown by the nearer and nearer approach of the raiders, of her own suspense, and her greater anguish when it became apparent that the raid had failed; she tells the detailed story—as it was told to her—of the killing of Colonel Dahlgren; and then of the events which followed.

"A coffin was made, and the body of Dahlgren placed in it and buried, where he was killed, at the fork of two roads, one leading from Stevensville and the other from Mantua ferry. After a few days it was disinterred by order of the Confederate government, brought to Richmond, and lay for a time in a box-car at the York River Railway station. It was buried, as the papers said, at eleven o'clock at night, no one knew where and no one should ever know. . . . The heart of every Unionist was stirred to its depth; . . . and to discover the hidden grave and remove his honored dust to friendly care was decided upon." (No word of Miss Van Lew's reveals that the plan from first to last was hers; it was she who incited the men to steal the body; her money purchased the metallic casket, which was concealed by her strategy.)

"Several endeavored to trace it, and Mr. F. W. E. Lohmann succeeded in doing so, willingly running the risk of its removal, which all knew here was perilous in no small degree. The discovery of the body was entirely accidental, or rather providential; would not have been made had not a negro been out in the burying-ground at midnight and saw them burying Dahlgren. . . . When search was made, this negro suspected that the person inquired for was sleeping in his care—and to this negro's [illegible word: intelligence?] it may be that Colonel Dahlgren's body was ever found.

"Arrangements had been made to convey it to the residence of Mr. William S. Rowley, some short distance in the country; and, accompanied by Mr. Martin M. Lipscomb, on the cold, dark, and rainy night of April 5th, Mr. Lohmann went to the ground, and with the aid of a negro took up the coffin, opened it, and identified the body by the missing limb—it having lost the right leg below the knee. It was then put into a wagon, and Mr. Lohmann drove it to Mr. Rowley's; the coffin was carried into an outbuilding—a kind of seed or work shop—where Mr. Rowley watched the rest of the night beside it. In the morning a metallic coffin was brought out. A few Union friends saw the body. Colonel Dahlgren's hair was very short, but all that could be spared was cut off and sent to his father. . . . The body was taken from the rough, coarse coffin and placed in the metallic one, the lid of which was sealed with a composition improvised by F. W. E. Lohmann, as there was no putty to be procured in Richmond. This coffin was placed in Mr. Rowley's wagon, which was then filled with young peach-trees packed as nurserymen pack them—the coffin, of course, being covered and concealed. Mr. Rowley took the driver's seat and drove all that remained of the brave young Dahlgren through the several pickets, one of which was then the strongest around Richmond; . . . at this very place the day before his death had Dahlgren fought for hours. Wary and vigilant were our pickets, and if one had run his bayonet into this wagon only a few inches, death would certainly have been the reward of this brave man; not only death, but torture to make him reveal those connected with him—his accomplices."

Rowley was chosen well; Miss Van Lew's account shows him to have been a man of iron nerve and a consummate actor. At the picket-post he listened without a quiver to the unexpected order that his wagon be searched; an inbound team drew up, and the picket, perceiving that Rowley gave no sign of being in a hurry, thoroughly searched it. The lieutenant of the post having re-entered his tent, and one of the guard at that moment having recognized in Rowley a chance acquaintance and recalled to him their former meeting, there at once commenced a lively conversation. More wagons came, were searched, and went on. The lieutenant, looking out from his tent for an instant, called, with an oath, to "search that man and let him go."

"It would be a pity to tear up those trees!" said the friendly guard. "I did not expect them to be disturbed," Rowley answered, "but"—nonchalantly—"I know a soldier's duty."

Then another wagon had to be examined, and a second time came the lieutenant's angry order to "search the man so that he can go!" The suspense must have been terrible; it seemed now that nothing could avert the discovery of the casket.

"Your face is guarantee enough," the guard said, in a low voice; "go on!" And so the body of Col. Ulric Dahlgren resumed its journey.

The two Lohmanns had flanked the picket, and presently joining Rowley, they directed the drive to the farm of a German named Orrick, near Hungary (now Laurel Station). The grave was quickly dug and the coffin placed in it; two faithful German women helped to fill it in and to plant over it one of the peach-trees which had so successfully prevented discovery.

It was perhaps unfortunate that the Unionists carried out their well-intentioned plan, for Admiral Dahlgren's recovery of the body of his son was thereby retarded until after the war. With Admiral Dahlgren's request for the return of the body the Confederate government made every effort to comply—an action which was a great surprise to the Richmond Unionists, who believed the Confederates to be too bitter against Dahlgren ever to accede to such a demand. But the body was gone, and the mystery of its disappearance remained—for the Confederates—long unsolved.

Close upon the heels of the Dahlgren Raid and its tragic ending came the opening of the spring campaign. "As the war advanced" (Miss Van Lew wrote) "and the army closed around Richmond, I was able to communicate with General Butler and General Grant, but not so well and persistently with General Butler, for there was too much danger in the system and persons. With General Grant, through his Chief of Secret Service, General George H. Sharpe, I was more fortunate." So "fortunate" that flowers which one day grew in her Richmond garden stood next morning on Grant's breakfast-table.

Great gaps occur in the "Occasional Journal" for 1864–5; the personal element had been destroyed, and there is left only description of general conditions—save for the story of Pole, the Englishman, who in February, when unseen Peace was but six weeks away, was piloted into Richmond from headquarters by a Federal agent to assist in obtaining information; Pole, the Englishman, who brought the shadow of death closer, blacker, more imminent than ever it had been before. For Pole, once he was in Richmond, immediately betrayed Babcock, who had brought him in, and White, with whom he was to have been quartered, and those Unionists by whom he and Babcock had been aided along their way.

Miss Van Lew read in the newspaper of the arrests, and there followed hours of suspense, until it became apparent that Pole had been unable to incriminate her, and that she had indeed escaped again.

Winter was hardly over when Lee's veterans—more gaunt, more grim, immeasurably more heroic—recommenced the now hopeless struggle. The despairing Confederacy was ransacking the South to obtain horses to send to its fighting-men; Miss Van Lew hid her last remaining horse in the smoke-house, until, finding it to be unsafe there, she stabled it in the study of the house, its stamping being deadened by a thick-strewn layer of straw.

The "Occasional Journal" contains many sentences: "Oh, the yearning for deliverance. The uncertain length of our captivity, now reckoned by years." Then at last there came deliverance—the fall of Richmond.

"Toward the close of the day [Sunday] the young soldiers could be seen bidding hurried farewells to their friends. . . . Word was sent to us that our house was to be burned—some Confederate soldiers had said so. . . . Midnight passed; the door-bell rang—two fugitives came in from Castle Thunder. . . . The constant explosion of shells, the blowing up of the gunboats and of the powder magazines seemed to jar, to shake the earth. . . . The burning bridges, the roaring flames, added a wild grandeur to the scene." And then in a burst of exultation, "Oh, army of my country, how glorious was your welcome!"

She does not tell how the mob did come to burn the house before the arrival of the first troops, and how she went out alone on the portico and defied them. "I know you,——, and you,——, and you, Mr.——," she cried, calling them by name and pointing to them. "General Grant will be in this city within the hour; if this house is harmed, your houses shall be burned by noon!" One by one they turned, muttering, and slunk away.

Nor does she tell—but it shall not be forgotten!—how with her own hands she raised over the old Van Lew mansion the first Federal flag that had been seen in Richmond since the other April morning four long years before. When she had seen that the fall of Richmond was inevitable, she had written to General Butler for a flag; when, and how, and by whom it was brought to her it will probably never be known; but in some way a great flag eighteen feet long by nine wide came through the Confederate pickets into the beleaguered city, and was treasured till it might be raised to greet the entering Union army. Before even the advance-guard was in sight she had raised the flag; and as the long, dusty line of men in blue swung into Main Street there waved from the Van Lew mansion on the hill above them the first Federal flag to tell that the capital of the Confederacy had fallen.

The special guard under command of Colonel Parke, sent by General Grant for Miss Van Lew's protection, found her in the deserted capitol, seeking in the archives for documents which might otherwise be destroyed; to the very end her every thought was for "the government."

And for a time the government remembered. President Grant, fifteen days after his inauguration, appointed Miss Van Lew postmistress of Richmond. She knew that it would be heralded throughout the South that she had demanded the office in payment for services rendered against the Confederacy; but her family was in great financial straits, and she made the sacrifice. For eight years she conducted the office with competence, even skill; her business relations with the people of Richmond were for the most part amicable, but socially she paid, she paid!

"I live—and have lived for years—as entirely distinct from the citizens as if I were plague-stricken," she wrote. "Rarely, very rarely, is our door-bell ever rung by any but a pauper, or those desiring my service. . . . September, 1875, my mother was taken from me by death. We had not friends enough to be pall-bearers."

Six weeks after General Grant had left the Presidential chair Miss Van Lew was writing to Mr. Rogers, private secretary to President

Hayes: "I am hounded down—I am hounded down. . . . I never, never was so bitterly persecuted—ask the President to protect me from this unwarranted, unmerited, and unprecedented persecution." In May came her successor.

After her removal from office there followed years of distressing poverty and unavailing efforts to procure any sort of government appointment. Her salary during office had been spent without regard for the morrow—chiefly in charities to the negro race; it was, to the very last, her dogmatically performed activities in behalf of the negroes—characterized by her neighbors as "pernicious social-equality doctrines and practices"—much more than her war record, which so ostracized her in her community. Utterly unable to dispose of her valuable but unproductive real estate, she was reduced to great distress—absolute need. "I tell you truly and solemnly," she wrote, "that I have suffered for necessary food. I have not one cent in the world. . . . I have stood the brunt *alone* of a persecution that I believe no other person in the country has endured who has not been Ku-Kluxed. I honestly think that the government should see that I was sustained."

And finally there did come the long-sought appointment—a clerkship in the Post-office Department at Washington. Then after two years the war party was overthrown, and the change brought bitter days to Miss Van Lew. Perhaps—as her superiors fretfully reported—she did owe her place to "sentimental reasons," perhaps her "peculiar temperament" did make her "a hindrance to the other clerks," perhaps she did "come and go at will." It was recommended that she be reduced to "a clerkship of the lowest salary and grade"—and it was done; but she mutely clung to her only means of livelihood. Two weeks later there appeared in a Northern newspaper a sneering editorial. "A Troublesome Relict," it began, and closed, "We draw the line at Miss Van Lew." And *then* she wrote her resignation, and, a heartbroken old woman, she returned to the lonely house on Church Hill.

There, in desperation, and stung by the taunt made to her that "the South would not have forsaken her as the North had done had she espoused the Southern cause," she wrote to Northern friends for help. To send the letter, she was obliged to borrow a stamp from a negro. The letter brought a response that was quick and generous; Boston men—

those friends and relatives of Col. Paul Revere[1] whom she had helped in Libby Prison—gave an ample annuity, which for her remaining years procured those comforts which money could buy; but there was that for which money had no purchasing power.

"I live here in the most perfect isolation. No one will walk with us on the street, no one will go with us anywhere [Miss Van Lew and an invalid niece were all that were left of the family]; and it grows worse and worse as the years roll on and those I love go to their long rest."

And so, at last, in the old mansion with its haunting memories, nursed by an old negress to whom she had given freedom long years before, Miss Van Lew died.

There is but one paragraph more to be written—to be copied from a torn scrap of paper among her manuscripts:

"If I am entitled to the name of 'Spy' because I was in the Secret Service, I accept it willingly; but it will hereafter have to my mind a high and honorable signification. For my loyalty to my country I have two beautiful names—here I am called 'Traitor,' farther North a 'Spy'— instead of the honored name of Faithful."

---

1 George Higginson, Col. Henry Lee, J. Ingersoll Bowditch, Frederick L. Ames, F. Gordon Dexter, Hon. John M. Forbes, William Endicott, and Mrs. G. Howland Shaw.

Young

When the pages of this memoir have been read, and laid aside, and then in the course of time have been all but quite forgotten, there shall yet linger a memory that will stir when chance brings some passing mention of his name, or maybe at mere reference to the Secret Service. A confused memory perhaps, a memory of countless desperate chances, of services that weigh heavy in the balance scale of Victory; remembrance of his youth and courage, and, at the last, an ever-questioning memory, vague as in the telling, of that final unrecorded battle; but outlasting all other recollections of the man there shall be this one concrete impression—admiration.

Who can quite forget such tributes as were paid him by his generals?—Sheridan's "I *want* him!" and the reply of General Edwards, "I would rather you would take my right arm than to have you take him from me." Best of all, the splendid profanity of one among his soldiers— a tribute rugged and imperishable as rough-hewn granite, "*We* think God A'mighty of him."

It is like a picture—that first story that begins before he was a soldier: the dusty chaise in which there stands the boy Young—he was scarcely more than a boy even when he was commissioned lieutenant-colonel four years later—and at his side the solemn-eyed little girl of ten, breathlessly watching brother Henry as he talks, watching him to the forgetting of the horse she holds, and the place her finger marks for him in the book of *Military Tactics,* forgetful of the very crowd that hems them in and that stands with upturned, troubled faces. For background to the picture the street of a New England village—elms, and white houses, flecks of sunlight on the dusty road, and the unclouded May sky; but none of these must be seen very plainly, for they do not count in the picture.

The nation is at war and must have men—must have men. And the crowd presses closer about the chaise and restlessly listens, until its occupants drive away without looking back, for the boy is already deep in *Tactics* and the little girl is driving.

So, through the Blackstone Valley; in every village the boy calls a crowd about him, and at the end of one day's haranguing sixty-three men have volunteered to enlist with him.

But Rhode Island's quota had been already filled when he took the list to Colonel Slocum; and so he went back to his work in Providence, with God knows what of disappointment, and settled down again at the high stool and the ledgers in Lippitt & Martin's. But already he had left behind him that unforgetable impression—admiration. Colonel Slocum sent for him, and on June 6, 1861, he was mustered in with the regiment as Company B's second lieutenant—so pale, so office-stamped, such a slender little lieutenant, that Wright, his robust captain, growled: "He will be flat on his back after the first march! What does that young man expect to do in the army?" Yet it was the second lieutenant that very night who silenced the angry, mutinous men in the bare, empty barracks of the Dexter Grounds. He might have stayed in the comfortable quarters of his brother officers, but instead, grasping the situation at a glance, he shouted, "It's about time to turn in, boys," and he spread a blanket, wrapped himself in his coat, and lay down on the hard floor among them. "Lie right down," he called, cheerfully; and the men, abashed, yet pleased and touched withal, lay down good-humoredly about him. That was the beginning, and it was like that till the very end—always, where he led, men followed with implicit confidence.

Six weeks later, at Bull Run, they—the men of Company B— followed like veterans where he led them—he, the second lieutenant, who was to have been flat on his back; it was Captain Wright, the prophet, who occupied the cot bed in the hospital, ill; the first lieutenant was absent. The acting captain of Company B did not escape notice that July Sunday. One eye-witness says, "I can remember how small he looked, his sword trailing on the ground, his slight figure so full of fire and energy." And it is said that fighting soldiers of other regiments paused and turned to look again at "such a boy in command of a company." Had he been a great, strapping fellow, the fewness of his years might have passed unnoticed, but he was not five feet five in height, and very slender; it seemed that a child had come out to lead them. That he led them well is shown by a first lieutenant's commission, dated July 22d.

In a letter to his mother a short time after this he wrote:

You say you should think it [the suffering] would discourage any one from going to the war. The fact is, no one knows what fighting is till they have seen it; and they that have, after it is over and they think about it, would like to see it over again. There is an excitement about it, there is a longing for it again that no one knows who has not experienced it.

Much of his character will be understood that could never be understood without those pregnant sentences. Read them again, for they contain that sentiment which was to be the lodestar, the north toward which the needle of his life was to point unswervingly till the end—the love of fighting and of danger.

General Oliver Edwards—and no one knew Young better—has written:

It was very rare to find a man who found in the most deadly peril his greatest pleasure, and who sought out danger, not only in the line of duty, but because he reveled in it. Colonel Henry H. Young and General Phil Kearny possessed this trait of character. . . .

Perhaps his crossing of the Rappahannock at Fredericksburg had something to do with his first staff appointment—Fredericksburg, where Captain Young led Company B (since November 13, '61, his own company) over the pontoon bridge in the face of the fire of the sharpshooters. And with this appointment, which detached him from his regiment, there ended his relations with the men of his old company. What the men thought of him one of them had told unwittingly to the mother of his captain. It was in the hospital at Portsmouth Grove, where Mrs. Young and her little daughter—the little girl who drove that day in the Blackstone Valley—had gone to carry comforts to the men of the Second Rhode Island. She had had shown to her the cot where lay a man of Company B—*his* company. To the man, who had never before seen her, the question, "Do you like your captain?" must have seemed an idle one, but it roused him as could no other.

"*Like* him, ma'am?" he cried, vehemently. "We think God A'mighty of him! There never was any one like him; the men would lay down their lives for him any day." It was admiration—idolatry—like that that he had left behind him.

It may be that in the staff appointment he foresaw the opportunity to commence the work that Sheridan has called "invaluable"; or perhaps, once on the staff, he merely drifted into it; but however it was, he began then his self-taught, self-sought apprenticeship to the Secret Service. Camp life grew irksome, and he went out between the lines to quicken it.

Once he saved a supply train from certain capture by raiders whose plans he had discovered. Discovered how?—at what personal hazard? If ever he told, it was in some such unsatisfying manner as the story of fighting his way out of a guerrilla ambush is told in a letter to his mother:

> I went out the other day on a little expedition over the mountains—three of us, all mounted on mules. We went some six miles outside of our picket-lines, and got in among the guerrillas after we had crossed what is called Carter's Run. We were fired on, but made out to get away. One of the boys lost his mule and equipments. The mule balked when they commenced firing, and would not stir a step, and they pressed the man so hard he had to take to the woods afoot. I think that I shall explore that section again at an early date.

And in another letter:

> A scout's life is a dangerous one to a certain extent, but I don't know, after all, that it is more so than a great many other positions.

Well indeed might he say that!—he of whom his brigade commander wrote:

When you wished an order carried to any part of the field he [Young] did not look about for the safest route but took the most direct one, no matter how the bullets whistled. He was always ready to dash through the hottest place, to cheer on a wavering regiment or to rally a disorganized one. While the battle [Marye's Heights] was at its height he discovered a wounded soldier of the Second Rhode Island in such a position that he was exposed to the fire of both sides. Leaping from his horse, amid a shower of bullets, he was himself wounded in the arm, but dragged the poor fellow to the shelter of a tree; it was but the work of a moment, yet amid the noise and confusion of battle seemed wonderfully cool and deliberate.

And all this time the duties of a staff officer continued, varied only by free-lance scoutings to gratify the longing for excitement; the other life was beyond him still, but he was reaching out to grasp it. Chancellorsville, Gettysburg, Rappahannock Station, Mine Run, Wilderness, Spottsylvania, Cold Harbor—he was of the brigade headquarters staff at all of them.

And then the Shenandoah, the valley in which the name of Major Harry Young was to be known and dreaded and respected in every household throughout its length and breadth: the place and the man were together; the time was almost upon them. After the battle of the Opequon—September 19, 1864—Col. Oliver Edwards was left in command of Winchester, and Young was his Inspector-General. It was part of his staff duty to familiarize himself with all the roads round about Winchester, and he was almost daily in Confederate uniform scouting through the Valley; he was now on that intangible border line which separates the army scouts from men of the Secret Service.

At this time there was in the Valley a body of scouts from General Crook's command—a hundred men on detached service commanded by one Captain Blazer—who were engaged in a war to the death with the partisan battalions of Gilmor, McNeill, and Mosby. Captain Young at every opportunity rode out at the side of Captain Blazer, and from him learned much of the methods of such irregular warfare, much that must afterward have proved of incalculable value when he was head of Sheridan's Secret Service. Later on, Mosby's Captain "Dolly" Richards all but wiped out Blazer's little command in a savage hand-to-hand battle, in which Captain Blazer's career was closed by his capture. After that Captain Young adopted different methods. At one time he induced three of Colonel Edwards's men to apparently desert from the Union army and enlist with Mosby, to whom one of them got so close as to be even orderly at the partisan leader's headquarters; but they must have been the wrong men for their opportunity, for nothing seems to have come of it, and Young restlessly turned to other schemes. A well-planned trap was inadvertently sprung by a detachment of Federal cavalry not in Young's secret. Soon after this, Sheridan lifted Young up to so broad a field of endeavor that such work shrank to secondary importance. But that was not until he had outfaced Death in two desperate personal encounters. Once was on the Front Royal road in the late afternoon of a summer day—one of those hot, dusty, breathless days when the great pallid cumulus clouds heap up, mountain upon mountain, then flush, then dull and darken into presagers of the coming storm. Young, alone, miles outside the Federal outposts, was galloping back to Winchester from another of his lonely, restless scoutings—he seems always to have preferred to be alone; other scouts went out in pairs, he seemed fascinated by the desolation of unshared dangers. In the thick hush before the breaking of the storm, he should have heard—but perhaps the muttering thunder drowned the drum of the approaching hoofbeats; they turned in from a cross-road close behind him—a party of Confederate cavalry. In an instant the pursuit began. He tried to outdistance them, but the little gray—so often mentioned in his letters home—was tired, and Young knew it; he suddenly stopped, turned at right angles, and put him at the wall; with a supreme effort the gray cleared the ditch, cleared the wall, and began the struggle up the long slope to the dense woodland that crowned it. Two only, on the fleetest mounts, took the wall, and followed; the rest refused it, and after a moment's confusion raced down the road to head him off should he come back to the road where it turned along the second side of the forest. The two, shouting, were overtaking him; he turned on them and charged furiously down upon them, shooting as he rode; they fled, yelling for their comrades. Then he rode into the shelter of the wood, and, but a few rods from its edge, he hid the trembling gray, and flung himself face down, burrowing into the leaf mold.

The storm broke; day was stripped of an hour by the darkness; the trees grew loud in the rush of the wind, and the earth trembled with the unusually violent thunder. The Confederates came back; he could hear them above the lash of the rain—calling to each other and crashing about in the thickets. He had stopped so near the point where he had entered the wood that they did not search there; but they passed perilously close, and once he was sure they would find him. They gave it up at last and went away; he learned afterward from a prisoner that the leader, blinded by the lightning's glare, had been dashed against a low bough and seriously injured.

After a while he led his horse out from the dripping trees, and rode unmolested back to the army.

The Valley was scourged with a plague of bushwhackers—robbers and murderers who had deserted from regular commands of both armies and had turned war to their own advantage. There were verbal orders from General Sheridan to hang all those that were proved bushwhackers, and Young compiled a "blacklist" of all such in the vicinity of Winchester—their names and haunts and habits. On days when no other duties were pressing he would go out with one or two men and hunt down some of the blacklisted. The record of one such day's hunting is still remembered—as much, perhaps, for the personality of the hunted as for the unusual courage of the hunter. It was known of the hunted that he had been a member of a Virginia cavalry regiment, had had a sixty-day furlough in order to procure a body-servant, but that he had been absent from his command for more than nine months and was a deserter and a bushwhacker—a murderer of prisoners; indeed, by his own boasts, known as the "Prisoner-Killer"; yet he could count on a score of houses in the Valley for help and shelter, for he was a tall, handsome fellow, cool and audacious. Captain Young in some way found out that day's hiding-place of the "Killer," and, hurrying to headquarters, he asked of Colonel Edwards a detail of two men; with his men he galloped away up the Valley. The "Killer "in some way escaped, barely escaped, and they followed, rapidly overtaking him. The "Killer" fired once, and a horse went down in a wild tangle of flying hoofs; the other riders leaped clear of their fallen comrade with never a look behind them. A bend in the road, and then out upon a mile-long straightaway; Young and the "Killer" fire almost together; the second soldier pitches backward, and the "Killer's" horse goes down in a heap in a ditch at the roadside; the "Killer" is down, then up again, and in a second is into the thicket. . . . When consciousness came to the wounded soldier he found himself alone; the faint sounds from the distant thicket told of a terrible struggle, and he stared stupidly at the point nearest the fallen horse of the "Killer."

After a long time, when there had been a protracted silence, the bushes parted, and there came forth the "Killer," white-faced and bruised and bound, with Captain Young, carrying two heavy revolvers, grimly urging him forward. Neither had been able to use his weapons, but they had fought it out there in the underbrush, and by some marvel of fighting the fierce little New-Englander had conquered a man over six feet tall, and heavy in proportion. Somehow he got his prisoner and his two wounded men back to headquarters, and there the trial of the "Killer" was a short one; perhaps it had been better for him had he been killed there in the bushes! There were papers found on him that proved him beyond doubt to be the murderer of prisoners. Colonel Edwards sternly told him that he might live just so long as it took to dig his grave, and asked him if he did not want to see a chaplain.

"I do not want to see a chaplain," he answered, with as little concern as though the matter in no way affected him. "Every man has to die once, and it makes but little difference to me when my time comes." He was so wonderfully cool and brave about it that Young impetuously interceded for his life, as did the other staff officers. And just here the story told by General Oliver Edwards—for it is General Edwards who tells the story— comes to an abrupt end, to leave one with an ever-haunting question that is to be never answered.

And now the years of preparation were at an end, and the long, gradual up-grade lay behind him; in front rose a mountain of labor—a mountain perpendicular with hardship and danger; its peak a pinnacle, to which he climbed and carved his name there.

The Northern Presidential election of 1864 was watched eagerly. The success or defeat of the Democratic party with its platform "The war is a failure" meant life or death to the Confederacy, and they did more than watch the election. Kenly's Maryland brigade, with Sheridan's army, had been permitted to vote in the field; to Colonel Mosby was given the order to capture the ballot-boxes and prevent the vote, *en route* to Martinsburg, from ever reaching Baltimore. The two companies of cavalry serving as escort were fiercely attacked by Mosby when but two miles out of Winchester and driven back; it required an entire regiment to carry the commissioners and the ballot safely through to the railroad.

At the same time a citizen rode into Winchester and excitedly told Colonel Edwards that Breckinridge was advancing on the town with an army, and already was within twenty miles. Edwards forwarded the report to Sheridan, and then sent out scouts and prepared for battle. Sheridan in reply sent the message:

> I am aware of the movement but do not know what it means. My scouts fail to bring me reliable information. If the enemy attacks Winchester, fight him if you feel strong enough; if not, start your trains for Harper's Ferry, put your back on your trains, and fight for them. Find out if possible what the movement means; the whole secret-service fund is at your disposal for this purpose.

Colonel Edwards answered that he did not believe Winchester to be the objective point, but if it were that he was ready. Then he waited. When his scouts came back with no definite information of the enemy's movements, it was then that Captain Young begged Colonel Edwards for permission to try to obtain this vital information, and Edwards reluctantly let him go. He asked only for three picked men and four Confederate cavalry uniforms—no horses, even, for he said that he preferred to mount himself and his men after leaving Winchester. Captain Young proposed to attempt one of the most desperate of all military necessities—to join the enemy's marching column and ride with them until he had gained the information. To pass pickets and enter an enemy's encampment is, so it is said, easy; to join a column on a march—and such a march!—has been found well-nigh impossible. Jack Sterry had tried it at the second Manassas, and Jack Sterry had been hanged for it. Henry Harrison Young tried the impossible and succeeded. How he did it would be told here, should be told here, with every detail of every danger met and overcome, for no achievement of the Secret Service is more worthy of record—only that the story is not known. He was one who reported results, not details, and if he ever related the hidden history of that journey it has died with them to whom he told it. But this is what he did—it shall be written simply, that every word may be remembered by all who love to honor American heroes: For two hours he rode with Lomax's cavalry or marched with the infantry of Breckinridge. Forty-five miles they rode—he and his three men, riding down three sets of horses, which they seized for reliefs as they needed them.

Yet it was all done in the short space of six hours, and when he dismounted at Edwards's headquarters he bore full information of the plans of the enemy. There had been ample time to have frustrated these plans, but that Breckinridge's return was so threatened that even then he was in hurried retreat with an abandoned purpose. Winchester had been but a feint; Hancock, Maryland—there to destroy the vote or to break up the election— had been the real objective.

Colonel Edwards himself took the report to General Sheridan.

"That is true, every word of it, I believe," Sheridan cried, vehemently. "Now, where did you get it?"

Edwards told him how his own professional scouts had failed in the same degree as had his, and that his inspector-general, Young, had volunteered and had succeeded.

Sheridan became greatly excited: "I have been looking for that man for two years, and I want him."

Colonel Edwards spoke slowly: "I would rather you would take my right arm than to take him from me."

Sheridan's answer was quick, impetuous, eager: "I will make him a major and a personal aide-de-camp on my staff; I will let him pick a hundred men and arm them and command them as he likes, and report only to me. I will not take an officer of your staff from you without your consent, but—I want him!"

For a time there was silence, Edwards weighing the offer, Sheridan waiting.

Then, "I will urge him to accept the offer," Colonel Edwards answered. He had to urge him. For, though he loved the life held out to him, Captain Young refused decidedly to leave Edwards, until convinced that it was indeed a duty to accept a position offering greater opportunities for more valuable work for the Union.

The war was within five months of the end; but into that time there was crowded more work by the Secret Service than had been done in all the years that preceded. They say of him that Major Young never rested; to have done what he has done confirms it. It was as though there had been drawn a sword, keen, high-tempered, brilliant, that for the first time left its scabbard and for the first time discovered its mission.

Major Young at once commenced the organization of his new command; the men he carefully selected from those he knew best in Colonel Edwards's brigade; also, he retained the seven who had served as scouts for Sheridan. The corps never numbered the even hundred; the roll-book, which was kept by and is still in the possession of Sergeant McCabe, shows but fifty-eight names all told. There were few enough to answer "present" when the five months were ended. That there were any at all is the wonder after service such as this, which must have been for the trying-out of their courage; after such a test there could never again be doubt of it!

This expedition was made within a few days after the men had been selected, dressed in the gray uniform, and armed with two revolvers each—carried in the tops of the high boots—and the short, terrible Spencer carbines. Night had fallen when they left the camp, and for a long time the men rode without knowing where they were going or the work that lay before them; then Young halted and carefully instructed them and told them his purpose. Sixty men were to attack an entire brigade of Confederate cavalry! They rode on again in the darkness—perhaps blacker now to each man as he considered the desperate chances. After a time they halted and drew off into the edge of a forest bordering a road on which Major Young had learned the Confederate column would travel; there followed a wait that must have seemed endless—the dreaded inaction just before battle. The well-trained horses stood with drooping heads, like statues; the raw

November night-wind chilled as though a corpse had suddenly risen and breathed upon them; and still the Confederates did not come; the strain must have been horrible. Then above the dry-bone knock and creak of the bare branches of the forest behind them there came a new sound—the sound of a distant cavalry column, trotting; the low rumble and jar of thousands of hoof-falls; the tiny jangles and tinklings of countless metal accoutrements. The advance passed in a shadowy flitting; the tired men riding in silence—only the noise of the now-galloping horses.

Young gave a signal, and the men stole out from among the trees, leading the horses; at the roadside they mounted, and waited. The head of the column approached, and they fell in with it and jogged along, slouching in the saddles as did the worn, sleepy Confederates, to whom they seemed but a returned scouting party, dully noted, instantly forgotten.

Major Young gave a shrill signal, whirled his horse about, and fired his carbine in the faces of the Confederate troopers. His men followed him; the carbines roared like artillery; bullets raked the column, down whose bloody lanes the Yankees rode at the charge, firing their revolvers on either side without mercy. The attack coming out of their midst was a blinding shock to the Confederates; to them it was mutiny, treason, murder. The rest is all told in one word—pandemonium. And all but one Union soldier came through that charge down the entire length of the column.

After that night terror came to the Confederates in the Valley—not to the army, but to the army's soldiers: pickets rode to their stations, and were not there when their comrades rode to relieve them; guards fired at shadows; men about outlying camp-fires huddled together closer than the cold could have driven them; from nerve-racked vedettes would come a "Halt-who-comes-there!"—and then an instant volley; Confederate patrols and scouting parties rode back to their own lines with more trepidation than up to the lines of the enemy. Yankees in gray were known to be hovering about the army always—were known to be in the lines, within the encampments; some were captured; there were always others who took their places. Most secret plans were found sooner or later to have a hole in them.

Back at Sheridan's headquarters there was one man doing it all. It can never be told, for it was never known—the details of organizing the Secret Service of Sheridan's army of the Shenandoah, for it was all done in the head of that one man, who was ever tirelessly planning, quietly directing, inspiring. Of the work of the Service for the first two months, General Sheridan wrote in his *Memoirs:*

> I now realized more than I had done hitherto how efficient my scouts had become since under the control of Colonel Young, for not only did they bring me almost every day intelligence from within Early's lines, but they also operated efficiently against the guerrillas infesting West Virginia.

He might have sat in a tent and from there merely directed—that in itself would have been work enough for any man; but instead, with every opportunity he was out with some party; fighting was his "leave of absence," his recreation. But there were other ways in which he was to the enemy more deadly. Woodbury (historian) says of him, "In the peculiar service in which he was engaged during the last year of the war he had no superior in the Northern armies." Most of all, that sentence meant the obtaining of information. At one time he lived for two weeks within the Confederate lines, boarding at a house near Winchester—as an invalid! Through acquaintances made there he obtained the information he was seeking, and one day rode quietly away with it.

Imperturbably cool, patient, shrewd, with a quiet, easy way about him, yet frank and ingenuous—it seemed that there was nothing he could not accomplish. It must be, too, that he had a mighty sense of humor; witness the fate of the Confederate recruiting-office. He came upon it quite by accident, at a little hamlet, while on one of his restless, lonely scoutings. It was in full blast—doing a good business. He rode up and, dismounting, looked on in bucolic placidity.

"Come here!" called the sergeant. "You're a likely lookin' young feller—how about enlistin'?" Young listened to the sergeant's pleadings—"didn't know but what he would some day—well, mebbe he would then." More argument: suddenly the sergeant had him— enlisted. He swore to show up at the appointed day, and there was great applause—for the sergeant. Did he disappoint the sergeant? Never! Brought him more recruits—Young's own men—who "enlisted" the sergeant and all the sergeant's soldiers and all the assembled, hard-earned recruits, and the entire contents of the office.

So often was he outside the lines that his disguises had to be changed and varied constantly; now it was one role now another—private soldier, deserter, countryman, peddler, Confederate officer. Once, to test a disguise—that of a Confederate colonel—just before starting on a particularly dangerous mission, he allowed himself to be captured by men of his own old brigade, who marched their great prize back to camp in triumph. He demanded an interview at headquarters, and they took him there; the rebel colonel never again was seen. For a long time it was a matter of much talk and speculation as to why the escape of so important a capture should go so unregarded by the General.

There was another side to him besides the fun-loving; a seldom-seen, terrible side of cold wrath and pitiless judgment.

A prisoner had been taken by Young and his men on one of the countless night incursions into the enemy's country; on the ride back the identity of the man was discovered by some of the men guarding him, and the whisper ran through the troop and grew into a deep, savage mutter as story after story of his cruelties and cowardice was repeated. One of the men spurred ahead to Major Young's side.

"Do you know who your prisoner is, Major?"

"No."

At the answer Young reined in his horse sharply.

"What's *that!* That man is—"

The soldier repeated the name—the name of the leader of the most infamous guerrilla band in all that valley; a man whose name brought to mind the memory of crimes unmentionable for their atrocity.

Major Young rode back through his ranks. . . . No execution, ponderous, formal, lawful, could have been more solemn, more awe-compelling, than that swift blotting out, there in the night in the silence of the lonely country.

Was it only chance that, a short time later, Young was given the opportunity to snatch back from certain death unreckoned scores of Union soldiers, condemned that hour to lay down their lives for their flag? There would be given the name of the skirmish (which in any other war would be dignified by the name of battle), but the name is lost in the crowded memories of the few who knew the story. But perhaps there will be of those who wore the blue one who will read this story to whom there will come back the memory of a morning with the regiments that lay on their faces at the wood's edge, galled and torn by the shells constantly bursting among them, while they awaited, restive, the order for the charge across the open and the attempt to scale the hillside from whose all but impregnable crest the battery thundered. Others there are, of the South, who will recall with heartburnings the loss of an all but won engagement. Here, perhaps for the first time, they will learn the reason. Some may now recollect having seen in the driving smoke a boyish, gray-clad officer who, in the name of their commanding general, ordered the battery to take immediate position on the left flank—there to be utterly useless. Perhaps they recall the way he sat his horse, there amid the flying Federal bullets, until he saw the carrying out of his order; then that they had seen him gallop away—forever, leaving them, the dupes, to face their angered general.

Young had carried to the Federal regiment the order to take the battery—the key position of the engagement; he had seen the terrible slaughter which must be the price of success, and he had not given the order. Instead he had formed a plan and told it, then swiftly donning his gray uniform, and making a detour, had entered the Confederate lines—at no one knows what hazard—and had come up behind the battery, to whose captain he had given a false order. The astonished Federal soldiers rushed the abandoned hill crest before the Confederates could replace their guns; but as for Major Young, an unexpected shift in the position of the army compelled him to remain within the Confederate lines for hours in imminent danger of detection and capture—and death.

Capture and Death (they should be written as one word for the case of Harry Young) never had far to come, for he was always at least half-way to meet them. Once he reached too far and fell in their path, and it seemed that at last they had him; it was only the gallantry of his men which that day saved him—nothing that he himself did for himself, except that he had won the devotion of the men who saved him.

It was on one of those nights in January when the army was in quarters but *he* was not. There was a Confederate picket reserve at the Edinburg bridge, another at Columbia Furnace—isolated detachments far in advance of their army. It is no story to tell of their capture; there was a dash out of the night, a few scattering shots, and they had surrendered—sixty-five men in all, and many horses. There were nearly as many prisoners as captors; for of the Federals there were but a score of the Secret Service men, some in Confederate gray, some in their blue uniforms, and a troop of fifty cavalry—on their first detached service and very nervous about it. The crest of Massanutten Mountain was black and sharp against the brightening sky before they turned for the long ride back to the Union lines near Kernstown. At a little village they stopped for breakfast; Young was jubilant over the capture—it had been so easy; he was merry at the breakfast, and joked with the men about him. Rowand, one of the scouts, finished his meal and restlessly wandered out to the street; a butcher named Kuhn passed close to Rowand and whispered, "Three hundred on the 'Back Road,' coming!" The scout hurried in with the tidings, but Major Harry Young that day was foolhardy. "I'll not budge till I finish my breakfast," he said, laughing. Campbell, one of Sheridan's oldest scouts, added his unavailing protests; Young ate on placidly. When he finished he leisurely gave the order to mount, and then saw that he was indeed too late—that he had overtarried; the Confederate cavalry was sweeping into the upper end of the mile-long village street. At almost the first fire the raw Federal cavalrymen abandoned their prisoners, broke, and fled. The scouts galloped after them more slowly, fighting coolly for the safety of the whole party. Young was his old self again; the elation was gone with his once-prisoners; he was fighting recklessly to redeem himself for his blunder.

"Rowand," he yelled, "for God's sake stop the cavalry and bring them back."

But they would not stop; Rowand rode among them and fiercely tried to turn them—he caught the sergeant's bridle rein, and drawing his pistol swore to kill him if he did not help to turn them; the sergeant was beyond further fear and paid no heed to him.

There was a shout from his partner, Campbell: "Rowand, come back; Young is down!" He looked and then spurred his horse to a run. He saw Major Young beside his dead horse, on foot, fighting savagely; he saw Campbell and "Sonny" Chrisman charging in the very faces of the yelling Confederates; Campbell passed Young and swung his horse across the road and stood there behind it firing over its back with both revolvers; Chrisman, without dismounting, caught Young up behind, turned, and rode bounding toward Rowand.

Together, Campbell and Rowand held back the enemy until others of the scouts were able to join them; step by step they retreated until Young and Chrisman had a good start; after that it was just a race, and the Federals won it! Had Young in his gray uniform been captured there would never have been a chance for him.

So close a call might have shaken the nerve of some men, but if Young thought of it again at all he was not much affected by it, for within two weeks he was engaged on one of the most desperate of all his missions— not the taking of Gilmor, but that which almost immediately followed.

February 5th he and his scouts captured Maj. Harry Gilmor at Moorefield, West Virginia. The story of that terrible ride of sixty miles in the dead of winter, over the mountains and down into the South Branch Valley, and of the surprise and the capture of Gilmor, has been told in the story of "Rowand"; but it has not been told how Young saved his prisoner from the vindictive mob at Harper's Ferry—how he held them off with his revolver, and whispered to Gilmor, "In case of attack, take one of my pistols and shoot right and left: they will have to walk over my dead body to get you!" And further along on their way to Boston and the prison of Fort Warren— when the warning came that the people of Baltimore were prepared for Harry Gilmor (he had at one time raided to within four miles of Baltimore)—Young told him that he should have arms, and added laughingly, "I should enjoy a skirmish amazingly; I think you and I could whip a small crowd by ourselves."

They were much alike, those two Harrys, and they seem to have developed a great admiration for each other. Long after the war Gilmor wrote of the man who not only captured him, but who took him to the very doors of the prison that held him till the end of the Rebellion:

He was a bold, fearless cavalry soldier, a man of remarkable talents for the duty he was selected to perform, possessing the qualities of quick discernment, good judgment, and great self-reliance, rapid execution of plans, made to suit circumstances as they presented themselves. Those are the essential qualities of a good scout. We never knew when or where to look for him, and yet we knew that he or some of his best men were constantly inside our lines. I have known him to pass our pickets on an old farm-horse with collar and hames and a sack of corn, as if on his way to mill, fool our pickets, and go out again without being suspected.

But it is not alone to give one on the other side the chance to pay tribute that Harry Gilmor has been mentioned; it was because his capture indirectly brought about the most audacious of all Major Young's adventures.

When he stood in the sleet that February night, alone—sixty miles from the Federal army—as sentry at the door of the headquarters of General Jubal Early, commander of the Confederate army in the Shenandoah, he was the master adventurer of the war.

In retaliation for the capture of Gilmor, Jesse McNeill, at the head of a band of sixty-five rangers, had captured Generals Crook and Kelly from their beds in hotels in the heart of the large town of Cumberland. That, like Gilmor's capture, was done by an armed party of men—a performance all dash and excitement, and with the penalty, if taken, of merely an enemy's prison. When Major Young set out alone for Staunton, a few days later, to capture General Early from his headquarters in the midst of his army, it was a deed that was akin to madness. By every rule of war he was a spy, and nothing could have saved him. What a story could be told by the man who faced death each moment of those six days and nights! It could be told by that man and by him alone.

What a story—of the difficulties met; the quick turns, both ways, of chance; of the unforeseen and the unexpected that leaped out and menaced him everywhere; of the moments of elation when success seemed certain, and the lonely times when it was pit-blackness to be so very much alone with the dangers! There is little enough that he ever told. He could have taken Early; for two nights he stood sentry at his very door while the faithless Confederate guard—with whom he had changed places—went into the town sweethearting! But with nearly sixty miles to travel in an enemy's country, winter-bound, and hampered by a prisoner, he realized that some time in the ensuing pursuit he must either free Early or kill him, and he would not wish to do either—once he had him. Young afterward said to General Edwards, "Had Early been guilty of murdering prisoners or of sanctioning it, I could and would have taken his life, but I did not consider it civilized warfare to kill him under the circumstances." Did General Jubal Early ever learn who had guarded him as he slept?—and ever after see in each sentry at his door a living sword of Damocles?

Young swung from plan to plan, but at last gave back the Confederate musket, and returned as quietly as he had come, empty-handed as to prisoners, but with much very valuable information.

The spring campaign began; the end of the war was almost at hand. Sheridan and his ten thousand cavalry commenced the Second James River Canal Raid. The war in the Shenandoah was ended. It was monotonous work for the army—the wrecking of railroads and the ruining of canals; the rain fell constantly, the roads were sloughs, the fields bogs; but all knew now that the end was coming, and it gave them heart to endure anything. Though there were no battles for the army to fight, there was desperate work for the men of the Secret Service. Not in many pages could the stories be told, but in two-score words Sheridan has written an imperishable record:

> To Maj. H. H. Young, of my staff, chief of scouts, and the thirty or forty men of his command who took their lives in their hands, cheerfully going wherever ordered, to obtain that great essential of success, information, I tender my gratitude. Ten of these men were lost.

March 27th the cavalry joined Grant, and very soon there commenced a whirlwind of fighting; not a day without its battle, not an hour without a skirmish; night-time and dawn and noonday, fighting, fighting. There was one chance for Lee and the Army of Northern Virginia—one chance to prolong the life of the Confederacy; to join Johnson in Carolina. And then Sheridan's ten thousand troopers at Dinwiddie Court House suddenly blocked the only way to the south;

April 1st at Five Forks they drove them back, turned them west, ruined them. Petersburg fell on the 2d; the capital, Richmond, was next
day evacuated; the Confederacy was down; Lee's army futilely struggled westward—a fugitive army. All the time there was fighting going
on, every move meant fighting, there was always fighting. It was no
rout; when the Confederates turned on their pursuers, and the forces
were at all equal, the Federals were nearly always driven back until
reinforcements—always the inevitable reinforcements—came up; then
the pursuit would begin again.

Neither seemed to know exhaustion. One was nerved by desperation;
the other, exultant, buoyed up by triumph. Troops that had marched
all day marched again nearly all night, and fought at dawn; and there
were days of that. There were troops—night marching they were, too—
rushing to the support of a single corps that had been turned on and
was being crushed by Lee's army, who made the night aglare with
their improvised torches of straw and pine knots and great fires by the
roadside; and as they marched they sang and cheered like mad, and the
marching bands crashed and blared to their singing. God! Was there
ever such a war with such an ending!

And here, if never before, Young and his men served the army. There
were a dozen roads the Confederates might follow, a score of turns
to take that might lead to no one knew what objective; but fast as
the fugitives moved, there were on each road, at every turn, always the
gray-clad Federal scouts, hidden, watchful; they all but lived with the
Confederates; so close did they keep they might as well have marched
with them, slept with them; for they returned to their own lines only to
report newly discovered movements. They had ever been brave, these
scouts; now they seemed the personification of courage. It was not
because of any change in the Confederates—the peril was as great or
greater than ever: witness—on the very morning of the surrender two
of Young's men were condemned to be hanged, and only the surrender
saved them.

Humorous incidents there were, too—comedy cheek by jowl with
tragedy, because it was life, not a story. There was the capture of
Barringer—Brigadier-General Rufus Barringer of the North Carolina

Brigade—who was captured behind his own lines the day after Five Forks. Dignifed General Barringer!—who drew himself up so haughtily and replied so coldly to Confederate-private Young's cheery, "Good afternoon, General," with a, "You have the advantage of *me,* sir."

"You're right I have, General!" laughed the Major, as he drew his revolver and demanded the astounded Confederate's surrender. The whole Southern army was between Young and the Union lines, yet he and his men led General Barringer and his staff to a Federal prison, although it took from two o'clock in the afternoon until dark to reach safety. And the very next day Major Young and party—the major resplendent in the captured uniform of a Confederate colonel—met in the enemy's lines a colonel from North Carolina and his orderly, and, as was fitting for two officers of such high rank, he stopped to pass the time of day with him. The colonel from North Carolina told of General Barringer's capture by the Yankees—one of the staff had escaped and spread the tidings. He, the colonel, did not exactly bewail the fate of Barringer, "for," said he, "I am to command; I take his place."

"Oh no!" said Harry Young. "You do not take his place; you go to the place where he is!" And, sure enough, he joined his general.

It is the last night of the war, but no one knows it. The countryside is full of aimlessly wandering soldiers, lost from their regiments by the rapid man<oe>uvers, lost from their very armies. A small party of Federal officers struck the railroad—the great foot-path for the strayed Confederates—and in the dusk sat watching the passing groups of stragglers—weary, dejected men without arms for the most part, who had flocked together for company; here and there were cavalrymen, armed and mounted, yet they, too, rode as dejected and listless as any part of the procession. The officers drew nearer; the cavalrymen eyed them with uneasiness, and finally in the growing darkness one of them stole up to the officers.

"Get back a little—you might spoil it," he said. "We're some of Major Young's men, and we're leadin' these Johnnies down the road a piece to where the Major's got a whole corral of 'em." The staff party, hugely amused, circled into the woods and soon came upon Major Young and some twenty of his men with cocked carbines—holding passive and silent several hundred prisoners, to which the decoys constantly added.

Farther down that very railroad—at Appomattox Station—others of Young's scouts had discovered the Confederates' four lost supply trains. Men of the Secret Service found them—that is repeated, because it is usual only to remember that Custer fought for the trains and took them. Sergeant McCabe was in charge of the detachment that found them; he sent Jim White to report the find, and White has had the credit! Perhaps White saw the supply trains first, and so claimed the honor of reporting them. But Sergeant McCabe was in charge of the detachment, and this is written that he may read it, and in it see an attempt to induce history to give him the place that, forty-seven years, he has grieved for.

It has been said that Lee surrendered because of the capture of those supply trains—that their capture fixed the day of the surrender. General Lee did not know of their capture until after he had written and signed that last letter. To General Grant he then said:

> . . . . "I have, indeed, nothing for my own men. . . . I telegraphed to Lynchburg, directing several train-loads of rations to be sent on by rail from there, and when they arrive I should be glad to have the present wants of my men supplied from them." At this remark all eyes turned toward Sheridan, for he had captured these trains with his cavalry the night before. . . . —GENERAL HORACE PORTER, in *Battles and Leaders.*

Presently, at about four o'clock of that April Sunday, General Lee rode away from the McLean House; rode back to his men after signing the letter in which he surrendered the Army of Northern Virginia, from signing away the existence of the Confederate States of America.

Thus was the end of the Civil War; and as an end to Major Henry Harrison Young's Civil War service there stands this record—no, not as an end, but framing it, just as a simple frame of dull gold completes and focuses a picture, so with these words of Sheridan's:

CAVALRY HEADQUARTERS,
PETERSBURG, VIRGINIA, *April 19, 1865.*
To HONORABLE E. M. STANTON,
Secretary of War, Washington, D. C.

SIR,— . . . I desire to make special mention of the valuable services of Major H. H. Young, Second Rhode Island Infantry, chief of my scouts during the cavalry expedition from Winchester, Virginia, to the James River. His personal gallantry and numerous conflicts with the enemy won the admiration of the whole command. In the late campaign from Petersburg to Appomattox Court House he kept me constantly informed of the movements of the enemy and brought in prisoners, from brigadier-generals down. The information obtained through him was invaluable. I earnestly request that he be made a lieutenant-colonel by brevet. . . .

Very respectfully,
Your obedient servant,
(Signed) P. H. SHERIDAN,
Major-General, Commanding.

What remains to be told is all too brief. He did not go back to Providence with the men of the Second Rhode Island; there came the chance to prolong for a few months the life of adventure, and he hailed it gladly.

With the end of the Civil War, the administration turned its attention to the French in Mexico. The Liberals, defeated at nearly every point, impoverished, split into factions, were in a desperate plight; Maximilian and the Imperialists were everywhere in the ascendant.

Sheridan at the head of an army of observation was sent to Brownsville at the mouth of the Rio Grande; and Colonel Young, taking four of his most trusty men, went with him.

In Brownsville, Sheridan met Caravajal, wily and subtle and old, then leader of the Liberals; and to him he recommended Young "as a confidential man, whom he could rely upon as a 'go-between' for communicating with our people at Brownsville, and whom he could trust to keep him informed of the affairs in his own country as well." Caravajal saw Young, and, first assuring him that his plan had the concurrence of General Sheridan, proposed a scheme which, God knows why, won him; it was that Young should raise, equip, and command a band of picked men to act as body-guard for Caravajal. Perhaps the plan awoke in him the sleeping spirit of a soldier of fortune; perhaps it was a nobler, more Quixotic desire to aid the struggling Mexican patriots. But he took the seven thousand dollars furnished him and hurried to New Orleans, where he quickly raised and equipped his company.

Then Sheridan, who for a fortnight had been in the interior of Texas, came back to New Orleans. Of their interview Sheridan writes in his *Memoirs:*

> I at once condemned the whole business, but . . . [he] was so deeply involved in the transaction, he said, that he could not withdraw without dishonor, and with tears in his eyes he besought me to help him. He told me he had entered upon the adventure in the firm belief that I would countenance it; that the men and their equipment were on his hands; that he must make good his word at all hazards; and that while I need not approve, yet I must go far enough to consent to the departure of the men, and to loan him the money necessary to provision his party and hire a schooner to carry them to Brazos. It was hard, indeed, to resist the appeals of this man, who had served me so long and so well; and the result of his pleading was that I gave him permission to sail, and also loaned him the sum asked for; but I have never ceased to regret my consent, for misfortune fell upon the enterprise almost from its inception.

At Brownsville, over across the Gulf, Young and his men, about fifty in number, were met by the first hot breath of disaster. Caravajal had been deposed, and his successor, Canales, refused to accept their services. After that all is confusion to the very end. Young was without money to take his men back to New Orleans, without money to buy even food for them. He and his men pushed on desperately to reach the camp of General Escobedo, leader of another faction; they kept on the American side of the Rio Grande, proposing to cross into Mexico near Ringgold Barracks.

Far in advance there had been spread their story—who they were and what they did there, and where and why they were coming. They stood absolutely alone; the law of neutrality cut them off from all succor from their countrymen as completely as though they were outcasts; for the time they were men who had no country.

Renegade Mexican rancheros, ex-Confederates, mercenaries, bandits—all swarmed down to the river to head off the desperate little band. From the ensuing battle there came back—rumor, only rumor. Whether they were at last attacked and turned on their pursuers, whether in despair they tried to cross to cut their way through—it is told one way, it is told the other.

The little girl who drove that day in the Blackstone Valley has written of the years that she and the mother waited for tidings. They had seen the report first in a newspaper—had read it together; neither would believe it, and for years each buoyed up the other.

> It was a sad time indeed when his letters ceased coming, and when all efforts to find him proved unavailing. . . . Although I know that no tidings of him have cheered us in thirteen years, still I cannot conscientiously say that I believe him dead. I have no foundation on which to build hope, indeed, unless it be the private conviction of General Sheridan.

Sheridan, indeed, seems to have been as stubborn as they in his belief that Young had in some way crossed the river. He had immediately contradicted the first report that he had been killed: Young had been seen in Monterey. To General Edwards he wrote, "I cannot bear to think of him as dead, and yet hope to see him."

And even after more than two years, in a letter to the mother, he said: "Still . . . I am inclined to the belief that he is living. I merely state that as my conviction." But as the years passed and brought no definite tidings he gave up, and in his *Memoirs*, written some twenty years later, he sets down the siftings of rumor:

> They were attacked . . . Being on American soil, Young forbade his men to return the fire and bent all his efforts to getting them

over the river; but in this attempt they were broken up and became completely demoralized. A number of the men were drowned while swimming the river. Young himself was shot and killed, a few were captured, and those who escaped—about twenty in all—finally joined Escobedo.

But there are other versions equally positive as Sheridan's—only different. And thus it must remain, perhaps till the end of time—like an unfinished picture, abandoned, forgotten by the artist. There is the hot, glaring sand, and the hot, empty sky; between, the cruel and sparkling river; but of the figures that were to have peopled the painting and given it life and told its story, there is but a blur of meaningless paint and raw, uncovered canvas.

Bowie

A man lay prone in the dust of a sunlit road—dying. Above the red sumac bushes at the roadside there yet lingered the telltale smoke fast melting into the grayer blue of the autumn haze. The narrow road curved and curved again; it was between the two curves that the man lay—dying. A scant quarter of a mile away, around the first bend, a small party of men in gray—*his* men—were shouting and laughing, calling from one to another humorous details of the fight. For they had just repulsed an attack of four to one, and the enemy had fled, terror-struck—made ridiculous—at the first volley, leaving behind their horses, their arms, and their honor. As the men saddled their horses and led them down the steep knollside—down which they had so lately charged—they laughed and shouted boisterously; perhaps he heard them, for he was sitting now, beyond the bend—still in the middle of the road—with his torn face in his hands.

Beyond the man in the road, beyond the second bend, there ran two men, gray-clad; they were running forward, one at each side of the road, long-barreled revolvers in each hand swinging here and there toward every stirring leaf, every rustling bough. As they ran they stooped and peered through each opening in the tangled undergrowth, down every woodland aisle; in their red, sweat-bathed faces there was savage anger, and in their eyes dull grief and pain. The man who was a little ahead at last stopped and faced about. "We might as well go back," he said.

They holstered their revolvers, and, stride for stride, retraced their steps in silence. As they reached the bend, they sprang forward with glad, excited cries. He whom they had believed dead was sitting in the road with his face in his hands. They ran to him and knelt at his side, supporting him in their arms and asking if he were much hurt.

"I've got to die," he said, simply. "I know. Get the boys together and get out; the whole country will be up; they will double the patrols at the fords. Leave me and get out." They waited a moment for him to speak again, but they had heard the last that he was to say to them—the order that was for their safety; with the effort, he had slipped lower in their arms and lay quite still. The elder of the two motioned with a backward nod of his head.

"Go tell the others, Charlie"; and the boy stood up, and then ran heavily down the road. To the man who was left there came clearly the jangle of the accoutrements of men swinging into their saddles, the hoof-falls of restive horses, the hilarious shouts of the raiders, and then a sudden silence that made the tiny noises of the woods and fields seem loud. The elder man, who knelt in the road, listened grimly. "He's told them," he said.

Down in Montgomery County, near a village called Sandy Spring, in the State of Maryland, there should be a stone set at the side of a narrow road to mark the spot where Wat Bowie fell. Whether there be a stone or no, his memory will not soon be forgot by the South, whose son he was and who loved him; or by the North, on whom be turned his back, and who hated and feared him for the harm he did, yet could not but admire his sheer bravery, and the reckless daring that was an insolence to his foes.

He was thirty, and a lawyer in a dusty little red-brick office next the county court-house of Upper Marlboro, Prince George County, Maryland; and then the great war broke out, and Bowie went with the South.

He was thirty, and a lawyer; student days were over—the serious business of life had begun. From the age-yellowed photograph of that time there looks out a student, a mild man, grave and sober—handsome in a refined, quiet way; with high, broad forehead, higher and broader by the frame of thick, smooth-parted brown hair; small, straight nose between two deep-set, gray-blue eyes, mild and thoughtful; the whole expression made melancholy by the droop of the long, limp, fair mustache.

And then the great war broke out, and Bowie went with the South. It was the spirit of the school-boy who had settled down to the endlessness of a long term, and who suddenly is reprieved by the closing of the school— back into playtime, into the world of out-of-doors. This is the Wat Bowie that his old comrades tell of with a brightening of their eyes and a softening of their voices.

"It wasn't just that he didn't know what it was to be afraid and that he loved to fight—there were some of the rest of us who were that way, too, those days—but he got such fun out of it. Would go out of his way for miles to get into trouble, and always come back laughing about it, an' joke over the way he had fooled 'em again.

"He was a handsome fellow, but it was always the laugh in his eyes that folks remembered first of all. Tall he was, and thin, and there was a bit of a stoop to his shoulders, like he'd had too much of the law-books. Lord, how the people loved him!—the Southern people of Maryland, that is. He knew every man, woman, and child in Prince George County, and they all called him Wat. And the girls—"

There was one Maryland girl— Perhaps that is why, when he closed the little law-office in Upper Marlboro, he did not go over into Virginia and enlist, preferring to stay in Prince George County and serve the South in the most hazardous capacity as spy. Perhaps it was only his love for greater danger, or dislike for discipline and routine; but certainly the girl was there, and certainly there were the dangers. And work! There was work to be done in Prince George—with Washington itself cutting deep into the northwest corner of the county, and Annapolis, the State capital, over next door in Anne Arundel; and the movement of Federal troops to watch, and the forwarding of three-fourths of all the mail for Richmond from sympathizers in the North—it was taken over the Potomac, where the Secret Service men and the patrols had to be outwitted in a new way every night.

Down in Prince George County there are scores of houses to-day where they will tell you something of Wat Bowie, but of those first months of the war there will be little that they can tell. He was here, there, back again, then gone for days and weeks at a time; long, lonely

night rides, nights along the river, days of hiding, days of planning—
of spying; trips into Washington itself—in the early days of the war
before he was a marked man; to Richmond, perhaps, with tidings; or
with reports to army headquarters over in Virginia, then back across
the storm-swept Potomac ere the dawn. It was hard, desperate, quick-
wit work; and as the months passed it grew harder, more dangerous
still. He was doing great work for the South—it was too good to escape
attention; the War Department in Washington grew irritated, and said
that Maryland might as well have joined the South. Secret Service men
overran Prince George, and soon the report went back that of all disloyal
Marylanders one Wat Bowie was the man.

At last, one autumn night, after months of search, they caught him—
at the home of the girl. The house was surrounded, then they burst in.
Wat Bowie dashed though the second-story window and fell, literally,
into the arms of the men outside.

They took him to Washington to the Old Capitol Prison, and there
they sentenced him to be hanged. Even President Lincoln, the "Merciful
Man," approved the sentence, they say. His people did everything to
have him freed; they planned and plotted, bribed and bought. At last
the plans were complete; but they could not get word to him, until his
aunt, Mrs. Tyler, pleaded so hard to be allowed to bid her boy good-by
that they let her in, a day or two before Friday—it was to be on Friday,
the hanging. And, though they searched her and watched her vigilantly,
yet as she kissed him good-by for the last time she slipped a tiny note
from her lips into his. When she had gone he read that that very night
a negro servant would be sent to him with food, and that the door of
his cell would not be locked again after the food had been handed in;
and at exactly seven o'clock the light in his corridor would be put out;
and that there would be a ladder to the skylight of the roof.

It was all made as simple as a child's game, and as simply carried
out. By a few minutes past seven he was lying on the roof of a wood-
shed, resting in the rain and waiting for the passing of the sentry along
his beat beyond the wall. When he heard the measured pacing grow
fainter, he climbed to the top of the wall and dropped down. But the
dark and the slime of the roadway made him land wrong, and he fell
heavily, wrenching his ankle. He lay breathless for a minute, expecting

the guard to rush back and seize him, or the alarm to be raised in the prison. The guard had stopped, and was listening too, pausing in doubt; with hesitation, he began to walk back. And then Bowie, the aggrieved citizen, commenced to swear loudly; he cursed the city and the city fathers, the wretched sidewalks, and the lampless street, the darkness of the night, and the rain; and then he yelled lustily for help. The guard hurried now.

"Help me up, my good fellow," Bowie cried. The guard was a stupid oaf, and asked him, with lulled suspicion, what he did in that place.

It was dark, and he had blundered over to the wrong side of the road—any fool should know that; if ever he got safe home he would never come that way again. Perhaps if he were helped a bit to the end of the sentry's beat— And so, half cajoling, half commanding in his insolent fashion, wholly making a fool of him, Bowie beguiled the sentry into aiding him on his way, and morning saw him back in Prince George with a tale to tell over which they chuckle to this day—down in Prince George. So they tell the story, Bowie's old comrades in arms, "just as Wat told it to us."

The Official Records of the War Department have their own way of telling such tales: "Walter Bowie, Maryland, confined Old Capitol Prison, Oct. 14, 1862, by order Secretary of War. Charge: 'Disloyal Practices.' Escaped at 7.00 P.M., November 17, 1862." But perhaps the sentry never told!

For weeks they kept hot on his trail—little details of cavalry and many Secret Service men. He blundered into a small camp of them one morning at dawn, and saw instantly that retreat was impossible; with a dozen revolvers they were ready to open fire. Without hesitation, he strode up to the men and shouted, indignantly:

"You make mighty free with my rails! With all this wood around, you did not need to burn my fences." He was very angry.

"Who are you?" a corporal stammered.

"The owner of the rails, of course." And then, becoming somewhat mollified, he went on: "Well, well. War is war; but don't do any more damage than you can help, boys." He sat down with them to their breakfast and chatted with them pleasantly. One of them asked if he had seen Wat Bowie, and described him accurately. At the description, they all stared at him and moved uneasily, in doubt as to what was to be done; he tallied with the description in every respect. But his insolence in walking up to them and cursing them for burning "his" rails made them doubt their own eyes.

"Why, yes," he drawled, "Wat Bowie was in these parts last week—I know him well. They say he has gone to the north part of the county, where he hails from. I don't know, though, as to that."

Then, rising and stretching himself, he looked down into their doubt-filled eyes and laughed at them—laughed in their very faces.

"I'm glad you-all met me on m' own land—you might have made trouble for me elsewhere, for they all say I look like him a lot. Good-by, boys. Good luck!"

He turned back a moment as he strode away. "If you would like a drink, any of y', come to the house about dusk, when I shall be home."

"Thank you, sir," they chorused.

Spring came, and passed, and summer began—the summer of '63. Secret Service men dogged his heels, always but one jump behind. Across the face of the orders for his arrest is invariably written, "Not to be found." Colonel Lafayette Baker, then Provost Marshal of the War Department, reports to Secretary of War Stanton, July 9, 1863, that the "notorious rebel and spy, Walter Bowie, succeeded in evading the search for him"; he does not say how.

But Wat Bowie told, laughing; and the story is a favorite in Prince George to-day. The house was surrounded, and they would not give him even the chance of darkness, in case he should break through the line; they waited for dawn. When the gray light came they closed in on the house; the door opened, and two negro women, their teeth chattering from fear of the Yankees, came shambling out with pails to go to the spring for water.

"You're a mighty tall nigger," a soldier called, as they passed him in the shrubbery; the girl dropped her bucket and rolled her eyes in fear, and the man laughed and let them by. The fat old negress came back, and they asked her where the wench was.

"Yo'-all scairt her so, she done run away," she said. Suspicion flamed in their eyes; several rushed to the spring—she was gone. They charged into the house; his coat and hat were there, and the corks with which he had blacked his face, but the mighty tall nigger they never saw again.

Perhaps it was the girl's doing; she may have begged him to leave the State, where each month saw him more hard pressed by the Secret Service men, where vindictive Unionists reported his movements day after day; the State where the shadow of the noose fell upon him at every turn. Perhaps it was only his restless nature that demanded change, that sought the other side of war. Or it may be that the wild deeds in "Mosby's Confederacy," where warfare was waged in the methods he had so long used single-handed, drew him irresistibly over the Potomac.

And so, in the early spring of '64, Wat Bowie joined the Forty-third Battalion of Virginia Cavalry, Mosby's Rangers—the Partisan Battalion they called themselves; to the North they were "Mosby's Guerrillas," hated and feared.

Colonel Mosby—now a hale, vigorous old man of seventy-nine— tells of him: "Wat Bowie, of Maryland? To be sure I remember him. He was a brave fighter." Perhaps he was thinking of that day at Mount Zion Church when they captured the raider Major Forbes; that day when he and Bowie and a handful of the Rangers fought side by side and hand to hand against a band of desperate Federals, hemmed in and at bay. Or of the night at Belle Plain when he and Bowie, scouting together, rode for their lives before the hotly pursuing Union cavalry. It was that same night, later, that they and a squad of Rangers captured the train of fifty wagons between Fredericksburg and Belle Plain. These and a score more adventures must Colonel Mosby recall at the memory of Bowie of Maryland.

It was by such deeds as these that he fought his way to the first lieutenancy of Company F before that same summer was gone. He had scarce won to his command when he went to Mosby with a plan that made even Mosby pause. But he talked and argued and pleaded eloquently, enthusiastically, giving detail after detail, point by point, of his great plan—shrewdly conceived, keenly thought out, and backed by a courage known to all.

"He was always after me those days," Colonel Mosby tells, with a twinkle in his eye, "to let him go over and 'stir things up in Maryland.' So this time I let him have twenty-five men, and told him to go ahead and make the try." Then, gravely, "He was a gallant young man."

He picked his men, the largest force that had as yet been intrusted to his individual command. Through Fairfax they rode, though Prince William and Stafford, to King George Court House in King George County, and there they turned toward the Potomac; and at the house of Mr. Tennant he quartered his men, while he and Jack Randolph and Jim Wiltshire went scouting over the river. They had a wild crossing of the Potomac—four miles wide there at Matthias Point—but they made the passage safely in the yawl of Long, the blockade-runner. The men lolled about on Virginia's shores, waiting.

Through the mist over the bottom-lands around Tennant's house could be seen the Potomac, green and sullen—white-capped; sometimes, even beyond, to the long low shores of Maryland. About eleven of the third night young Wiltshire came back.

"Charlie Vest, O'Bannon, George Smith, and George Radcliffe and Haney are wanted—dismounted. The rest are to report back to Colonel Mosby in Fauquier," he said. It had been found too hazardous to operate with so large a force as twenty-five, and none of the horses could be ferried across.

On the way to the river Wiltshire told them how Long had tried to turn back when part way across with him, because of his fear of the many passing boats, and how he had had to urge him on, at the point of his pistol, and swear that if Long did not wait for them that he would hunt him down and kill him, wherever found. But the blockade-runner was waiting, and sullenly ferried them across to "the Walnut," where Bowie and Randolph joined them; and they all trudged across the fields to a sheltering wood a mile away. There they slept. Bowie was gone again, soon after sunrise, on one of his lone scouts, and they waited in the woods all that day for his return. They dozed and woke, and dozed again, till the watery sun broke through the thin clouds and warmed away the chill; and they grew gay again and jested what they would say to his excellency Bradford, the governor of Maryland, when, a prisoner, he should ride back with them to Virginia and the Confederacy.

This army of eight, without mounts, clad in rebel-gray, armed only with revolvers, cut off from supplies and the succor of their friends, meant to penetrate to the heart of a hostile state and snatch its chief executive from Annapolis, or, failing that, to rob the State bank and dash with the spoils or the captive to the fords of the upper Potomac.

It was not such a hopeless plan—to them. They were boys, all, from the stripling Charlie Vest, aged seventeen, to Bowie, thirty-one. Boys, sanguine, gay, whom thee years of a bloody war had not made grim nor old.

Men they were, too, in trained skill, in resource, in aggression, and in the experience of successful raid after raid in one of the most daring cavalry commands the world has ever seen, a command led and inspired by that genius of partisan warfare, Mosby. And at their head now was Mosby's lieutenant, Bowie.

They cheered him when he returned at twilight to tell them that he had horses for them—good horses, United States government horses—"if they could lick long odds." It was twelve or fifteen miles to the horses, which belonged to a provost guard of a cavalry camp at Port Tobacco, and they walked all the way.

As described by a newspaper writer,[1] this is the Port Tobacco of those days, the home of Atzeroth, hanged accomplice of John Wilkes Booth:

> If any place in the world is utterly given over to depravity, it is Port Tobacco . . . a rebel port for blockade-runners, and a rebel post-office general. Gambling, corner-fighting, shooting-matches. . . . The hotel here is called Brawner House; it has a bar in the nethermost cellar, and its patrons, carousing in that imperfect light, look like the denizens of some burglar's crib talking robbery between their cups. The court-house is the most superfluous house in the place—except the church. It stands in the center of the town, in a square, and the dwellings lie about it closely, as if to throttle justice. Five hundred people exist in Port Tobacco: life there reminds me, in connection with the slimy river and the adjacent swamps, of the great reptile period of the world.

Such was Port Tobacco; Bowie knew it well. It was in a little room behind the bar in the nethermost cellar of Brawner House that they

---

[1] Quoted the *History of the United States Secret Service,* by General L. C. Baker.

waited, smoking, drinking, telling stories, unconcerned for the coming hour, waiting till the town should grow silent in sleep. It was in the superfluous court-house that the provost guard was stationed; the cavalry camp was on the outskirts of the town. They strolled over to the court-house, and in the dark Bowie and Wiltshire throttled the single guard; then they all tiptoed into the wide, empty hall. In the doorway Vest was stationed.

"Shoot the first man out, Charlie," Bowie said.

There could be no retreat by Confederates, no escape for Federals—Charlie Vest was a certainty when it came to shooting the first man. Just inside the hall there were two doors, one on either side—both rooms might be filled. Wat Bowie and Wiltshire, lighting a match, flung open the door on the right-hand side and went in; the floor was filled with men—twenty of them.

"If any one fires a shot, we'll murder you all," Bowie yelled. The rest of his men rushed in; the match went out, and in the dark and confusion it seemed that the entire Confederate army was charging into the room. Outside, Charlie Vest was waiting to shoot the first man. But none came; the Federals were each giving a parole not to leave the room or give information till morning, "when we will be safe across the river," Bowie shrewdly said. The Union men kept their parole, though they had to listen to the raiders riding off on their horses.

And so they galloped gleefully away from Port Tobacco, Bowie riding a big raw-boned gray, his choice, though not the best; a fitting horse for a leader who always led, a horse to guide by, night and day, in battle or in retreat. Thirty-six miles they rode, and Bowie was in Upper Marlboro again. He must have pointed out to them the little red-brick office as they passed; must have drawn deep free breaths as they galloped by. They were hungry, and there was no food; the people dared not feed them. The shadow of the Old Capitol Prison stretched out from a dozen miles away, and lay like a blight upon the faint hearts of the Southern sympathizers.

They took a side road and came to a cabin, where Bowie ordered them to dismount. An old negress came to the door. At the sound of his voice she rushed to him as though to throw her arms about him, laughing and weeping, her old voice quivering with joy and surprise.

"Ma's' Wat! Ma's' Wat! Ah thought yo' was daid—they done tole me yo' was daid." He soothed her, patted her stooped shoulders, and stroked her gnarled, fumbling old hands, caressing her gently, as he stood with bared head before her out there under the stars.

He looked up at his waiting men. "She's m' 'mammy,' boys," he said.

More than forty-eight years have passed since that night, but the men who saw it have not forgotten it today. Both Jim Wiltshire and Charlie Vest told of it when they told the story of that last raid. "It was beautiful—that old woman's joy; a mighty affectin' sight to see."

And *she* fed them! Lord love you, yes—would have fed them though "Bull-dog" Stanton and his whole Secret Service howled around her door. Ham and cornbread and bacon—it was scarce those days, but— Marse Wat hungry! Marse Wat! She would have given them all she had if they had allowed it. She cried when he rode away.

It was a strange raid—more a pleasure ride of friends through a sunny, smiling land—that next day. Dawn brought them to Bowie's home, and they hid their horses in the wood and stole into the house. His mother and sisters were to be greeted after a long absence, and perhaps even the Girl was there. And then he must present his men—he led them forward one by one; this was the first chance for the mother and the girls to meet the men of his command. The servants had been sent away lest they carry tales, and so the girls themselves served the meal. And later, when the shyness had passed away, the sturdy campaign-stained cavalrymen and the slender white-clad girls, there in the cool parlor with the low-drawn shades, clustered about the piano and sang— "Maryland! My Maryland!" "Dixie," and "The Bonnie Blue Flag"—a dozen more, and all over again—with their host and leader, proud of his men, more lightheartedly gay than ever before.

In the twilight they rode away again—a swift journey back to war. Brune Bowie, a brother, convalescent of a wound, had joined them, making nine.

The story runs swift to the end. No one but Bowie could have led such a band into the very heart of Maryland—and not a shot fired, no alarm, no pursuit. He knew the country, but better still, the people— whom to trust, whom to fear; and he made only one mistake. And so at last they reached the vicinity of Annapolis, and Bowie, Wiltshire, and

Vest left the others hid in a wood and rode into town to reconnoiter—perhaps to bring off the governor if the chance offered.

O'Bannon, Radcliffe, Smith, Haney, Randolph, and Brune Bowie waited, and the strain grew greater with each passing hour. They were at tension every moment, expecting the order "Forward," perhaps shots, or else to hear from the others, dashing by, the signal calling them to join in the wild ride for the ford—the signal that meant success, that the governor was in their power. And so they waited beside their horses while hours passed. Then out of the dark three men rode up slowly—only three. They were sullen, crestfallen; the expedition had ended in flat-footed failure. The governor—the devil take him!—was in Washington for a day, a week, ten days—no one knew. Worse, Annapolis was crowded with recruits, with armed troops; it had been turned into an enrolment camp since their plans had been made; the very streets were bivouacs.

They turned toward Virginia; they had failed. None pursued, and they rode leisurely back a different way. A night or two later they were in Montgomery County, and the road led by the village of Sandy Spring. The one mistake was here. The cross-roads store attracted them; they were hungry.

"We'll dine here," Bowie said. One or two tried to dissuade him. "It'll only start trouble, Wat," they said. Perhaps his failure rankled, for he would not heed, but ordered them into the store. They broke in and rifled the shelves of canned goods—whatever they fancied, or could carry away with ease; and the helpless owner fumed and glowered. Then, deliberately, they rode away; a few shots were fired from the roadside; they answered with a careless volley and indifferently galloped on. Not far—a few miles at most—and then a pine-clad knoll thrust itself up from the fields, and they climbed its dark slope and camped; joyously they broke open their stolen tins and feasted, then lay down and slept in the circle of pines. . . .

Voices down on the road—hoofbeats. A sleepy raider awoke and sat up; the sun was an hour or two high. He aroused his comrades; the voices in the road grew louder, became an angry, ominous roar. Startled, they crept to the edge and looked down. A boy's voice shrilled, "They're

Rowand in his Confederate uniform

Miss Van Lew

Harry Young

John Y. Phillips

Mrs. Greenhow and her daughter

Timothy Webster

there—I seen 'em!" The road seemed filled with men and horses; more were riding up every moment. There were thirty—forty—maybe even more—they kept moving about so. Some dismounted and left their horses to be held by boys or by old men. The citizens had armed; the storekeeper of Sandy Spring had done his work well. There were home guards and conscripts, convalescent regulars, old graybeards, and excited, shrill-voiced boys.

They eddied about in the road aimlessly; muzzles wavered toward Bowie's men from all sides—old muskets, shotguns, squirrel-rifles; one or two loud-mouthed citizens had great rusty swords that they valiantly waved. It was a mob. Now and then a nervously aimed musket was fired, and the bullet whined amid the pines. The raiders began to laugh. They held a hasty council. "They are too many," several urged.

Bowie shook his head. "We'll fight," he said. They lined up on foot, Bowie in the center, four on either side. He had a little silver whistle between his teeth, a revolver in either hand. "Ready?" he asked, bending forward and peering along his battle-line. They in the road had become strangely, ominously still. Would they stand? Charlie Vest, then aged seventeen, says he was afraid.

"This is about all, Jim—they are too many this time!"

Wiltshire gripped his hand an instant. "Never give up the ship while the flag flies."

The little silver whistle blew. They rushed down the slope into the road, yelling and firing the revolvers in each hand. Whirlwinds of fallen autumn leaves; stumps, clusters of low bushes to leap over; stones that rolled and turned underfoot; and then in a brown fog of dust, a mad tangle of plunging, riderless horses that galloped back and forth, and reared, and kicked, and fell; a tumult of fear-crazed men who fired their guns in the air, then threw them away and ran, and fell in the dust and leaped up and screamed, and ran on. And above all other sounds rose the guffaws of the raiders as they seized the horses or wantonly fired at the little figures that scurried, cravenly, across the sunny fields.

One or two of the home guard ran down the road; Bowie leaped out after them, laughing, shouting joyously like a boy; Wiltshire and Vest followed, less fleetly, but running too. They saw two horsemen, too late for the fight, ride up and stop uncertainly across a little stream. They saw them raise their guns, heard Bowie shout and fire and miss; saw the horsemen turn and gallop furiously away, and heard Bowie shout with laughter.

"Come back," they called; "let them go—come back, Wat!"

But he sped on. They heard him still laughing as he ran beyond the bend of the road. There was the report of a shotgun, from the roadside, close at hand; then silence. Wiltshire and Vest sprang forward. Their vengeance never fell, for they could not find the man.

The Phillipses—Father and Son

Men made the great war. Thoughtful, prayerful men, of mighty intellect and soul-deep conviction, they strove together and drew a scratch upon the ground from east to west, a line to divide South from North. Together they kindled a fire, and into a vast and devastating flame they together fanned it.

Some, that by it the line might be fused into an imperishable barrier; some, that the line might forever be consumed. The war was made by men.

But the children, too, were drawn by the draught of this terrible fire. More than six hundred thousand of the Federal enlistments were by lads not yet twenty-one. There were thousands of children in the ranks of the North from thirteen to fifteen years of age.

But of all this blood-stained army there is none of whom there is record who served as did Charles H. Phillips, aged fourteen, who for four years was a Federal spy in the city of Richmond.

Some time early in the winter of '61 John Y. Phillips was sent to Richmond by his employers, R. M. Hoe & Co., of New York City, to set up and put in operation one of their newspaper-presses for the Richmond *Dispatch*. Four and a half years later he returned, and there gathered about him old friends and former neighbors.

"What did you do, John, in Richmond all through the war?" said they. And John Phillips would draw himself up and, with dignity and pride, slowly say, "I furnished the government with a lot of important secret information."

"What!" the old friends would chorus. "What, John! Secret service! How?"

"That," John Phillips would answer, "is a very long story to tell." But he never told the story. Perhaps he but faithfully kept some pledge of silence; perhaps in Richmond and the South comrades of those perilous days were living to as ripe an age as he. He had his reasons—and he never told.

No high resolve to aid his country in the coming war kept John Phillips in Richmond when the work which took him there was done. He stayed because he was offered a better position, greater earnings in his peaceful trade.

He was to work as pressman for the *Dispatch,* but his real work was to repair the press of any newspaper in Richmond when it should break down. As for the war—what war? This was but the cry of "Wolf, wolf!"—there would be no war!

And so in March he brought his family down—his wife, and Charlie (whose story is to be told), aged fourteen; Jim, aged eleven; and the two little girls. They took a house on Shockhoe Hill, on the very outskirts of the city; and there Charlie became for the first time a country lad—hunted and fished and "just rammed 'round," learning, boy-like, every foot of the country for miles; also such lore as telling time by the sun, and north by the moss on trees. One thing more he learned—to "talk 'Dixie'" like the other boys, black and white, with whom he played. He little dreamed what he should do with the knowledge later on.

Then down in South Carolina a cannon was fired. The war was begun. The Phillipses could have gone North at first, but Mr. Llewellyn, of the *Dispatch,* urged John Phillips to stay, and promised to "see them through." After a while it became too late to go. For the most part those schools taught by men teachers closed, and sweet holidays came to little Charlie Phillips and cloyed his appetite before he had gulped down a month of them. Then he volunteered to tend fly (the rack where the printed sheets come off the press), and night after night he stood amid the clanking presses of the *Dispatch* office delightedly sniffing the acrid smell of damp paper and fresh ink, of spring midnights, and, in the late telegrams, the pungent smell of war.

And there, one night, his father quietly called him from his work. He was to carry a note, he was told. He remembers to-day how his father looked at him with grave, piercing eyes, and—

"'Don't ask questions,' father said. 'Don't be gabby. Keep your mouth shut and your eyes open—now and always.'"

He was to go down by the Old Market until he met a man (described, but not named), to whom he was not to speak unless the man asked if father had sent him. That, then, would be the right man, and he was to give him the note and go home to bed.

Without direct words he was made to understand that this was no ordinary note, and the thought sent him out into the deserted streets thrilled and proud.

From the shadow of the Old Market itself a man stepped out. "Did y' pa send ye down here to me?" he drawled.

The boy fished out the scrap of paper, which he had concealed about his clothes.

"Where was y' pa when y' left him?" the man innocently questioned.

The boy hesitated. "I don't know," he said, desperately.

"I reckon you'll do," chuckled the man.

It was the first lesson in the new school, a lesson repeated until the test was many times complete: To do what he was told to do—no less, but of a greater certainty—no more!

They, his teachers (those men whom he found by their descriptions, but never from their names), hammered in the lesson by mental assaults full of feints and twists and trips and all manner of unfair advantages— simulated anger, jocose friendliness, flattery, surprise—but he always kept his wits, and to no questions that they asked (once he had delivered the message that he had been told to give) did he ever know an answer.

"Don't be a fool, boy," they would say. "You know you can trust us—*we* are all right."

"Sure!" he would answer. "But how can I tell you if I don't know?"

And thus the lesson went on, a lesson with a twofold purpose: they were teaching him that he was only a sharp little tool, dangerous to himself and to them unless under their control; and they were preparing him—for his sake and theirs—against the day when he should be caught.

The despatches or messages were written usually on narrow strips of thin paper and rolled into little wads, which Charlie carried in an inner seam of his trousers. Where the messages came from, where they went, who wrote them, who read them ultimately, he will never know. Sometimes the man to whom he had carried a message read it, rerolled it, and bade him take it to another of the spies. As for what the messages said, how should he know? . . . "Open them? What! *Open* them! You never knew my father. Father would 'a' killed me—I do believe he would 'a' killed me. Some way he would have known—but it never entered my head to open one of those little wads. My father was a great big man. He had a brown beard and no mustache, so that you saw his straight, thin-lipped mouth. To me my father was a god that I worshiped, like I was a little heathen and him the sun. My father knew everything, and was never wrong, always dignified, an' kind o' cold; but he had the warmest heart—and the heaviest hand—of any man I ever knew." So that was it—idolatry! That queer, rare blending of love and fear that makes for perfect, blind obedience: we shall understand little Charlie Phillips better now.

There came time for the learning of a second lesson in a sterner school. When his father asked the simple question, "Would you like to sell newspapers, Charlie?" the boy answered: "Yes, sir. Sure!" He knew he would not have been asked to sell papers if selling papers were all. And so he was given a stock in trade and told that he "had better go sell 'em down at the Rocketts' at the early boat." To the Rocketts' (the boat-landing) he went, and joined the small army of newsboys that gathered to sell first-editions to the many passengers leaving at the early hour of four in the morning. He was small and slight and fair-haired, and of a singular whiteness of skin, so that he looked delicate and younger than his actual age. For this reason he was imposed upon and bullied and thrown aside; and then, just as his father had known that he would, he turned and fought his way. He delights to-day to tell of some of those fights, in the gray half-light of dawn: berserker fights of boyhood they were—fierce, bare-fist, rough-and-tumble battles with half-grown negroes, who made up nine-tenths of the "newsies" of Richmond. It was a Spartan school which at last turned him out hard and sharp ("fly," he calls it), agile and vigilant, self-reliant, confident—a finished product.

He was not told what he was to do later on, but if he did not guess he soon learned that his bundle of newspapers was a badge more potent than is the Red Cross of the non-combatant of to-day, a passport by which he entered prisons and crossed picket-lines, a commodity which made him welcome in camp and arsenal, in rifle-pit and department office.

There was that first trip out of Richmond—a simple affair, merely the delivery of a message. It was so easily done that he has forgotten all except that it was to Petersburg that he made his first trip "outside." "Was told to do something and did it." He made the forty-five miles in less than one day. It was this statement that drew from Charles Phillips another story—that of how he had learned to ride. The cavalry stables were out along the old Baconquarter branch road, and scores of horses—raw young levies—in charge of a few cavalrymen passed the Phillipses' house each day. "Us boys" would dash out and vault onto the bare backs of the wildest of the plunging horses and, clinging by their manes, ride in triumph to the stables amid the cheers—or jeers (for there were hard falls some days)—of the delighted cavalrymen. In time he learned to ride "anything."

Then came the Lynchburg trip, when for the first time he acted as a spy. But it is not the spy part which looms large in his own story; it is the never-to-be-forgotten glamour of that first long trip alone, the tang of traveling on a first-class ticket on a first-class packet of the James River Canal. His "uncle" met him at the wharf and took him home and told him (for the first time) what he was to do. Few points in the story of this child strike so sharply home as the blind obedience which sent him to do he knew not what. Next day he was on the Lynchburg streets selling Richmond papers, and presently—a spy—he was in the arsenal selling his papers there.

" 'Newsies' can get in almost anywhere—you know that," he explains. "And once in, it wasn't so hard as you might think. Every one was thinking of nothing but the war, so, 'Gee!' I'd say, 'ain't ye got a lot o' cannons here!' An' workmen would say something like 'Ain't them the guns, though! Won't they just blow the Yanks to hell! Forty o' those six-inchers!' And that would be something worth remembering right there."

In a few days he found out "more than a lot," though the man—his "uncle"—never told him what was done with the information that he gave. But let it be remembered that information regarding the extent of military stores was of prime importance those days, and that Lynchburg was one of the chief storehouses.

He was sent home afoot to Richmond, making most of the journey at night; and this was not because it was safer then, but in order to save his complexion! That pallid skin and the appearance of being extremely young and innocent were the only disguises which he ever needed or ever wore. And when he had reached home again, and the curiosity of playmates must be stilled, the satisfying explanation was, "Oh, been sick!" And the white face and an assumed languor did the rest. He spent four very "sickly" years.

The autumn passed into winter; the war was fairly begun. Now and then, as dusk fell, a guest would ostentatiously ring at the Phillipses' front door to cover the arrival of stealthy shadows who stole in at the back from the open fields. The boy never was present at those secret meetings. His father's quiet "I want you to leave the room" would send him impassively to bed. He never questioned, never sought to know; but he tells now that in his heart he ceaselessly wondered at it all.

Father and mother set an example which taught that the very walls had ears, and in the Phillipses' household the war was never mentioned at all. But his mother knew, for now and then she would stroke his hair and softly say, "Be careful, Charlie, be very careful!"—just that—to show him that she knew.

Mid-afternoon of a winter's day he rode out of Richmond in one of the procession of market carts and wagons that was returning to the outlying farms. Dusk fell, and still they drove on westward, he and the grim, silent man on the jolting seat beside him. That night they spent with a negro family in a wretched one-room cabin. In the morning before the sun had risen they were on the road again. The wagon had been left behind; they rode the two horses and carried with them only their blankets. All that day they rode westward, always westward; and the next and the next day, and so on and on till the boy lost all count of time. The road at last ended on the bank of the Cumberland River at the little village of Dover. They did not enter the town together, and after that when they passed in the village street the two were to each other as utter strangers.

It was a straggling, dull little village; but on the hill to the north, looking sullenly down on town and river, were the raw clay ramparts of heavy fortifications, above which, a dark speck against the leaden sky, fluttered the Confederate flag of Fort Donelson. By instruction the boy rode to a described house and, slipping wearily from his horse, knocked at the door. It opened suddenly, and a man hurried out. He gave the boy no chance to speak.

"Well, if here isn't brother John's boy at last!" He turned genially to the gaping villagers. "Him as I was telling you about." Then to the boy: "I'm your uncle Peter. But come in! Come in!" Few actors could have done it as well. But when the door had closed on them, how they must have looked each other up and down!

At first there was the old newsboy game of selling papers in the fort, but the boy quickly felt that that was not to be all, that something else was hanging over him. After a while they told him what it was: he was to make friends with a certain young woman in the town. He was "what you would call a pretty boy." Women always tried to pet him—which he, boy-like, had hated. But he was nearly fifteen now, and here was a girl but four or five years his senior, just such a "first girl" as boys of his age adore. Here was the woman who might pet him all she pleased. It was no time before she was calling him her little beau and flaunting him at a red-faced captain from Donelson.

Presently she sent a note by the boy. He was to be careful and give it to the captain himself. He promised, and kept his word—but not until he had turned aside into a thicket and given the note first to the man by whom he had been brought to Dover. The man read the note, which he hastily copied, resealed, and gave back to the boy. There were other notes (despatches?) in the next few days, and they all were read and copied, but it was Charlie Phillips himself who spoiled the smoothly working plan.

There had been too much petting of this too large boy to please a jealous captain. Some one had been taunting or tale-bearing, and the captan in a rage met the boy one day in the road before he had reached the fort. "I'd like to shoot off your blank young head!" said the captain. He drew a revolver, and the boy snatched up a stone. As the captain stood there blustering and threatening ("It wasn't that I was scared that he would shoot such a kid," Charlie Phillips explains, "but I just never liked him!") the boy suddenly threw the stone with all his might. It struck the man on the temple, and he crumpled down on the road. The boy stared for an instant, then turned and ran. That night he impudently told the girl of it. "Served him right," she said. "I can get another captain easy."

When the fort fell, Charlie Phillips saw the captain marched from the hospital a prisoner. But he saw many things before that time. He saw Dover village wake up and find itself invested by Grant's army. From behind the Federal lines he saw the three days' fighting when the earth shook with the thunder of cannon from hill and fort and river. He saw Grant. He was taken to headquarters by the man who had brought him to Dover, and there General Grant and the man talked together just beyond his earshot. They looked over at him often, and the General several times thoughtfully nodded at what the man said. And the next day, when the fort and the town had been taken, the boy saw (though she did not see him) "his girl" arrested by a file of soldiers and marched away: his handiwork.

Twelve years after the war, when Charles H. Phillips, a policeman in New York City, was patrolling his beat, he met and recognized "his girl" again. She had been taken North—to prison in Illinois—but had soon been released, so she told him. After that the war was never mentioned. Next evening the young policeman called at her home to be presented to her husband and the children—which all goes to prove that the story must be truth. Romance would indubitably have had him marry her.

Spring had come before Charlie saw Richmond again. His was a home-coming that he has never forgotten. For once his father's reserve gave way, and he caught both his boy's hands and wrung them, and his voice trembled as he said, "I had begun to believe that my son would never again come home!" Perhaps he feared, too, that even should his son return the boy might find his father gone, for two Federal spies from the Army of the Potomac, Lewis and Scully, had been taken in

Richmond and were condemned to hang. Those were anxious days for the Unionists. Detection of any of their number was like a plague broken out in their midst. Where all had been exposed to the contagion, no man might say who would be stricken next. But when the blow fell it was upon one man, Timothy Webster, and only he was hanged. Charlie Phillips saw the execution. From the branches of the trees outside the fence of the old Fair Grounds he and scores of other boys watched it, then went home to dinner, excitedly discussing each detail among themselves. Charlie Phillips had already done that which might within the fortnight send both him and his father out upon the very road he had idly watched another take.

But the despatch-bearing and the paper-selling were kept up un-flinchingly until there came the order once again to leave Richmond. There had come the battle of Gaines's Mill, the second of the Seven Days. Lee had saved Richmond. From Gaines's Mill on the north to Harrison's Landing on the south the whole country-side was covered with freshly made graves and still unburied dead, with abandoned munitions of war also; and for weeks the agents of the Confederacy gathered in the spoils. It was into this hell-swept country that Charlie Phillips was sent to meet a man who would "use" him.

He took fishing-tackle, "borrowed" a boat, and quietly paddled about, fishing here and there, drifting with the current down the river. Four or five miles below Richmond he rowed ashore and struck inland cross country, heading for the line of the Federal retreat. At the desig-nated place he met his man, who seemed unprepared yet to "use" him, but instead asked if he would be afraid to sleep alone that night in the woods. "No," the boy answered, simply. When the man had left him he moved farther in among the trees, groping about in the darkness to find a sleeping-place. Few recollections of the war equal in sharpness his remembrance of the birds that night: every manner of carrion bird perched, glutted, upon every branch, it seemed, of every tree in the forest. Wherever he went he disturbed them, heard the beating and flapping of unseen wings above him. All that night he was fretted by their noises, sickened by the very thought of them.

Dawn came, and with it the man. "Come on!" he said, brusquely. For hours they trudged along the line of the Quaker Road down which the sullen Army of the Potomac in retreat had marched and fought and had flung away or destroyed at every pause all they could no longer transport or carry. The man and the boy wandered among the wreckage, all for the purpose, the boy gathered, of forming an estimate of what munitions would fall into the hands of the Confederates. At last, toward midday the man wrote out a message and curtly told the boy to take it and start home to Richmond.

That night he spent in a negro cabin. At sunrise he pushed on again. He still followed the general line of the chain of battles, but far to the side, to give wide berth to parties of wreckers or of straggling soldiers; yet even here were waifs of the battle, dead men out of bounds for the burying-parties.

And then, in a clump of bushes, the boy came upon a soldier. The man was kneeling beside a uniformed figure rifling the pockets. He looked up startled, but, seeing it was only a boy, bent again over the body. Charlie Phillips, telling of it, speaks in awed wonder of the madness that fell upon him, rage such as he never since has seen or known. He snatched up a rusty musket, and the man, reading in his eyes a purpose of which the boy himself was hardly conscious, sprang to his feet with an oath and caught up a broken saber, then struck as a snarling animal strikes. The blow, ill parried, glanced down the musket-barrel and gashed open the thumb that held it; but the boy swung the musket under the man's guard and felled him, then in blind fury made many times sure that he had killed him.

Back in Richmond his father asked, "What happened to the thumb, Charlie?"

"Oh," he said, "I cut it." The scar is there to-day, a memento of the man who gave it.

Winter came again, the winter of '62–'63, when conscription began to grow more rigorous. John Phillips concocted, in what purported to be the Family Bible, a new register of ages for himself and his sons. He beat the conscription laws, but there was still the home guard, which at last he refused to join; then the soldiers came and marched him away. Charlie remembers the terror he and his mother were in lest it be on a graver charge. But the newspapers (which they have kept to this day) brought reassurance that, after all, it was but the simple accusation: "John Y.

Phillips, Castle Godwin; committed March 20th; charge, disloyalty."
For sixty-four days John Phillips lay in Castle Godwin, that had been
McDonald's negro jail before the war. It was while his father was in
prison that the boy accomplished, a bit of service unequaled for sheer
impudence and audacity—in short, stole a Confederate despatch out
of the office of Provost-Marshal-General Winder.

There came to him one day as he was selling papers one of those men
whom he recognized as having authority over him, for it was as though
he had been presented body and soul to the Secret Service. He was a
communistic tool for the use of any member. He was told to go to the
neighborhood of Winder's office and watch for a certain (described)
man, one of General Winder's force. He was to follow this man into
the office and "get" the paper which he would lay on the table; and that
was exactly what he did. He followed the man into the busy, crowded
office, saw him lay a folded paper on the table, and immediately he went
over and laid his newspapers down on top of it. When he picked them
up again the despatch was with them, and he went out of the office
with it pressed close to his side. Perhaps there was a high-and-low hunt
and a hue and cry when the despatch was missed—he never knew; nor
does he know whether the man who brought the despatch to the office
was a Federal spy who had worked himself in there or whether he was
one who had sold himself for Secret Service money. The Unionist who
had sent him for the paper passed soon after. The boy deftly slipped
the despatch to him, and after that he did not care even if he were
searched, and he loitered in front of the office long enough to set at rest
any suspicions.

There is the story of how at last Charlie was conscripted—"got
the collar." Not much of a story, he says; then swiftly sketches it in
until a picture has been made complete—the soldiers at the door when
he unsuspectingly opened it to their knock. The sight, as he looked
back, of his mother standing framed in the doorway bravely waving
to him, the crying children clinging to her skirts! It wouldn't have
seemed so bad if there had just been a little sun, but that had been
such a dispiriting day—slush and mud, the slowly falling snow, and
the lowering, unbroken clouds. The soldiers had turned him into a big,
gloomy room, stiflingly overheated and crowded with sullen men and

boys. He had wandered about for a time, then, with suddenly formed purpose, made his way to the door. "Say, I'm sick t' my stomach. Le' me go to the wash-room," he begged. The sentries hesitated. There were other guards at the outer doors, and this was such a young, white-faced kid; they nodded. "No tricks, mind!" one said. Once around the turn of the corridor, he assumed a jaunty air. At the front door he motioned the guards to one side. "Ta, ta, boys—the jedge said I was to go home an' grow some." They laughed good-naturedly and let him by. For days after that he was afraid to go home, but for some inexplicable reason they never came for him again.

There came a night when, on his way to the office for his newspapers, he suddenly met his father and another man. His father made a sign to him to stop, and he stepped back into the shadows and waited. He overheard the man say, "But it has got to be done!" And after a moment's hesitation his father's seemingly reluctant answer, "All right— here's the boy." John Phillips motioned to his son, and then they moved away, Charlie following at a little distance. At the river's edge close to Mayo Bridge they stopped, and he joined them. The night was cloudy; heavy rains had fallen, and the river was swollen and noisy. It was here that they told the boy for the first time what he was to do. He was given the despatch, and the man untied a flat-bottomed, square ended boat, into which Charlie Phillips climbed and lay down. The two men covered the boat over with brush and debris until the gunwale was brought down within a few inches of the water, and the whole looked like some tangled mass of wreckage; then Charlie's father carefully pushed it out until it was caught by the swift current.

Of that ride details like these stick in his memory: the sound of the water against the boat-sides and the smell of the wet, rotten wood above him; the penetrating chill as his clothes soaked up the seeping water, and the twinges of pain from his cramped position; the loudness of the river foaming round some rock or snag, dizzy spinnings in whirlpools, or the rocking and bobbing in eddies where portions of the driftwood blind tore loose with loud raspings and crackles. There was the ever-present thought that the boat might sink and he be entangled and held down by the heap of driftwood; but worse than any sense of danger was the feeling of utter loneliness. He trailed an old broom to steer with, and, when the flying wrack of clouds blew away and it grew lighter, he wabbled the broom to make the too straightly drifting boat better simulate a pile of wreckage borne by the current. There were obstructions—old ships and the gunboat *Jamestown*—that had been sunk to block the channel, and the river was studded with torpedoes; but he had been warned and instructed, so hugged the left-hand shore and thus avoided them. A shot brought his heart into his throat as he drifted past Fort Darling on Drewry's Bluff, but it was followed by no others. At last he went ashore on the north bank, and there, by comparison with what had gone before, the adventure seemed ended. He slept in the woods all next day. At dusk he swam across and "delivered the message."

The second time he saw Grant is very different from that of the first meeting in front of Donelson. He had been given a message to deliver; he had his passport—the bundle of Richmond papers—and he had his disguise— his fair skin and the face of a child, hardened and sharpened, keener than that of the boy of three years ago; and he had his unbounded self-assurance, and so (not the only newsboy, you must remember) he passed through the Confederate army to the outermost picket-line. There was no fighting just then; the armies lay within half-musket-shot, watching each other, cat-and-mouse fashion, with their picket eyes.

"Mister," he said, with his broadest Southern drawl, "let me go and sell my papers to the Yanks over yonder."

"Bring us back some Yankee papers and y' kin go," they bargained.

But within the Union lines something for once went wrong. He was arrested and locked up until they could overhaul his story. He "played baby"—whined and begged—but they would not let him go; then, as a last resort, "Corporal of the guard," he bawled, "take me to General Grant. He won't let you keep me in the guardhouse." At last an officer was called, and he must have reported to the General. Grant sent for him. The officer led the way to the tent, saluting. "Here is that boy, General." Charlie Phillips, barefooted, coatless, his torn trousers held up by one suspender, stood unabashed before the general-in-chief of the Union armies. In the tent were half a dozen officers.

"I'd like to see you alone for a couple of minutes, General," the boy boldly said.

Grant turned to his officers: "Retire, please, gentlemen." When they had gone the boy fumbled at one of the many rips in his trousers and drew out a small wad of paper which he handed without a word to Grant, who read it, then stood looking thoughtfully at the messenger.

"Where did you get this?" he asked, impassively. To the boy's answer his rejoinder was another question: "How did you come through the lines?" Then: "How are you going back?" That was all; no comments, only questions; for commendation, only a quick, pleased nod that thrilled the boy as no outpouring of words could have done.

General Grant went to the tent door and beckoned to the waiting officer. "This boy is doing no harm," he said, mildly. "Let him sell his papers in the camp."

As he walked exultantly away the boy glanced back for one more look at the tent where he and Grant had talked together. The General was still standing in the tent door, still smoking and biting on the short, thick cigar, still thoughtfully watching him. Did Grant remember their other meeting? Charlie Phillips says that he has wondered about that from then till now. "Maybe yes, maybe no, but I've always thought he did."

"The next thing that I mind—after Grant and I had our little visit together," says Charlie Phillips, "was the time I stole old Dill's horse, and killed it, an' blame near got killed m'self." On this occasion another despatch was to be delivered, not to General Grant in person this time, but just to the Union army. There were no instructions except to get it there. For some reason he did not use the way of openly passing the pickets by the newsboy dodge. Instead, he headed for the Federal army and tramped out of Richmond by the shortest road. In a field by the roadside a pastured horse put its head over the fence and whinnied to him; he recognized it as "old Dill's—the government hardtack baker's horse—one of the best horses left in Richmond." Perhaps some devil of recklessness seized him, perhaps a too strong desire to be mounted on that glossy back and to feel beneath him the bird-like glide of a thoroughbred. He whistled softly, and the horse neighed an answer. He says it seemed to say to him, "Steal me, Charlie, steal me!" Tempted and slowly yielding, he climbed the fence. The moment he was mounted the horse stole him; they were over the fence and going like mad down the road before he had made up his mind or realized what had happened.

He rode at an easy gallop cross country until he reached the point where he believed that he had passed, by blind luck, between the guards and patrols and pickets, out of the Confederate lines, and into the no-man's land between the two armies. Then came a sudden shout from a little patch of woodland which he had just skirted, and without looking back he began to ride for his life. By the time the vedettes had mounted he had gained the start which saved him. His only fear, he says, was that in some way his father would learn of his folly. He was riding the better horse, and his slight weight was as nothing compared with that borne by the cavalry horses. He began to draw away from them rapidly. One after another of his pursuers fired at him, and their shots told that they had almost given up hope of taking him. He was looking back over his shoulder when the end came, and never saw the gully at all. He had an instant's sensation of flying, of a terrible jar, then of being whirled end over end. He had staggered to his feet and had instinctively commenced to run before he comprehended that his horse had fallen short in its leap and had struck with its forelegs, breaking both of them against the gully's edge. He heard the yells of the cavalrymen and a sputter of pistol-shots, but that from which he tried to flee was the sound of his wounded horse's screams. It was a long run to the strip of woods toward which he had intuitively headed, but he was almost there before the Confederates could cross the gully and resume the chase. By the time they reached the wood he was in a tree-top safely hidden. Twilight was nearly done. He could hear the clanking of the cavalrymen's sabers as they stamped about beating the undergrowth for him. When it was quite dark they went away, and he climbed stiffly down and pushed on for the Union lines, still grieving for his horse.

The war wrought horrors upon the bodies of children who fought in it, but there was not one who escaped unscathed of body that was not the greater maimed by the callousing of heart and mind. Charlie Phillips before he was seventeen had killed two men, not in battle as a soldier kills impersonally and at long range, but face to face, almost within arm's reach; and he gave to their deaths no heed. One, the ghoul, he killed in a frenzy that lifted him out of himself; the other he killed coldly, deliberately, because the man living menaced him, but, dead, was safely out of his way. Justifiable both, and to his war-scarred mind instantly and forever justified.

Scores of negroes aided Charlie Phillips during the war; fed him, sheltered him, gave him information and warnings, guided him; few of them did he ever see again; but the only negro whom he could not trust was sent across his path time after time. The other negroes all were secretly for the North and freedom; this man was for the South and his master—"the only secesh nigger," Charlie Phillips says, that he ever knew. The man was branded by his own race; negroes who had never seen him knew of him and grew silent and ill at ease at his approach; they warned the boy that here was one negro who would do him harm. The man was a Confederate officer's body-servant, a swaggering fellow, a mulatto with arrogant eyes and a sneering face. At each chance meeting the man's suspicions and the boy's fears grew.

There came an evening in late summer when the boy was stealing out of the city on secret service; he had left the town some distance behind him and was walking swiftly along one of the back or little-traveled roads. Something had prompted him to carry a revolver, which he seldom dared to do, since it was not in keeping with his part.

He recognized the negro almost at the moment that he saw him coming across the fields; their converging courses would bring them face to face. It was not yet dark, and the dying light in the west shone full upon the negro. Something of a dandy he was, in his cavalry boots and parts of cast-off uniforms; perhaps he was coming on leave into Richmond, courting; perhaps merely on an errand for his master. The field sloped up to the road, fringed with sumacs and alders; as the man mounted the rise the boy on the road was but a few yards from him. Without a word having been spoken, Charlie Phillips drew the cocked revolver from under his jacket and shot the man between the eyes; the body pitched face down into the bushes. The boy gave a quick look around, then threw the revolver from him as far as he could throw. Then he ran a few rods and crawled into the bushes and lay there, breathing quickly, for a long time; when it was quite dark he went on upon his mission.

"Tell father of it? No, I didn't—why should I? It was *my* business—I knew I had to kill the fellow."

There is one story that is mere fragments. It would take a cement of the forbidden fiction to join them together. These are the fragments: A despatch was to be delivered to the Federals north of the Rappahannock, several days' journey from Richmond. Charlie remembers stopping for food and shelter at a house in Caroline County, and being taken in and fed and given a chance to dry his clothes, for it was sleeting. Not many months later another traveler, a fugitive, John Wilkes Booth, was to seek at this same Garrett farm a vain shelter. After the boy got warm and dry he pushed on. He crossed the Rappahannock, for he remembers sculling a boat through the floating ice; and that night or the next—he does not remember—he came to the end of his journey, but not to his destination.

"Lord, Lord," he says, "what a night!—as bright as day it was, and cold, *cold!* There was a crust on the snow, and the fields made better traveling than the roads, and so I was going cross country when two men jumped out from behind a tree. They said, 'Hands up!'—like robbers—not 'Halt!'—like soldiers would—and I hands upped." But he was able to get the little wad of despatch into his mouth, and he swallowed it. So all that they got was money. He had in his pocket a good big roll of Confederate bank-notes—mighty little good those days!—and, sewed in the lining of his vest, a roll of Federal Secret-Service money, greenbacks.

They found this, too, and were about to rip it out, but he pretended he was afraid that they would cut him, and he was such a little chap and so terrified that, with unwise kindness, they let him wield the knife himself, and he managed to slash the greenbacks into bits. They were going to hang him for that, but instead they marched him to a farm and locked him into an outbuilding. There are only two more fragments of the story left in his memory: one, that he escaped, and another that he made his way back (for, since his despatch was gone, there was no use to go farther) to the house of a "sympathizer," a Unionist, where he had stopped by instruction on the way out. There they told him that he must have been captured by Mosby's men, and was lucky to be able to tell of it.

And then at last (at the very last, for it was in January, '65) the Confederates got him, but not red-handed in a hanging matter. Many people in Richmond had tired of starving; also the spring campaign was coming, and conscription would be harder to escape than ever. Every man who left Richmond, especially if he were a skilled workman, weakened the Confederacy, already hard pressed to fill such places. It became the duty of the Secret Service agents to make up and pilot parties of malcontents into the nearest Federal army. It was in this work that Charlie Phillips was taken. A party of nineteen mechanics had been formed, and the boy and two others of the service were to lead them. The story is hardly worth the telling: there was no resistance, only a tumult of cries and a wild scramble when they found themselves surrounded by detectives and soldiers. One man broke away and escaped—probably the stool-pigeon who had baited the trap for them. Then it was just Castle Thunder, days of fretting and of waiting, days of being a prisoner, with all that that meant during the Rebellion.

The boy made desperate plans for escape, plans which might have succeeded had it not been for the dog Nero, the bloodhound of Castle Thunder. With that dog there—and he was always there—no escapes were even attempted. Months afterward, back in New York City, the boy renewed his acquaintance with Nero, now fallen—or risen?—to be star exhibit in P. T. Barnum's old museum on Ann Street.

But, after all, there was but a month of prison for Charlie Phillips, and then came a parole and freedom, a freer freedom than the laws of parole ever sanctioned. For a time he was compelled to report each day at noon. It was too hampering. He petitioned to be allowed to report but once a week. His business—his business!—was being ruined by this daily restriction. Once a week would do, they told him. When one is a spy the violation of a parole is a small matter—one can be hanged only once, anyway, so Charlie Phillips each day "cut a notch" in a meaningless piece of paper. Before he had redeemed it Richmond had fallen.

With the Federal occupation there was at once government employment for the Phillipses in the post quartermaster's department, work which to Charlie was a sharp and sudden contrast to the days of Secret Service—work that gave abundant promise of fast becoming routine, and that, too, while there still was fighting, desperate fighting, to the west of Richmond. He had "gone everywhere on God's footstool for others," now just this once let him go somewhere for himself! He "borrowed a horse from 'Uncle Samuel,'" and rode off to his holiday. For the last time he would see a battle!

He was hunting for it when he slowly rode into the little town of Appomattox; he had come too late for battles. He saw General Grant and a large party of officers ride up to one of the houses and enter. Scarce knowing why, he lingered. The front yard and the roadway were filled with horses held by orderlies. "Gen'ral Lee's in there!" they told him. Some of the citizens of the town had come over to see what was going on. One or two of the bolder, perhaps friends of Wilmer McLean, the house-owner, went up on the porch, and then, the front door standing invitingly open, entered the hall and peeped into the room which that day became historic. Charlie Phillips followed. He saw a small room crowded with officers; he saw General Grant seated at one table, at another General Lee. An officer to whom he had once carried a message recognized him and nodded. In his excitement the boy scarcely saw him. It is one of his most poignant regrets that he could never remember which officer had nodded to him. He dared take but one hurried look about the room, then tiptoed out into the yard again and waited. After a long time General Lee and another gray-clad officer came out, followed by the Federals. The boy watched them ride away. It was over! He turned his own horse toward Richmond and rode, now sober, now exultant.

It was late the next day when he reached the post quartermaster's office. He scarcely knew his father, who stood with a young Federal lieutenant, talking and laughing like a man suddenly grown years younger. His father's greeting was as though to a comrade.

"Where you been, Charlie?" and then, without waiting for an answer, "Did you know about Lee's surrender?" The boy's rejoinder is the epitome of his service:

"Sure!" he said. "I was there. I saw it."

Mrs. Greenhow

These pages record the story of the woman who cast a pebble into the sea of circumstance—a pebble from whose widening ripples there rose a mighty wave, on whose crest the Confederate States of America were borne through four years of civil war.

Rose O'Neal Greenhow gave to General Beauregard information which enabled him to concentrate the widely scattered Confederate forces in time to meet McDowell on the field of Manassas, and there, with General Johnson, to win for the South the all-important battle of Bull Run.

Mrs. Greenhow's cipher despatch—nine words on a scrap of paper—set in motion the reinforcements which arrived at the height of the battle and turned it against the North. But for the part she played in the Confederate victory Rose O'Neal Greenhow paid a heavy price.

During the Buchanan administration Mrs. Greenhow was one of the leaders of Washington society. She was a Southerner by birth, but a resident of Washington from her girlhood; a widow, beautiful, accomplished, wealthy, and noted for her wit and her forceful personality. Her home was the rendezvous of those prominent in official life in Washington—the "court circle," had America been a monarchy. She was personally acquainted with all the leading men of the country, many of whom had partaken of her hospitality. President Buchanan was a close personal friend; a friend, too, was William H. Seward, then Senator from New York; her niece, a granddaughter of Dolly Madison, was the wife of Stephen A. Douglas. It was in such company that she watched with burning interest the war-clouds grow and darken over Charleston Harbor, then burst into the four years' storm; she never saw it end.

Among her guests at this time was Colonel Thomas Jordan, who, before leaving Washington to accept the appointment of Adjutant-General of the Confederate army at Manassas, broached to Mrs. Greenhow the subject of a secret military correspondence. What would *she* do to aid the Confederacy? he asked her. Ah, what would she not do! Then he told her how some one in Washington was needed by the South; of the importance of the work which might be done, and her own special fitness for the task. And that night before he left the house he gave her a cipher code, and arranged that her despatches to him were to be addressed to "Thomas John Rayford."

And so he crossed the river into Virginia and left her, in the Federal capital, armed with the glittering shield, "Justified by military necessity," and the two-edged sword, "All's fair in love and war"—left her, his agent, to gather in her own way information from the enemy, her former friends, where and from whom she would.

It was in April, '61, that she took up her work; in November, Allan Pinkerton, head of the Federal Secret Service, made to the War Department a report in which he said—in the vehement language of a partisanship as intense as Mrs. Greenhow's own:

It was a fact too notorious to need reciting here, that for months . . . Mrs. Greenhow was actively and to a great extent openly engaged in giving aid and comfort, sympathy and information; . . . her house was the rendezvous for the most violent enemies of the government, . . . where they were furnished with every possible information to be obtained by the untiring energies of this very remarkable woman; . . . that since the commencement of this rebellion this woman, from her long residence at the capital, her superior education, her uncommon social powers, her very extensive acquaintance among, and her active association with, the leading politicians of this nation, has possessed an almost superhuman power, all of which she has most wickedly used to destroy the government. . . . She has made use of whoever and whatever she could as mediums to carry into effect her unholy purposes. . . . She has not used her powers in vain among the officers of the army, not a few of whom he has robbed of patriotic hearts and transformed them into sympathizers with the enemies of the country. . . . She had her secret and insidious agents in all parts of this city and scattered over a large extent of country. . . . She had alphabets, numbers, ciphers, and various other not mentioned ways of holding intercourse. . . . Statistical facts were thus obtained and forwarded that could have been found nowhere but in the national archives, thus leading me to the conclusion that such evidence must have been obtained from employees and agents in the various departments of the government.

Thus she worked throughout the opening days of the war. Washington lay ringed about with camps of new-formed regiments, drilling feverishly. Already the press and public had raised the cry, "On to Richmond!" When would they start? Where would they first strike? It was on those two points that the Confederate plan of campaign hinged. It was Mrs. Greenhow who gave the information. To General Beauregard at Manassas, where he anxiously awaited tidings of the Federal advance, there came about the 10th of July the first message from Mrs. Greenhow. The message told of the intended advance of the enemy across the Potomac and on to Manassas *via* Fairfax Court-house and Centreville. It was brought into the Confederate lines by a young lady of Washington, Miss Duval, who, disguised as a market-girl, carried the message to a house near Fairfax Court-house, occupied by the wife and daughters (Southern born) of an officer in the Federal army. General Beauregard at once commenced his preparations for receiving the attack, and sent one of his aides to President Davis to communicate the information and to urge the immediate concentration of the scattered Confederate forces.

But still the Federal start was delayed, and the precise date was as indefinite as ever. It was during this period of uncertainty that G. Donellan, who, before joining the Confederates, had been a clerk in the Department of the Interior, volunteered to return to Washington for information. He was armed with the two words "Trust Bearer" in Colonel Jordan's cipher, and was sent across the Potomac with instructions to report to Mrs. Greenhow. He arrived at the very moment that she most needed a messenger. Hastily writing in cipher her all-important despatch, "Order issued for McDowell to move on Manassas to-night," she gave it to Donellan, who was taken by her agents in a buggy, with relays of horses, down the eastern shore of the Potomac to a ferry near Dumfries, where he was ferried across. Cavalry couriers delivered the despatch into General Beauregard's hands that night, July 16th.

And the source of Mrs. Greenhow's information? She has made the statement that she *"received a copy of the order to McDowell."* Allan Pinkerton was not wrong when he said that she "had not used her powers in vain among the officers of the army."

At midday of the 17th there came Colonel Jordan's reply:

Yours was received at eight o'clock at night. Let them come; we are ready for them. We rely upon you for precise information. Be particular as to description and destination of forces, quantity of artillery, etc.

She was ready with fresh information, and the messenger was sent back with the news that the Federals intended to cut the Manassas Gap Railroad to prevent Johnson, at Winchester, from reinforcing Beauregard. After that there was nothing to be done but await the result of the inevitable battle. She had done her best. What that best was worth she learned when she received from Colonel Jordan the treasured message:

Our President and our General direct me to thank you. We rely upon you for further information. The Confederacy owes you a debt.

When the details of the battle became known, and she learned how the last of Johnson's 8,500 men (marched to General Beauregard's aid because of *her* despatches) had arrived at three o'clock on the day of the battle and had turned the wavering Federal army into a mob of panic-stricken fugitives, she felt that the "Confederacy owed her a debt," indeed.

In the days immediately following Bull Run it seemed to the Confederate sympathizers in the city that their victorious army had only to march into Washington to take it. "Everything about the national Capitol betokened the panic of the Administration," Mrs. Greenhow wrote. "Preparations were made for the expected attack, and signals were arranged to give the alarm. . . . I went round with the principal officer in charge of this duty, and took advantage of the situation. . . . Our gallant Beauregard would have found himself right ably seconded by the rebels in Washington had he deemed it expedient to advance on the city. A part of the plan was to have cut the telegraph-wires connecting the various military positions with the War Department, to make prisoners of McClellan and several others, thereby creating still greater confusion in the first moments of panic. Measures had also been taken to spike the guns in Fort Corcoran, Fort Ellsworth, and other important points, accurate drawings of which had been furnished to our commanding officer by me." Doubtless it was these same drawings concerning which the New York *Herald* commented editorially a month later:

> . . . We have in this little matter [Mrs. Greenhow's arrest] a clue to the mystery of those important government maps and plans which the rebels lately left behind them in their hasty flight from Fairfax Court-house, . . . and we are at liberty to guess how Beauregard was so minutely informed of this advance, and of our plan of attack on his lines, as to be ready to meet it at every salient point with overwhelming numbers.

Poor Mrs. Greenhow—from the very first doomed to disaster. Her maps and plans (if these, indeed, were hers) were allowed to fall into the enemy's hands; despatches were sent to her by an ill-chosen messenger, who, too late, was discovered to be a spy for the Federal War Department; her very cipher code, given her by Colonel Jordan, proved to be an amateurish affair that was readily deciphered by the Federal War Office.

She never had a chance to escape detection. Concerning the cipher, Colonel Jordan wrote to Confederate Secretary of War Judah P. Benjamin, October, '61 (the letter was found in the archives of Richmond four years later): "This cipher I arranged last April. Being my first attempt and hastily devised, it may be deciphered by any expert, as I found after use of it for a time. . . . That does not matter, as of course I used it with but the lady, and with her it has served our purpose. . . ." It had, indeed, served their purpose, but in serving it had brought imprisonment and ruin to the woman.

When the War Department began to shake itself free from the staggering burden placed upon it by the rout at Bull Run, almost its first step was to seek out the source of the steady and swift-flowing stream of information to Richmond. Suspicion at once fell upon Mrs. Greenhow. Many expressed their secession sentiments as openly as did she, but there was none other who possessed her opportunities for obtaining Federal secrets. Federal officers and officials continued their pleasant social relations with her, and she was believed by the War Office to be influencing some of these. Thomas A. Scott, Assistant Secretary of War, sent for Allan Pinkerton and instructed him to place Mrs. Greenhow under surveillance; her house was to be constantly watched, as well as all visitors from the moment they were seen to enter or to leave it, and, should any of these visitors later attempt to go South, they were immediately to be arrested. The watch on the house continued for some days; many prominent gentlemen called—men whose loyalty was above question. Then on the night of August 22d, while Pinkerton and several of his men watched during a hard storm, an officer of the Federal army entered the house. Pinkerton removed his shoes and stood on the shoulders of one of his men that he might watch and listen at a crack in the shutters. When the officer left the house he was followed by Pinkerton (still in his stocking feet) and one of his detectives. Turning suddenly, the officer discovered that he was being followed; he broke into a run, and the three of them raced through the deserted, rain-swept streets straight to the door of a station of the Provost-Marshal.

The pursued had maintained his lead, and reached the station first; he was its commanding officer, and instantly turned out the guard. Allan Pinkerton and his agent suddenly found that the quarry had bagged the hunters.

The angry officer refused to send word for them to Secretary Scott, to General McClellan, to the Provost-Marshal—to any one! He clapped them into the guardhouse—"a most filthy and uncomfortable place"— and left them there, wet and bedraggled, among the crowd of drunken soldiers and common prisoners of the streets. In the morning, when the guard was relieved, one of them, whom Pinkerton had bribed, carried a message to Secretary Scott, by whom they were at once set free. In his report Allan Pinkerton says:

> . . . The officer then [immediately after Pinkerton was put under arrest] went up-stairs while I halted and looked at my watch. Said officer returned in twenty minutes with a revolver in his hand, saying that he went up-stairs on purpose to get the revolver. The inquiry arises, was it for that purpose he stayed thus, or for the more probable one of hiding or destroying the evidence of his guilt obtained of Mrs. Greenhow or furnished to her? . . .

This report goes no further into the charge, but that very day, August 23d, within a few hours of his release, Allan Pinkerton placed Mrs. Greenhow under arrest as a spy.

Of the events of that fateful Friday Mrs. Greenhow has left a graphic record, complete save that it does not tell why such events need ever have been, for she had been warned of her proposed arrest—warned in ample time at least to have attempted an escape. The message which told of the impending blow had been sent to her, Mrs. Greenhow tells, by a lady in Georgetown, to whom one of General McClellan's aides had given the information. The note said also that the Hon. William Preston, Minister to Spain until the outbreak of the war, was likewise to be arrested. To him Mrs. Greenhow passed on the warning, and he safely reached the Confederate army. But Mrs. Greenhow—why did she stay? Did escape seem so improbable that she dared not run the risk of indubitably convicting herself by an attempted flight? Did she underestimate the gravity of her situation and depend upon "influence" to save her? Or was it, after all, some Casabianca-like folly of remaining at her "post" until the end? Whatever the reason, she stayed.

Day after day she waited for the warning's fulfilment. Though waiting, she worked on. " 'Twas very exciting," she told a friend long afterward. "I would be walking down the Avenue with one of the officials, military or state, and as we strolled along there would pass—perhaps a washerwoman carrying home her basket of clean clothes, or, maybe, a gaily attired youth from lower Seventh Avenue; but something in the way the woman held her basket, or in the way the youth twirled his cane, told me that news had been received, or that news was wanted—that I must open up communications in some way. Or as we sat in some city park a sedate old gentleman would pass by; to my unsuspecting escort the passerby was but commonplace, but to me his manner of polishing his glasses or the flourish of the handkerchief with which he rubbed his nose was a message."

Days full of anxious forebodings sped by until the morning of August 23d dawned, oppressively sultry after the night of rain which had so bedraggled Allan Pinkerton and his detective. At about eleven o'clock that morning Mrs. Greenhow was returning home from a promenade with a distinguished member of the diplomatic corps, but for whose escort she believed she would have been arrested sooner, for she knew she was being followed. Excusing herself to her escort, she stopped to inquire for the sick child of a neighbor, and there they warned her that her house was being watched. So, then, the time had come! As she paused at her neighbor's door, perhaps for the moment a trifle irresolute, one of her "humble agents" chanced to be coming that way; farther down the street two men were watching her; she knew their mission.

To her passing agent she called, softly: "I think that I am about to be arrested. Watch from Corcoran's corner. I shall raise my handkerchief to my face if they arrest me. Give information of it." Then she slowly crossed the street to her house. She had several important papers with her that morning; one, a tiny note, she put into her mouth and destroyed; the other, a letter in cipher, she was unable to get from her pocket without being observed; for the opportunity to destroy it she must trust to chance. As she mounted the short flight of steps to her door the two men—Allan Pinkerton and his operative, who had followed her rapidly—reached the foot of the steps. She turned and faced them, waiting for them to speak.

"Is this Mrs. Greenhow?"

"Yes," she replied, coldly. As they still hesitated, she asked, "Who are you, and what do you want?"

"I have come to arrest you," Pinkerton answered, shortly.

"By what authority? Let me see your warrant," she demanded, bravely enough except for what seemed a nervous movement of the fluttering handkerchief. To the detectives, if they noticed it, it was but the tremulous gesture of a woman's fright. To the agent lingering at Corcoran' s corner it was the signal.

"I have no power to resist you," she said; "but had I been inside of my house I would have killed one of you before I had submitted to this illegal process." They followed her into her house and closed the door.

"It seemed, but a moment," she tells, "before the house became filled with men, and an indiscriminate search commenced. Men rushed with frantic haste into my chamber, into every sanctuary. Beds, drawers, wardrobes, soiled linen—search was made everywhere! Even scraps of paper—children's unlettered scribblings—were seized and tortured into dangerous correspondence with the enemy."

It was a very hot day. She asked to be allowed to change her dress, and permission was grudgingly given her; but almost immediately a detective followed to her bedroom, calling, "Madam! Madam!" and flung open the door. She barely had had time to destroy the cipher note that was in her pocket. Very shortly afterward a woman detective arrived, and "I was allowed the poor privilege of unfastening my own garments, which one by one were received by this pseudo-woman and carefully examined."

Though wild confusion existed within the house, no sign of it was allowed to show itself from without, for the house was now a trap, baited and set; behind the doors detectives waited to seize all who, ignorant of the fate of its owner, might call. Anxious to save her friends, and fearful, too, lest she be compromised further by papers which might be found on them when searched, Mrs. Greenhow sought means to warn them away. The frightened servants were all under guard, but there was one member of the household whose freedom was not yet taken from her— Mrs. Greenhow's daughter, Rose, a child of eight. It is her letters which have supplied many of the details for this story. Of that day, so full of terror and bewilderment, the memory which stands out most clear to her is that of climbing a tree in the garden and from there calling to all the passers-by: "Mother has been arrested! Mother has been arrested!" until the detectives in the house heard her, and angrily dragged her, weeping, from the tree.

But in spite of the efforts of the "humble agent" who had waited at Corcoran's corner for the handkerchief signal, in spite of the sacrifice of little Rose's freedom, the trap that day was sprung many times. Miss Mackall and her sister, close friends of Mrs. Greenhow, were seized as they crossed the threshold, and searched and detained. Their mother, coming to find her daughters, became with them a prisoner. A negro girl—a former servant—and her brother, who were merely passing the house, were induced to enter it, and for hours subjected to an inquisition.

Night came, and the men left in charge grew boisterous; an argument started among them. Mrs. Greenhow tells—with keen enjoyment—of having egged on the disputants, pitting nationality against nationality—English, German, Irish, Yankee—so that in the still night their loud, angry voices might serve as a danger-signal to her friends. But the dispute died out at last—too soon to save two gentlemen who called late that evening, a call which cost them months of imprisonment on the never-proved charge of being engaged in "contraband and treasonable correspondence with the Confederates."

Soon after midnight there came the brief relaxing of vigilance for which Mrs. Greenhow had watched expectantly all day. She had taken the resolution to fire the house if she did not succeed in obtaining certain papers in the course of the night, for she had no hope that they would escape a second day's search. But now the time for making the attempt had come, and she stole noiselessly into the dark library. From the topmost shelf she took down a book, between whose leaves lay the coveted despatch; concealing it in the folds of her dress, she swiftly regained her room. A few moments later the guard returned to his post at her open door.

She had been permitted the companionship of Miss Mackall, and now as the two women reclined on the bed they planned how they might get the despatch out of the house. When Mrs. Greenhow had been searched that afternoon her shoes and stockings had not been examined, and so, trusting to the slim chance that Miss Mackall's would likewise escape examination, it was determined that the despatch should be hidden in her stocking; and this—since the room was in darkness save for the faint light from the open door, and the bed stood in deep shadow—was accomplished in the very presence of the guard. They planned that should Miss Mackall, when about to be released, have reason to believe she was to be searched carefully, she must then be seized with compunction at leaving her friend, and return.

Between three and four o'clock Saturday morning those friends who had been detained were permitted to depart (except the two gentlemen, who, some hours before, had been taken to the Provost Marshal), and with Miss Mackall went in safety the despatch for whose destruction Mrs. Greenhow would have burned her house.

But though she had destroyed or saved much dangerous correspondence, there fell into the hands of the Federal Secret Service much more of her correspondence, by which were dragged into the net many of her friends and agents. A letter in cipher addressed to Thomas John Rayford in part read:

> Your three last despatches I never got. Those by Applegate were betrayed by him to the War Department; also the one sent by our other channel was destroyed by Van Camp.

Dr. Aaron Van Camp, charged with being a spy, was arrested, and cast into the Old Capitol Prison. In a stove in the Greenhow house were found, and pieced together, the fragments of a note from Donellan, the messenger who had carried her despatch to Beauregard before Bull Run. The note introduced "Colonel Thompson, the bearer, . . . [who] will be happy to take from your hands any communications and obey your injunctions as to disposition of same with despatch." The arrest of Colonel Thompson, as of Mrs. Greenhow, involved others; it was all like a house of cards—by the arrest of Mrs. Greenhow the whole flimsy structure had been brought crashing down.

Of the days which followed the beginning of Mrs. Greenhow's imprisonment in her own house, few were devoid of excitement of some sort. After a few days Miss Mackall had obtained permission to return and share her friend's captivity. It was she who fortunately found and destroyed a sheet of blotting-paper which bore the perfect imprint of the Bull Run despatch! The detectives remained in charge for seven days; they examined every book in the library leaf by leaf (too late!); boxes containing books, china, and glass that had been packed away for months were likewise minutely examined. Portions of the furniture were taken apart; pictures removed from their frames; beds overturned many times.

"Seemingly I was treated with deference," Mrs. Greenhow tells. "Once only were violent hands put upon my person—the detective, Captain Denis, having rudely seized me to prevent me giving warning to a lady and gentleman on the first evening of my arrest (which I succeeded in doing)." She was permitted to be alone scarcely a moment. "If I wished to lie down, he was seated a few paces from my bed. If I desired to change my dress, it was obliged to be done with open doors. . . . They still presumed to seat themselves at table with me, with unwashed hands and shirt-sleeves." Only a few months before this the President of the United States had dined frequently at that very table.

Her jailers sought to be bribed to carry messages for her—in order to betray her; their hands were ever outstretched. One set himself the pleasant task of making love to her maid, Lizzie Fitzgerald, a quick-witted Irish girl, who entered into the sport of sentimental walks and treats at Uncle Sam's expense—and, of course, revealed nothing.

On Friday morning, August 30th, Mrs. Greenhow was informed that other prisoners were to be brought in, and that her house was to be converted into a prison. A lieutenant and twenty-one men of the Sturgis Rifles (General McClellan's body-guard) were now placed in charge instead of the detective police. The house began to fill with other prisoners—all women. The once quiet and unpretentious residence at No. 398 Sixteenth Street became known as "Fort Greenhow," and an object of intense interest to the crowds that came to stare at it—which provoked from the New York *Times* the caustic comment:

Had Madam Greenhow been sent South immediately after her arrest, as we recommended, we should have heard no more of the heroic deeds of Secesh women, which she has made the fashion.

Had the gaping crowds known what the harassed sentries knew, they would have stared with better cause. They sought to catch a glimpse of Mrs. Greenhow because of what she had done; the guards' chief concern was with the Mrs. Greenhow of the present moment. For during the entire time that she was a prisoner in her own house Mrs. Greenhow was in frequent communication with the South. How she accomplished the seemingly impossible will never be fully known.

She tells of information being conveyed to her by her "little bird"; of preparing "those *peculiar, square* despatches to be forwarded to our great and good President at Richmond"; of "tapestry-work in a vocabulary of colors, which, though not a very prolific language, served my purpose"; and she gives, as an example of many such, "a seemingly innocent letter," which seems innocent indeed, and must forever remain so, since she does not supply the key whereby its hidden meaning may be understood.

Then there is the story of the ball of pink knitting-yarn, a story which, unlike the yarn ball, was never unwound to lay its innermost secrets bare.

Among those prisoners in "Fort Greenhow" at that time were the wife and the daughter of Judge Philip Phillips. Mere suspicion had caused their imprisonment; "influence" was able to obtain their freedom, but not able to save them from being deported from Washington. They were released from "Fort Greenhow" and given three days to settle their affairs and prepare to be escorted to the south side of the Potomac. On the day before they were to be sent away (she who was Miss Caroline Phillips tells the story), what was their surprise to see Mrs. Greenhow, closely guarded on either side by Federal officers, passing their residence. To the still greater surprise of Mrs. Phillips, who stood at the open front window, Mrs. Greenhow suddenly tossed a ball of pink worsted in at the window.

"Here is your yarn that you left at my house, Mrs. Phillips," she called; then passed on, laughing and chatting with the gullible officers. Mrs. Phillips knew that she had left no yarn at "Fort Greenhow." She and her daughter carefully unwound the ball. Four days later—in spite of having been rigidly searched at Fortress Monroe—Mrs. Phillips herself placed in the hand of Jefferson Davis the ball of pink worsted's contents—one of Mrs. Greenhow's cipher despatches!

By such means she was able to outwit her many guards—though not as invariably as at the time she believed that she had done. Allan Pinkerton reports to the War Department, with a mixture of irritation and complacency:

> She has not ceased to lay plans, to attempt the bribery of officers having her in charge, to make use of signs from the windows of her house to her friends on the streets, to communicate with such friends and through them as she supposed send information to the rebels in ciphers requiring much time to decipher—all of which she supposed she was doing through an officer who had her in charge and whom she supposed she had bribed to that purpose, but who, faithful to his trust, laid her communications before yourself.

But Mrs. Greenhow evidently made use of other channels as well, for the copy of her first letter to Secretary Seward safely reached the hands of those friends to whom it was addressed, and by them it was published in the newspapers, North and South, thereby showing to all the world that a tendril of the "grape-vine telegraph" still reached out from "Fort Greenhow." It was not this alone which made officialdom and the public gasp—it was the letter itself. In tone it was calm, almost dispassionate—a masterly letter. The blunt Anglo-Saxon words which set forth in detail the indignities which she suffered from the unceasing watch kept over her came like so many blows. She pointed out that her arrest had been without warrant; that her house and all its contents had been seized; and that she herself had been held a prisoner more than three months without a trial, and that she was yet ignorant of the charge against her. The letter was strong, simple, dignified, but it brought no reply.

The heat of midsummer had passed and autumn had come, and with it many changes. Miss Mackall was one day abruptly taken away and sent to her own home; the two friends were never to meet again. Other prisoners were freed or transferred elsewhere, and yet others came—

among them a Miss Poole, who almost immediately sought to curry favor by reporting that little Rose, who for some time had been allowed to play, under guard, on the pavement, had received a communication for her mother; and the child was again confined within the four walls. "This was perhaps my hardest trial—to see my little one pining and fading under my eyes for want of food and air. The health and spirits of my faithful maid also began to fail." The attempt of several of the guard to communicate information was likewise reported by Miss Poole, and the thumb-screws of discipline were tightened by many turns. The kindly officer of the guard, Lieutenant Sheldon, was ordered to hold no personal communication with Mrs. Greenhow; the guards were set as spies upon one another and upon him; they, too, were forbidden under severe penalty to speak to her or to answer her questions. An order was issued prohibiting her from purchasing newspapers or being informed of their contents. At times it seemed as though her house, and she in it, had been swallowed, and now lay within the four walls of a Chillon or a Château d'If; it was added bitterness to her to look about the familiar room and remember that once it had been home!

Miss Mackall had been making ceaseless efforts to be allowed to visit her friend, but permission was steadily denied. Then the news sifted into "Fort Greenhow," and reached its one-time mistress, that Miss Mackall was ill, desperately ill; for the first time Mrs. Greenhow ceased to demand—she pleaded to see her friend; and failed. Then came the news that Miss Mackall was dead.

Among those friends of the old days who now and then were allowed to call was Edwin M. Stanton, not yet Secretary of War. Mrs. Greenhow endeavored to engage him as counsel to obtain for her a writ of *habeas corpus*, but he declined.

Friends—with dubious tact—smuggled to her newspaper clippings in which the statement was made that "Mrs. Greenhow had lost her mind," and that "it is rumored that the government is about to remove her to a private lunatic asylum." "My blood freezes even now," she wrote, "when I recall my feelings at the reception of this communication, and I wonder that I had not gone mad." When the Judge-Advocate, making a friendly, "unofficial" call, asked, "To what terms would you be willing to subscribe for your release?" she replied, with unbroken courage:

"None, sir! I demand my unconditional release, indemnity for losses, and the restoration of my papers and effects."

The day after Christmas Mrs. Greenhow wrote two letters. The one, in cipher, was found in the archives of the Confederate War Department when Richmond was evacuated; it was deciphered and published in the Official Records:

December 26th.

In a day or two 1,200 cavalry supported by four batteries of artillery will cross the river above to get behind Manassas and cut off railroad and other communications with our army whilst an attack is made in front. For God's sake heed this. It is positive. . . .

The "grape-vine telegraph-lines" were still clear both into and out of "Fort Greenhow."

The other was a second letter to Secretary Seward—a very different sort of letter from the first, being but a tirade on the ethics of the Southern cause, purposeless, save that "Contempt and defiance alone actuated me. I had known Seward intimately, and he had frequently enjoyed the hospitalities of my table." Unlike its worthy predecessor, this letter was to bear fruit.

On the morning of January 5th a search was again commenced throughout the house. The police were searching for the copy of the second letter. But, as in the first instance, the copy had gone out simultaneously with the original. When Mrs. Greenhow was allowed to return to her room she found that the window had been nailed up, and every scrap of paper had been taken from her writing-desk and table.

It was this copy of the second letter to Secretary Seward which sent Mrs. Greenhow to the Old Capitol Prison.

It was published as the first had been, thereby clearly showing that Mrs. Greenhow was still able to communicate with the South almost at will in spite of all efforts to prevent her. It was the last straw. The State Department acted swiftly. On January 18th came the order for Mrs. Greenhow to prepare for immediate removal elsewhere; two hours later she parted from her faithful and weeping maid, and she and the little Rose left their home forever. Between the doorstep and the carriage was a double file of soldiers, between whom she passed; at the carriage—still holding little Rose by the hand—she turned on the soldiers indignantly. "May your next duty be a more honorable one than that of guarding helpless women and children," she said.

Dusk had fallen ere the carriage reached the Old Capitol; here, too, a guard was drawn up under arms to prevent any attempt at rescue. The receiving-room of the prison was crowded with officers and civilians, all peering curiously. Half an hour later she and the child were marched into a room very different from that which they had left in the house in Sixteenth Street. The room, ten by twelve, was on the second floor of the back building of the prison; its only window (over which special bars were placed next day) looked out upon the prison yard. A narrow bed, on which was a straw mattress covered by a pair of unwashed cotton sheets, a small feather pillow, dingy and dirty, a few wooden chairs, a table, and a cracked mirror, furnished the room which from that night was to be theirs during months of heartbreaking imprisonment.

An understanding of those bitter days can be given best by extracts from her diary:

"*January 25th.* I have been one week in my new prison. My letters now all go through the detective police, who subject them to a chemical process to extract the treason. In one of the newspaper accounts I am supposed to use sympathetic ink. I purposely left a preparation very conspicuously placed, in order to divert attention from my real means of communication, and they have swallowed the bait and fancy my friends are at their mercy."

"*January 28th.* This day as I stood at my barred window the guard rudely called, 'Go 'way from that window!' and leveled his musket at me. I maintained my position without condescending to notice him, whereupon he called the corporal of the guard. I called also for the officer of the guard, . . . who informed me that I must not go to the window. I quietly told him that at whatever peril, I should avail myself of the largest liberty of the four walls of my prison. He told me that his guard would have orders to fire upon me. I had no idea that such monstrous regulations existed. To-day the dinner for myself and child consists of a bowl of beans swimming in grease, two slices of fat junk, and two slices of bread. . . . I was very often intruded upon by large parties of Yankees, who came with passes from the Provost-Marshal to stare at me. Sometimes I was amused, and generally contrived to find out what was going on. . . . Afterward I requested the superintendent not to allow any more of these parties to have access to me. He told me that numbers daily came to the prison who would gladly give him ten dollars apiece to be allowed to pass my open door."

"*March 3d.* Since two days we are actually allowed a half-hour's exercise in the prison-yard, where we walk up and down, picking our way as best we can through mud and negroes, followed by soldiers and corporals, bayonets in hand. . . . Last night I put my candle on the window, in order to get something out of my trunk near which it stood, all unconscious of committing any offense against prison discipline, when the guard below called, 'Put out that light!' I gave no heed, but only lighted another, whereupon several voices took up the cry, adding, 'Damn you, I will fire into your room!' Rose was in a state of great delight, and collected all the ends of candles to add to the illumination. By this the clank of arms and patter of feet, in conjunction with the furious rapping at my door, with a demand to open it, announced the advent of corporal and sergeant. My door was now secured inside by a bolt which had been allowed me. I asked their business. Answer, 'You are making signals, and must remove your lights from the window.' I said, 'But it suits my convenience to keep them there.' 'We will break open your door if you don't open it.' 'You will act as you see fit, but it will be at your peril!' They did not dare to carry out this threat, as they knew that I had a very admirable pistol on my mantelpiece, restored to me a short time since, although they did not know that I had no ammunition for it." The candles burned themselves out, and that ended it, save that next day, by order of the Provost-Marshal, the pistol was taken from the prisoner.

But it was not all a merry baiting of the guards—there was hardship connected with this imprisonment. In spite of the folded clothing placed on the hard bed, the child used to cry out in the night, "Oh, mama, mama, the bed hurts me so!" The rooms above were filled with negroes. "The tramping and screaming of negro children overhead was most dreadful." Worse than mere sound came from these other prisoners: there came disease. Smallpox broke out among them, also the lesser disease, camp measles, which latter was contracted by the little Rose. She, too, had her memories of the Old Capitol; in a recent letter she wrote:

"I do not remember very much about our imprisonment except that I used to cry myself to sleep from hunger. . . . There was a tiny closet in our room in which mother contrived to loosen a plank that she would lift up, and the prisoners of war underneath would catch hold of my legs and lower me into their room; they were allowed to receive fruit, etc., from the outside, and generously shared with me, also they would give mother news of the outside world." Thus the days passed until Mrs. Greenhow was summoned to appear, March 25th, before the United States Commissioners for the Trial of State Prisoners.

Of this "trial" the only record available is her own—rather too flippant in tone to be wholly convincing as to its entire sincerity. Her account begins soberly enough: the cold, raw day, the slowly falling snow, the mud through which the carriage labored to the office of the Provost-Marshal in what had been the residence of Senator Guin—"one of the most elegant in the city; . . . my mind instinctively reverted to the gay and brilliant scenes in which I had mingled in that house, and the goodly company who had enjoyed its hospitality." There was a long wait in a fireless anteroom; then she was led before the Commissioners for her trial. "My name was announced, and the Commissioners advanced to receive me with ill-concealed embarrassment. I bowed to them, saying: 'Gentlemen, resume your seats. I recognize the embarrassment of your positions; it was a mistake on the part of your government to have selected gentlemen for this mission. You have, however, shown me but scant courtesy in having kept me waiting your pleasure for nearly an hour in the cold.' " The prisoner took her place at the long table, midway between the two Commissioners, one of whom, General Dix, was a former friend; at smaller tables were several secretaries; if there were any spectators other than the newspaper reporters, she makes no mention of them. The trial began.

"One of the reporters now said, 'If you please, speak a little louder, madam.' I rose from my seat, and said to General Dix, 'If it is your object to make a spectacle of me, and furnish reports for the newspapers, I shall have the honor to withdraw from this presence.' Hereupon both Commissioners arose and protested that they had no such intention, but that it was necessary to take notes. . . ." The examination then continued "in a strain in no respect different from that of an ordinary conversation held in a drawing-room, and to which I replied sarcastically, . . . and a careless listener would have imagined that the Commission was endeavoring with plausible arguments to defend the government rather than to incriminate me. . . ." The other Commissioner then said, " 'General Dix, you are so much better acquainted with Mrs. Greenhow, suppose you continue the examination.' I laughingly said, 'Commence it, for I hold that it has not begun.' " Mrs. Greenhow's account makes no mention of any witnesses either for or against her; the evidence seems to have consisted solely in the papers found in her house. The whole examination—as she records it—may be summed up in the following questions and answers:

" 'You are charged with treason.' 'I deny it!' 'You are charged, madam, with having caused a letter which you wrote to the Secretary of State to be published in Richmond.' 'That can hardly be brought forward as one of the causes of my arrest, for I had been some three months a prisoner when that letter was written.' 'You are charged, madam, with holding communication with the enemy in the South.' 'If this were an established fact, you could not be surprised at it; I am a Southern woman.' . . . 'How is it, madam, that you have managed to communicate, in spite of the vigilance exercised over you?' 'That is my secret!' " And that was practically the end, save that the prisoner said she would refuse to take the oath of allegiance if this opportunity to be freed were offered her.

April 3d the superintendent of the Old Capitol read to her a copy of the decree of the Commission: she had been sentenced to be exiled. But the days passed, and nothing came of it. Tantalized beyond endurance, she wrote that she was "ready" to go South. General McClellan, she was then told, had objected to her being sent South at this time. (Federal spies— Secret Service men, who, under Allan Pinkerton, had arrested Mrs. Greenhow—were on trial for their lives in Richmond; it was feared that, were she sent South, her testimony would be used against them.) "Day glides into day with nothing to mark the flight of time," the diary continues. "The heat is intense, with the sun beating down upon the house-top and in the windows. . . . My child is looking pale and ill. . . ."

"*Saturday, May 31st.* At two o'clock to-day [Prison Superintendent] Wood came in with the announcement that I was to start at three o'clock for Baltimore." The end of imprisonment had come as suddenly as its beginning.

Disquieting rumors had been reaching Mrs. Greenhow for some time in regard to removal to Fort Warren. Was this, after all, a mere Yankee trick to get her there quietly? She was about to enter the carriage that was to bear her from the Old Capitol, when, unable longer to bear the suspense, she turned suddenly to the young lieutenant of the escort: "Sir, ere I advance further, I ask you, not as Lincoln's officer, but as a man of honor and a gentleman, are your orders from Baltimore to conduct me to a Northern prison, or to some point in the Confederacy?" "On my honor, madam," he answered, "to conduct you to Fortress Monroe and thence to the Southern Confederacy." Her imprisonment had, indeed, ended. There was yet the Abolition-soldier guard—on the way to the station, to the cars, in Baltimore, on the steamer; there was yet to be signed at Fortress Monroe the parole in which, in consideration of being set at liberty, she pledged her honor not to return north of the Potomac during the war; but from that moment at the carriage door she felt herself no longer a prisoner.

To the query of the Provost-Marshal at Fortress Monroe she replied that she wished to be sent "to the capital of the Condeferacy, wherever that might be." That was still Richmond, he told her, but it would be in Federal hands before she could reach there. She would take chances on that, was her laughing rejoinder. And so she was set ashore at City Point by a boat from the *Monitor;* and next morning, June 4th, she and little Rose, escorted by Confederate officers, arrived in Richmond. And there, "on the evening of my arrival, our President did me the honor to call on me, and his words of greeting, 'But for you there would have been no battle of Bull Run,' repaid me for all I had endured."

Could the story be told of the succeeding twenty-seven months of Mrs. Greenhow's life, much of the secret history of the Confederacy might be revealed. It is improbable that the story ever will be told. Months of effort to learn details have resulted in but vague glimpses of her, as one sees an ever-receding figure at the turns of a winding road. Her daughter Rose has written: "Whether mother did anything for the Condeferacy in Richmond is more than I can tell. I know that we went to Charleston, South Carolina, and that she saw General Beauregard there." Then came weeks of waiting for the sailing of a blockade-runner from Wilmington, North Carolina; quiet, happy weeks they were, perhaps the happiest she had known since the war began. She was taking little Rose to Paris, to place her in the Convent of the Sacred Heart, she told her new-made friends. One morning they found that she and little Rose had gone. A blockade-runner had slipped out during the night and was on its way with them to Bermuda.

Many have definitely asserted that Mrs. Greenhow went to England and France on a secret mission for the Confederacy. No proof of this has ever been found, but the little which has been learned of her sojourn in Europe strongly supports the theory of such a mission there. The ship which bore them to England from Bermuda was an English man-of-war, in which they sailed "at President Davis's especial request." Then there were President Davis's personal letters to Messrs. Mason and Slidell, requesting them that they show to Mrs. Greenhow every attention. In France she was given a private audience with Napoleon III.; in London, presented to England's Queen. A letter written to her by James Spence, financial agent of the Confederates in Liverpool, shows her to have been actively engaged in support of the interests of the South from her arrival in England. But of any secret mission there is not a trace—unless her book, *My Imprisonment, or the First Year of Abolition Rule in Washington,* may thus be considered. The book was brought out in November, 1863, by the well-known English publishing-house of Richard Bentley & Son; immediately it made a profound sensation in London—particularly in the highest society circles, into which Mrs. Greenhow had at once been received. *My Imprisonment* was a brilliant veneer of personal wartime experiences laid alluringly over a solid backing of Confederate States propaganda. Richmond may or may not have fathered it, but that book in England served the South well.[1] None who knew Mrs. Greenhow ever forgot her charm; she made friends everywhere—such friends as Thomas Carlyle and Lady Franklin, and a score more whose names are nearly as well known to-day. She was betrothed to a prominent peer.

All in all, this is but scant information to cover a period of more than two years. Only one other fact has been obtained regarding her life abroad, but it is most significant in support of the belief that she was a secret agent for the Confederacy. In August, 1864, Mrs. Greenhow left England suddenly and sailed for Wilmington on the ship *Condor*. Though her plans were to return almost at once, marry, and remain in England, the fact that she left in London her affianced husband, and her little Rose in the Convent of the Sacred Heart in Paris, while she herself risked her life to run the blockade, seems strong evidence that her business in the Confederate States of America was important business indeed. The *Condor* was a three funneled steamer, newly built, and on her first trip as a blockade-runner—a trade for which she was superbly adapted, being swift as a sea-swallow. She was commanded by a veteran captain of the Crimean War—an English officer on a year's leave, blockade-running or adventure—Captain Augustus Charles Hobart-Hampden, variously known to the blockade-running fleet as Captain Roberts, Hewett, or Gulick.

On the night of September 30th the *Condor* arrived opposite the mouth of the Cape Fear River, the entry for Wilmington, and in the darkness stole swiftly though the blockade. She was almost in the mouth of the river, and not two hundred yards from shore, when suddenly there loomed up in the darkness a vessel dead ahead. To the frightened pilot of the *Condor* it was one of the Federal squadron; he swerved his ship sharply, and she drove hard on New Inlet bar. In reality the ship which had caused the damage was the wreck of the blockade-runner *Nighthawk*, which had been run down the previous night. The *Condor's* pilot sprang overboard and swam ashore. Dawn was near breaking, and in the now growing light the Federal blockaders which had followed the *Condor* were seen to be closing in. Though the *Condor,* lying almost under the very guns of Fort Fisher—which had begun firing at the

---

[1] Many of the passages in this article have been quoted from Mrs. Greenhow's own narrative.

Federal ships and was holding them off—was for the time being safe, yet Mrs. Greenhow and the two other passengers, Judge Holcombe and Lieutenant Wilson, Confederate agents, demanded that they be set ashore. There was little wind and there had been no storm, but the tide-rip ran high over the bar, and the boat was lowered into heavy surf. Scarcely was it clear of the tackles ere a great wave caught it, and in an instant it was overturned. Mrs. Greenhow, weighted down by her heavy black-silk dress and a bag full of gold sovereigns, which she had fastened round her waist, sank at once, and did not rise again. The others succeeded in getting ashore.

The body of Mrs. Greenhow was washed up on the beach next day. They buried her in Wilmington—buried her with the honors of war, and a Confederate flag wrapped about her coffin. And every Memorial Day since then there is laid upon her grave a wreath of laurel leaves such as is placed only upon the graves of soldiers. Long ago the Ladies' Memorial Society placed there a simple marble cross, on which is carved: "Mrs. Rose O'Neal Greenhow. A Bearer of Despatches to the Confederate Government."

Landegon

"He was the bravest man I ever knew: General Kilpatrick also used to say that of him. But he will not talk about himself—so you may not get what you want; but come up and try." That was in the letter that sent me all the miles to see John Landegon.

He did not believe in getting into the papers—he said—and all that sort of thing; people would say, "Here's another old vet lying about the war"—more of that sort; he hadn't got into print, and he wouldn't now.

We led him on—or tried to—Captain Northrop and I.

"John, do you remember anything about the six Confederates you and one of the boys captured in a barn? What about that?" And old John Landegon, with never a smile, answered, dryly:

"I was there. That was in the spring of '62, and soon after that we broke camp and marched to—"

Campaigns and dates, and the movements of armies and of corps—but never an "I" in it all, and he would have it so. Evening came—the hours I had looked forward to all the long, profitless afternoon; but it seemed it was to bring only more dates, and the proper spelling of the names of officers long forgotten and long dead. Through it all, like a tortuous river-bed, empty, bone-dry, there ran his modest estimate of his service:

"I enlisted for three months in the First Regiment, Connecticut Volunteer Infantry, Company D, and there I got a little notoriety cheap. How? Oh, I got a prisoner; and so I was detailed as a headquarters scout under General Tyler; and because of that, when I reenlisted in

Company C of the Second Regiment, New York Volunteer Cavalry—better known as the 'Harris Light'—I was once more detailed as a scout, this time under Colonel Judson Kilpatrick. That was in the spring of '61, and I served with him until—" Discouraged, I threw the note-book down, and said that I had done. There were hours to wait until the train should come and carry my ruined note-book and myself away. The time dragged; we smoked, and talked in a desultory way, and then some chance idle word impelled John Landegon to tell me his stories.

It was as though an unexpected current had carried him out of his depth, and the tide had caught him and swept him back through nearly fifty years, until he rode again in the great war. And I was with him as though I rode at his side. Sentences were whole scenes; words were sensations, emotions. He had gone back into it—was living it over again, and he had taken me along.

There was the dry griminess of dust rising in clouds from the parched Virginia roads; . . . there was the acrid smell of sweating horses and of men . . . creak of rain-soaked saddles . . . the loneliness of wind in the trees at night along dark-flowing rivers; his words brought the shimmer of heat above unfenced, untended fields . . . brought, the feel of cool gray aisles in forests of Georgia pine . . . stiffened bandages . . . pungent whiffs of bluewhite powder-smoke . . . the confusion and absorption of men fighting at close range—fighting to kill.

It was such a simple, boyish beginning that he made! A story to be told with chuckles, to be listened to with smiles. So like those early, lost-to-memory days of the great war—the days when war was a pastime, a summer muster to end with a skirmish and a hoorah; the days when the first volunteers had not yet made the first veterans, and "Black-horse Cavalry," "masked batteries," and the "Louisiana Tigers" were specters that stalked round each camp-fire; the days before men had seen their comrades die.

They would not enlist John Landegon. He was too young, too thin, too poor food for powder. And so he saw the company of heroes march away in triumph from the little Connecticut village; they left him raging and grieving behind. He went to Waterbury; they were raising a company there. Would they enlist him? No, they would not. But the rush of the first enthusiasts slackened, applications became less frequent; the captain fumed—before he could get his company into the field the war would be over and done—would the quota never fill! The last few enlistments came in, hours apart, and the whole country-side fretted for the honor of the town—all but Landegon; each hour was bringing nearer to him his chance. At last they took him; he was under age and looked it; he had not the necessary parental consent, he was not even from Waterbury—but they took him; and it was thus that he went to war.

"Camp" was at Vienna, Virginia, a few miles out from Alexandria; it was just "camp"—not more. The army that was to be was then but companies of individuals, groups of neighbors, friends. The welding of war had not yet begun. Rumor was the one excitement of the dragging weeks; camp life palled; the three-months period of enlistment was nearly past.

Time after time Landegon was passed over when picket and scouting detachments were detailed. At last he went to the captain—a stout, fussy, kindly little man.

"Captain," he said, "*I* want to go out with the scouting party; I can scout as good as any of them."

The captain shook his head.

"I can't do that, John." Then, kind and confidential, he went on: "You see, it's this way: those fellows are all prominent citizens back in Waterbury, and they've got to have a chance. Waterbury expects a lot from some of us; the fellows have got to have something to write home; the papers up in our town have got to tell about our citizens doin' things, and scoutin' is the nearest to fightin' that there is just now."

Landegon protested earnestly that his town expected just as much of him.

"Oh, nothin' much is expected of you, John—you're too young." Then, with finality, "This war is nearly over; I got to give our citizens a chance."

"Scouting" consisted of a solemn, impressive march by ten or a dozen prominent citizens along the front of the camp, half a mile or so in advance of the pickets; but it was a deed filled with fine thrills.

Between the two camps—Federal and Confederate—there stretched four miles of no man's land, filled with all the terrors that go hand in hand with untried ground. But John Landegon found it to be a land of woods and fields and low, rolling hills—a land empty of friend or foe. He had gone out into it alone many times before he begged of the stout captain the privilege of making the dignified scouting. Something of latent daring, some restlessness within him, had sent him stealing beyond the pickets time after time to wander among the hills. He says he wanted to see a Confederate before he went home again! Sometimes he wandered far enough to see long black lines creeping along the side of a distant hill; but they never seemed to be coming his way, so he would go back to the camp, content and silent.

The day after he was rejected from the official scout he wandered out farther than ever before, driven perhaps a little by pique, a little resentful, a little sullen, maybe. At last he turned to go back. He had kept to the woods, and now among the trees he caught a glimpse of moving gray. He leaped behind a tree, and stood there trembling with excitement and, he says, with fear. Once he stole a look, and as quickly dodged behind again; the glimpse had shown him a man in full uniform—a very new, very elegant uniform—a hat turned jauntily up on the side, and with a highly polished musket lying across his arm. The young blade of the Confederacy was returning from some lone-hand scout of his own. Landegon pressed close against the bark of the tree and humbly prayed that the man might change his course; he came straight on. Behind lay the Confederate army—he could not run; from in front advanced the very devil of a fighter, one that would never surrender (camp-fire authority for that! "They'll never surrender; we'll just have to mow them down"). He would have to mow this one down; would have to kill him. He had never even seen a man die. Somehow it had never seemed that war would be like this. The man was almost to the tree. He would have to mow him down; he would have to—he leaped out, leveling his musket as he sprang.

"Sur-*ren*-der!" he screamed.

The brightly polished Confederate musket fell to the ground; the hands waved, beseeching to be seen. "I surrender!" screamed the gray-clad youth, in reply.

John Landegon says the reaction almost made him giddy, and he wanted to dance and yell. But he warily picked up the musket, and he marched the unhappy man the three long miles back to the camp. And on that march, in his elation, he evolved the philosophy that was to carry him to such distinction through the war: "The other fellow is just as much afraid of me—maybe more." I should like to have seen that home-coming! I think I can see it now: the prisoner stumbling in front; lank John Landegon stalking like Death behind; men running from regiments a mile away to see the captor and his prize.

"And after that," said he, in his dry, shy way, "*I* was the big fellow; *I* went on all the scoutings that were made." Waterbury claimed him for its own.

That philosophy did not always hold good. It was a rank failure at Bull Run. He climbed a tree there, and it was not philosophy that brought him down. The battle had been fought and lost. Long, late afternoon shadows lay heavy on the trampled, bloody grass; shadows from west and south, toward north and east, blighting the path, pointing the way to Washington.

In that portion of the field where Landegon was when the battle ended, he says that there seemed no cause to hurry away. The Confederates were in plain sight on the distant hillsides, but came no nearer, content to shell the fugitives from afar. Some distance back, he came upon a church, about which a score of abandoned, plunging cavalry horses were tied. He was plodding past, when an officer rushed to him.

"Take a horse!" the officer was urging all who were passing; many ran close by and never turned their heads; men were running everywhere.

"Take a horse! take a horse!" the officer kept calling, as they passed. "The rebels'll get them if you don't." He was a thrifty soul. Landegon stopped; he selected one, and tied his gun to the saddle, then galloped for the rear. The officer was still querulously calling, "Take a horse! take a horse!" as he rode away.

There came a great crowd, running. From behind them at the blocked ford—where they had been headed by some Confederate cavalry—there came the turmoil of fighting, mob-like fighting, so different from a battle's roar. Those who were running had been behind, or had broken away, and now, the forefront of the rout, came running, sheep-like, back in panic over the way they had just, in panic, gone. Some were running stolidly, mechanically, as though stiff with fear; others, plunging; others, running profitlessly—shoulders forward, elbows stiffly back, and ghastly, sweatless faces upturned to the blinding sky; of these, their mouths were gaping open like banked fishes sucking at the air. There was little sound save the pounding of the footfalls on the sun-baked Virginia fields. Cries of terror could have added nothing to the horror; the very sight of such is contagion of the plague—Panic.

Landegon slid from his horse, and, without untying his gun, turned and ran. The mob was scattering, each seeking his own hiding-place; Landegon ran for the woods. He says that just then he feared nothing so much as capture—death was not so dread.

He ran into a tree, staggered back, then began in frantic haste to climb it; if only they would not come till he could reach the top! Among the slender branches he screened himself with leaves, and clung there swaying in the wind, like some strange arboreal animal. In the great, hot dome of the sky there was no sign of the darkness whose coming should save him; through the maze of branches and the fluttering leaves beneath him he could see the earth, still sun-flecked and wholly light. Suddenly he began to scramble down. On the instant with his elated thought, "They'll never take me here," had come, "There's never a chance to be taken—I'll be shot. They'll not be able to resist the temptation to see me tumble from so high." It sent him sliding and swinging and dropping from branch to branch until he reached the ground and threw himself into a thicket.

It was a long, hard road from the top of the tree to the position of Sheridan's chief scout. What happened during that journey I shall never know; he was not telling me the history of his career, remember. What he told were just incidents plucked from here and there—a half-dozen days out of the thousand days and nights of his service.

I wanted him to tell me more about his work as scout—the messages he had carried, the information he had obtained.

"I can't do that," he said. "Why? because I don't remember it—how could I? I couldn't keep copies of despatches, and I can't remember the verbal messages—now. 'Landegon, take this to General So-and-so over back of Such-a-place.' Maybe I wouldn't ever know what was in the message, even though the result of an engagement had been decided by it; maybe it was in cipher; maybe I didn't care what was in it. My business was to get it there. Perhaps it was only such a message as an aide-de-camp would have been sent with if he could have kept in our lines while delivering it. But here's the thing: us scouts risked our lives to deliver those messages. We did it sometimes every day; sometimes only once every week. If we got caught we got hanged, or maybe only shot; if we got through without any close call that was out of the ordinary—like losing our chum or our horse, or something like that—why, then, that was just part of a day's work, and by next week we wouldn't remember anything about it except the roads we had been on and the fords crossed and the lay of the hills and ravines.

"Information, the same way. 'See if you can find out when Magruder is going to move'—something o' that sort. And I'd go out through the country between the lines—in just as much danger from our own scoutin' parties, mind, as from the enemy—and I would get through their pickets and mix in with any I'd find, and when I got what I wanted to know I'd come back and report.

"Maybe there would be a fight that day or the next, and maybe my report had something to do with it, but I wouldn't know that for sure. Like as not I wouldn't be able to see that my report had any attention paid to it. So why should I remember now about such things? But here's a letter that I'm going to let you read; I don't want you to think us scouts risked our necks for just nothing those days—even if we can't remember what reports we made forty-five years ago!"

He hesitated a moment, then drew from its envelope a single worn sheet. It was written from the Metropolitan Hotel, New York, under date of April 20, 1869. The contents were intimately personal, but there is this much which seems by right to belong in the pages that are to record John Landegon's service:

> . . . From the first time you reported to me as scout in 1861 until the close of the war I had frequent occasion to acknowledge your distinguished services, and I know of no man who has manifested more devotion to the cause of the Union or braved greater dangers than yourself. At Fredericksburg, on the Rapidan, and in the Shenandoah Valley, you displayed great courage and enterprise in obtaining within the enemy's lines intelligence of his intended

movements, and I can freely say that much of the success of my cavalry, in the campaign of General Sherman from Savannah to the surrender of Johnson's army, was owing to the information obtained by you for me as scout and spy. . . .

(Signed) JUDSON KILPATRICK.

When I had done, I looked with new eyes at the man whom General Judson Kilpatrick had freely accredited with much of the success of the brilliant cavalry campaign of the Carolinas.

It was characteristic of John Landegon at such a time to force an abrupt change of subject.

"I mind one report I made," he said. "My first report to General Sheridan. I'd been out for three days—somewhere in the enemy's lines, I don't remember where, or why—and when I came in to report to the General I thought it would be my last report. 'Well,' he says, 'what did you find?' 'Nothin',' I answered—just that. 'By Gee!' he yelled, and he jumped up from his chair. 'That's the best report I ever heard a scout make!' I thought he was mad and just making fun of me, and I stood still and didn't say anything. He walked close up to me. 'Do you know why I think so much of that "nothin'" of yours? It's because you didn't think you had to make up a lot of lies for fear I'd think you hadn't been working. If you saw "nothin'" in three days, that means there was nothing to see, and that's the one thing I wanted to know!'

"I remembered that little talk of General Sheridan's, and it helped me all the rest of the war. I never exaggerated anything, and soon they got to count on what I said. Well"—abruptly, as though he had again said too much—"there was only twice after that day I climbed the tree that I was as bad scared. There was often enough that I'd think: 'Well, by Gee! if ever I get back safe from this fool scout I'll never go out again. I'll go back to my regiment, *I*'ll stand guard, *I*'ll do picket, *I* will clean camp'—more of that sort—'but I'm darned if I go in gray out of the lines.' But I would get in all right, and loaf around a few days and watch the other boys work, and then I'd get restless or think of the big money, and then the order would come and out I'd go— like as not into worse than before. The next time I was so badly scared was the night after I had been shot. I was Sheridan's chief scout then, but when I got shot I was with Meade's scouts of the Army of the Potomac. I'd been sent to General Meade with despatches—I'll tell you about that.

"After we left General Sheridan at Ground Squirrel Bridge, on the South Anna—this was Sheridan's raid around Lee in May, '64—Patrick Myers, my best scout, and I rode around the flank of the Confederate cavalry where they were fighting with our rear guard. They had been fighting the rear guard ever since we had got in the rear of Lee's lines on the 9th. This day I'm telling you of was the 10th—late afternoon of the 10th—the day before Yellow Tavern, where Jeb Stuart fell, six miles from Richmond. We missed that fight.

"The country was so rough that, to make time, we swung into the road behind the Confederate cavalry, and ordered the stragglers forward to their regiments. Y' see, I was in the full uniform of a Confederate officer, and Patrick Myers was my orderly; we kept hurrying the stragglers forward, and all the time we were getting farther to the rear. It was the best fun I ever had!" It was the pinnacle of a jest. Landegon chuckled as he told of it; I chuckled as I heard. It seemed a jest in the telling; since then I have set it down as one of the shrewdest, coolest deeds that men have done.

They stopped at dark at a farm-house and asked for something to eat. The owner of the house was too old to go to war; he gave them a good meal, and gladly assented to put them up for as much of the night as they could remain. After the meal they all sat about the table talking. In some way they misunderstood their host—something he said; they believed him to be a Union sympathizer who, because of their gray uniforms, dared not come out and say that he was against the South.

"We're not Confederates," one of them blurted out; "we are Union soldiers." The old man rose from his chair.

"Ye lied to me," he said.

They both sprang, startled, to their feet at his sudden movement, and it must have been a dramatic moment as they faced each other across the lamp-lit table—the scouts with their hands on their revolvers, the white-bearded old man majestic in his indignation.

"I've given you food and offered you bed: and you have lied to me! You yourselves say that you have been telling me lies all the evenin'! I wouldn't have you sleep in my barn. It isn't which side you're on; ye *lied* to me!"

He drove them from his house by the sheer weight of his scorn. They sulkily rode away; but in the stillness of the night they heard a horse, hard ridden, leave the farmhouse, and they rode aside into the woods and waited. Presently a troop of Confederate cavalry swept by on the road they had just been on.

It was night of the next day—the 11th—when they got through the Confederate pickets and struck the Mattapony River some miles below the Army of the Potomac.

They stripped, and put their clothes on a bit of board, which they pushed before them as they swam the river; it was storming fiercely; in the dark the rain lashed the river into pale foam.

They made their painful way through the tangled thickets, now dazed by the lightning, now blinded by the streaming rain. Federal pickets made them prisoners, and finally, to their insistence, yielded and took them under guard to General Grant—to Grant, though they asked to be taken to Meade.

I wish that Landegon had told me more of that meeting; I wish that I had asked.

It was the night before that battle which was to surpass in its terrors all others of those terrible days of the Second Wilderness and Spottsylvania Court-house—the battle of the "Bloody Angle."

Of the meeting I learned only that Grant thanked them and praised them for bringing the message through Lee's army. Then Landegon swung off into a vehement panegyric of the great leader; it was as though he had lowered a curtain; I was left with but a dim-seen picture of the lantern-lighted tent; the Grant of my own imagination, bending low to smooth out and read by the flickering light a crumpled despatch . . . two dripping, gray-clad soldiers—just that, and an intruding consciousness of the confused beating of the rain outside.

This is the despatch that they had borne through the Confederate armies:

HEADQUARTERS, CAVALRY CORPS,
ARMY OF THE POTOMAC, *May 10, 1864.*
MAJ.-GEN. GEORGE G. MEADE,
  Commanding Army of the Potomac.
GENERAL:
  I turned the enemy's right and got into their rear. Did not
meet sufficient of cavalry to stop me. Destroyed from eight to
ten miles of Orange Railroad, two locomotives, three trains, and
a large amount of supplies. The enemy were making a depot of
supplies at Beaver Dam. Since I got into their rear there has been
great excitement among the inhabitants and with the army. The
citizens report that Lee is beaten. Their cavalry has attempted to
annoy my rear and flank, but have been run off. I expect to fight
their cavalry south of the South Anna River. I have no forage.
Started with half rations for one day, and have found none yet.
Have recaptured five hundred men, two colonels.

I am, General, very respectfully,
Your obedient servant,
P. H. SHERIDAN,
Major-General, Commanding.

He brought out a big book, and his long, thin fingers fluttered the
pages till he had found the place he sought; I watched him in surprise.
He handed me the book, open.

"There!" he said. "That won't surprise you like it did me the first
time I saw it!"

"Scouts and Guides with the Army of the Potomac," I read under the
picture.

"I bought that book about a year ago, and I was looking through it,
and all of a sudden, by Gee! there was I! I got shot the very next day after
the picture was taken—the only one I had taken during the war—and
I hadn't thought about the photograph from that day until I looked out
at myself after all these years. I had just about forgotten what sort of a
young fellow I was those days." He commenced a chuckle of infinite
amusement that ended in a sigh. He took the book gently from me and
closed it, shutting away the boy that had been. For a moment his thin

fingers fumbled the white beard. "That was a long time ago," he said. Then, abruptly, "The next day I made my last scout in Virginia."

Eleven of Meade's scouts, together with Landegon and Myers, were sent out to learn if Lee was being reinforced from the south. If, by the time the Army of the Potomac scouts were ready to return, Sheridan had not been met, then Landegon and Myers were to go on until they found him. Had he and Myers gone to Sheridan, the whole trip would have gone the way of a day's work; but, instead, every incident of the day is fixed sharp and clear in his memory; the De Jarnett's, where they stopped to get feed for their horses, and where they were "given" wine; the "contraband," who showed them a blind ford of the Mattapony, where Landegon and Knight (Meade's chief scout) crossed to interview the lonely figure on the distant hillcrest, whom they took to be a vedette, until the man, not knowing of his danger, unconsciously saved himself by raising a huge cotton umbrella that showed him to be a planter overseeing the hands at work in his fields.

They turned to ride back to their men, awaiting them on the river's bank, when there suddenly came out of a lane a man and a girl, who stared at them in surprise.

"Have you seen any troops come by?" the scouts asked, politely. It was the girl who answered:

"Oh, yes! More than I ever saw before at one time! South Carolina soldiers. How many? Why, they would reach from there to there!" The space indicated a brigade of four regiments. It was the information they had come out to gain; Knight was elated at the ease with which it had been obtained.

"We're Yankees!" he suddenly said. The girl looked at Landegon's gray uniform, at Knight's wheat-straw hat, his coat—purpled by the rain and sun; she laughed.

"About as much Yankees as we are!" she said.

"We are Yankees!" they sternly told her. Her eyes grew wide with fear.

"You shall not—I—you will, not take the Doctor—my husband?" she pleaded.

They reassured her—they would only take dinner, and pay for it, they said. But she still was very much afraid. Landegon waved a handkerchief, and the rest of the scouts came up at a gallop from the river. Young Doctor Dew and his wife fled in terror. The scouts shouted with laughter, and trotted after them to the house, where presently they had dinner. Trivial little details, these, but I dare say such things stick in a man's mind if he is shot that day.

They rode to Penola Station, not more than a mile away, and there lay the parting of the ways: Landegon and Myers must start south to find Sheridan, Knight and his scouts go back to the army of Grant and Meade.

A small band of Confederates dashed out of a crossroad, fired a bravado volley at them, and galloped away.

"Let's have a fight!" one of the scouts yelled, "before you fellows leave." In a moment they were riding hard after the Confederates, shouting and yelling like frolicking boys.

Landegon says he had the best horse of them all. As a brave man and a modest should, he lays it to the horse; I lay it to the man who rode. He drew farther and farther ahead; the road grew choked with dust that rose all about them like smoke-filled fog. The fleeing Confederates had been reinforced, had turned, and were coming back. In the dust Landegon flashed full tilt into them before he found what he had done. Horses reared and backed and shied; there was a tangle and confusion that sent up blinding clouds in which no man knew friend from foe. Landegon whirled his horse about and fired a revolver in a man's face, and then some one shot him, and his paralyzed hand dropped his pistol, and the whole thing grew confused. He knows that one man followed him, shooting at him at every bound; and when his revolver was empty, the man rose in his stirrups and threw the pistol whirling over and over, and it struck him, barrel end on; it seemed to break his spine.

He knows something of two of his scouts riding one on either side holding him in his saddle; and then all he knew was that he was back at Doctor Dew's under a tree in the yard, and all his men had gone; and he was quite sure that very soon he would be found and hanged. He told this to the Dews, and they took his gray clothes and buried them in the garden; but still he knew that very soon he would certainly be hanged.

He says that he had once before nearly gone by the rope route, and it was the memory of that other time that now filled him with such fear.

He thought that his men might have made some arrangement to take him away; he found afterward that they had stood off the reinforced Confederates until he had been gotten out of sight on his way to the Dews; then they had ridden for the safety of the Union lines. They had been sure, from his wound, that Landegon was to die; but they promised the Dews that they would come back for him in a few days. When they came he was gone.

The afternoon waned; the young doctor had managed to get him into the house; they wanted to put him to bed up-stairs, but he would not have it so; he begged to be left in the hall. It was a long, straight hall through the house; at one end the front door, at the other the back. He felt that unless the house were surrounded he had some chance there for his life. Yet when the time did come he was without the strength to raise himself from the couch. The night had grown threadbare gray and old before they came; he had known all along that they would come, yet when he heard the feet on the gravel walk he was more afraid than he thought he could ever be. The Dews had gone to their room for a little rest; Landegon lay alone in the long, black hall—alone, listening to the footsteps coming nearer; he heard them reach the door. He raised himself on one elbow—it was as far as he could go. The angry knocks on the door sounded like thunder; without waiting for a reply, the door was burst open by a booted foot, and a man stood for a moment black against the graying sky.

"Does any one live in this house?" he roared.

Landegon fell back limp and helpless; he answered almost hysteri-cally, "Yes, Jack, I do!"

It was Jack Williams, one of his own scouts with Sheridan—a com-rade from the "Harris Light," his own old regiment.

Sheridan was coming back that way; Williams had been sent ahead to find out about the roads, and he had stopped at the house to inquire his way. Within a few hours Landegon was in an ambulance, riding in safety in the midst of ten thousand blue-clad men.

He smoked for a time in silence, and I sought to set him talking again. "You said you were nearly hanged once—?" He shook his head and frowned slightly, but said nothing.

"When was it?" I persisted.

"May 12, '62," he answered, dryly. He lay back in his big chair, with his eyes closed as though to shut out something he did not care to see. For a long time neither of us spoke; suddenly he opened his eyes and sat sharply forward in the chair.

"Do you know that there are nights even yet when I dream of that day? Do you know—but of course you don't! Well, you've got me to thinking of it again, and I might as well tell you, even of that, too.

"There was a cavalry skirmish a couple of miles from Massaponax Church—about twelve or fifteen miles south of Fredericksburg; it was going hard against us, and I was sent back to bring up help. I was about half-way to the church when I saw a lot of dust, and I rode harder—thinking, you understand, it was the advance of some of our troops; there was so much dust that I rode right into them before I found that they were Confederates that had got round our flank and were coming up behind our men. It was just a scouting party . . . more coming, I learned. There wasn't a chance to get away, or even to fight; they had never made any mistake about me . . . grabbed me the minute I got in reach. I was in my gray uniform, mind! They were in a hurry, but they said they had time to hang *me*. They just hauled off to the roadside and said they would have a trial, anyway—that they always tried the men they hanged. So they got up a drumhead court that wasn't any more a court than is our talking here. There was a lot of laughing and joking—the rest of the men all sitting around on the grass at the side of the road, holding their horses by the bridles to let them graze; some of the men smoked their pipes—it was all good fun for them.

"Back around the hills I could hear the popping of the carbines of the men of my regiment—that I'd left not half an hour before.

"I didn't get five minutes of trial; they asked me again where I'd been going, and I told them again—lying the best I knew—that I was only a camp servant . . . it had got too hot for me up there at the front, and I was scared, and getting back to the camp where I belonged.

"Some one yelled, 'He's a spy; look at his clothes.'

"And I turned on him and says: 'I'm no spy. I'm just a servant, an' these 's all the clothes I have—*I* don't get a uniform; I got to wear just what I can find'—all that sort of thing. Anyway, if I wasn't a spy, one of 'em said, I was a 'damned Yankee, that had stole the clothes off some pore dead Confederate soldier.' And they all said: 'That's so, all right! Stole 'em off some pore dead soldier. He had ought to be hung!'

"The president of the court got up and said, 'You're guilty, Yank, and it is the sentence o' this court that we hang you by the neck until you're dead.'

"They all laughed at that, and got up and stood around to see me get hung. We all moved over a hundred yards or so to a tree, and some one started to climb up with a rope—they had a rope, all right—and then some one said 'they'd ought to have some grease for the rope—noose wouldn't slip good without the rope was greased,' and one of the men was sent riding hard across the fields to a farm-house to get some. They got the rope tied to a limb, then they kept showing me the noose . . . telling me how I'd dance on air—they weren't going to tie my hands and feet, they said; and they danced and waved their hands to show me how I'd do.

"These weren't guerrillas; they were regularly enlisted men. But it was '62, mind, and they were a lot more bitter in those days than they were later in the war; but I never did see, before or after, such ones as these.

"I had been seared nearly to death up till then, but when they got to talking like that I got mad—they might hang me, all right, but they weren't going to torture me that way before I died. I tried to pull away from the fellows holding me, and I cursed them all, and called them murderers and cowards, and I told them I'd fight any three of them— any five—any number at once, if they would give me my saber and pistol, but that I wouldn't be hung.

"Just then the man with the grease got back; he'd only been able to get some butter! 'Don't waste good butter hanging a damn Yankee; string him up without greasing the rope, and be quick about it,' some one said.

"So they dragged and lifted me onto a horse, and led it under the limb, and they put the noose around my neck. I didn't see anything or think anything from the time I got put on the horse, and I didn't see that some of them were standing in a little party off to one side. Just then one stepped out and said that I was not to be hung; that I was a brave man; and it wasn't so much that they didn't want me to be hanged, but the other fellows weren't going to do it; I was as much *their* prisoner as I was theirs—that *they* hadn't any of them been selected for the court . . . more of that sort of thing (they were from two regiments—do you understand?); and that *they* had decided to send me back to the main column and have me tried right! Some of the fellows drew their revolvers, and some got on their horses, and it looked as if there was going to be a fight right there. But they talked it over—with me sitting on the horse, and the rope around my neck all the time—and finally decided that they would send me on.

"They took the rope off, and I began to get some of my senses back, and It saw that the man who was to take me forward was a great, surly-looking devil—one of them that had been so anxious to hang me; he was standing talking to his officer, and they looked over at me, and he kind of smiled and nodded his head; I knew right there that he meant to kill me on the way—was getting ordered to just then.

"We started—he and I—and the others rode away. The whole business hadn't taken more than twenty minutes, but it was a month to me. They wouldn't give me a horse; the fellow rode, but I had to run along at the horse's head. The horse he rode was one of the biggest I ever saw—when it walked I had to trot, and when he rode at a trot I had to run. I had lost my hat, and the sun hurt my head, and the dust choked and blinded me; I was so sick and weak—mind you, the reaction from such fear is a sickening thing—that I staggered as I ran, and the fellow kept leanin' over and prodding me with his saber to make me go faster; that began to make me mad when I got conscious of it, and I felt my strength coming back again.

"I kept on the off side of the horse, so that he would have to cut across with his saber instead of down, when the time came for me to try to run. I can see that road now—long and straight, with the unfenced fields sloping down to the road on either side, and sumac bushes along where the fences had been before the war; ahead, the road ran like a tunnel into a big woods that looked all hazy and blue. Beyond the woods a little way was Massaponax Church; I made up my mind that what was to be would take place in that woods, and I sort of felt that the Confederate had made up his mind to end it in the woods, too.

"Just then he called to me: 'Halt, Yank! Till I tighten the girth—saddle's slippin'!'"

"He was dismounting—you know, of course, how a man gets off a horse? his left foot in the stirrup, and swings his right leg back over the horse—for just a second his back was toward me, and at that moment he dropped his drawn saber to the ground. . . . He died right there!

"My three years' term of enlistment was just about up before I got out of the hospital at Portsmouth Grove, Rhode Island—that time I got shot and left at the Dews', remember?"

There was scarcely a moment's pause in his story; he seemed to be hurrying on to efface something from his mind and mine. I scarcely heard his words; I could see nothing but the sprawling figure that lay like a blot under a pall of slowly settling dust in a long, straight, sunlit road—a road that ran like a tunnel into a great woods all blue with haze.

"Sheridan was a few miles west of Harper's Ferry when I found him"—so the story was going on when I heard it again—"and when I walked up to his tent he ran out and put his hand on my shoulder—impulsive, like he always was—and he said: 'Landegon! I'm *glad* you're back! I've got a *lot* of work for you to do!' And then I told him that I wasn't coming back to him—that I was through. Ye see, Sheridan was now in command in the Shenandoah Valley, and he had reorganized the scouts, and put them on a strictly military footing, with Major H. H. Young in command.

"Then, too, General Kilpatrick—whose chief scout I had been for two years before Sheridan had got me to go with him—and Captain Northrop here, who now was 'Kil's' chief scout, had both written for me to come to them; they were with General Sherman down in Georgia, and I had made up my mind to go. Sheridan was very angry—said something about deserting in the face of the enemy—more of that sort of thing—and turned and walked away from me. I never saw General Sheridan again.

"I did not march to the sea. General Sherman, with 'Kil' in command of his cavalry, was at Savannah before I joined him there. What?—tell you of the 'most important, most dangerous' work I did in the war? It wasn't in the war—it was after the war was done!"

He told of a period which history has so abridged that it is now well-nigh lost to men's minds—a time that is dwarfed by the war just past, that is overshadowed by the black period of reconstruction that was to come. Peace had been declared. But the great, all-wise Lincoln was dead. The one hand which could have beckoned and led the turbulent victors home, which would have reached out to guide and guard the broken, gloomy South, was gone. There were weeks in the South when anarchy reigned.

For days before there came the inevitable end to the Confederacy, men—bitter, broken-hearted men, who foresaw the swift coming of that end—had deserted the Southern armies, in order that they might never desert their Cause. In twos and threes and little bands they streamed through the country, swearing to commence, from the mountains, a guerrilla warfare that should not end until they died.

Others with less high principles joined them on the way; men who had abandoned all and lost all to the war were now abandoned by the war, and they stood bewildered by the double loss; they had nowhere to turn but to the weapons in their hands; they, too, fled for the mountains.

From the Northern armies, chiefly those in the Middle South, hundreds deserted. Men who would never have deserted in the face of the enemy, now, dreading months of inactivity before being mustered out, or for the first time permitting the longing for home to come between them and discipline, stole out between the considerate pickets and, with their arms in their hands for protection on the way, began the long journey.

From the armies of both sides, the dissolute and the vicious, the discouraged and unreconciled, fled from peace as from a pest; armed, skilled in war, calloused to war's horrors, they swarmed out over the country and turned it into hell.

Truculent bands going north met sullen parties coming south, and they fought for the sheer love of fighting. There was no discipline anywhere; worse, there was the license and liberty that came as a reaction from the sudden removal of strict military law. From simple foraging, in order to live, it was but a step to pillage and murder.

Men who under good officers had fought bravely in the ranks now turned cowardly assassins—became common cutthroats and thieves. For them there was now no North or South; by twos and threes they joined themselves to partyless bands of marauders that turned aside for nothing but more powerful bands. Dejected, paroled Confederates, making their best way south to their ruined homes; buoyant Federal deserters going north—blue or gray, it was all one to these bandits; they robbed and killed on every hand.

And into this land of lurking, ignominious death, John Landegon, alone, except for little black Ben, rode for three hundred terrible miles.

The distracted Federal government, at last heeding the persistent rumors of organized guerrilla bands in the Blue Ridge, demanded authentic information, and Landegon was chosen by Kilpatrick to find out the truth.

In the tent with General Kilpatrick when he gave Landegon the order was a Negro boy whom Landegon had picked up—or, rather, who had picked up Landegon—at Barnsville, South Carolina. He had pleaded to be taken North; and Landegon, unable to care for him himself, had taken him to Kilpatrick, whose body-servant he had become. But the boy's admiration for Landegon had never swerved; he heard the order that was to send Landegon away from him—out of his life—and he sprang forward, and with all the abandon of his emotional race he begged and pleaded to be taken along.

"Doan leave me, Marse Landegon," he cried. "Y' said y' would take me when yo' went Norf, an' now you're goin' to leave little Ben, an' I'll never see yo' again. Take me with yo', Marse Landegon—take me Norf with yo'!"

General Kilpatrick nodded.

"Take him, John; you're to go as a Confederate officer returning to Maryland—it will be a good thing for your story to have your servant along."

That night the two rode out of Lexington on their way to the Blue Ridge Mountains.

There followed days of steady riding over and around and between mountains—always mountains.

Now for miles along some wind-swept range crest from which on either hand it seemed that the whole world had wrinkled itself into endless chains upon chains of mountains. Now through some valley— scarce a rift in the heaped-up, tree-clad walls. Nights when they slept under the stars; solemn, lonely nights, such as come only in a waste of mountains; nights when the boy sobbed in his sleep from the loneliness, and from homesickness for his "cousins," and for the South he was leaving behind.

For the most part Landegon's skill and watchfulness kept them out of grave peril, but there was once when they nearly met the end. Darkness was coming on, and they had obviously mistaken the road; the road they were on led up and ever up the mountain-side, until they were above the evening mists of the valley. They passed a barn, and a few yards farther, topping a steep rise; came suddenly upon a house close by the roadside. On the porch and in the yard were a dozen men, waiting, with their guns across their arms; to have hesitated or to have turned to run would have meant certain death. There were several faded blue uniforms among the butternut and gray; it was one of the cutthroat bands. Landegon rode forward to the fence; he asked for supper; the men avariciously eyed the fine horses, and half a dozen lounged down to the fence and gathered round him. He dismounted coolly and asked for a lantern that he might find feed for the horses. It completely disarmed the suspicions of the men; one of them brought the lantern and walked beside Landegon down the road toward the barn. At the top of the steep grade he struck down the man, and he and Ben rode for their lives—the drop in the road saved them from the volley that passed over their heads.

They had trouble in Maryland at a ferry, but they braved it down; and at last the futile ride came to an end; futile, for there was nothing found, no organized resistance to the Union. The war was over.

John Beall, Privateersman

In Toronto, Canada, one September day in 1864, two men, rounding a street corner from opposite directions, met suddenly face to face, stared in astonishment for a moment, then warmly clasped hands, and turned into a near-by hotel. Captain John Beall thus met the man whom he had least expected to meet—Bennett Burley, one of his old privateersmen, the man who now was about to become second in command in the historic raid on Lake Erie.

When they had shut the door of Beall's room, "Burley," said Beall, slowly, "I want you. I want you for my lieutenant. My old plan at last—my big chance. I am to capture the *Michigan,* free the Johnson's Island prisoners, burn Sandusky, Cleveland, Buffalo—all the rest! You know the old plans. Will you come?"

Burley nodded. "I am with you," he said. "When do we begin?" The plans, Beall explained, were not yet complete, but that very night he was to confer with "Captain Carson," and the final details were to be arranged. Until then there was time for a good old talk. Since leaving his, Beall's, command, what had he and Maxwell done? How came he to be in Canada?

And so Burley told how he had privateered on the Potomac and the Chesapeake until May 12th, when his partner, John Maxwell, had been killed at Stingray Point in a fight with negro troops that were removing the torpedoes that he and Maxwell had planted. For himself, since then, a Yankee prison, Fort Delaware, until he swam out of it through a drain pipe into the river! And now, Captain John Beall, what is the story of your year?

Much of Captain Beall's story needed no detailed explanation to Bennett Burley, for Beall's had been the parent organization from which Burley's and Maxwell's had sprung. They had been, on the Potomac and the Chesapeake, what Mosby was beginning to be on land, what Raphael Semmes in the *Alabama* already was upon the sea—rangers, partisans, privateers. The Confederate government by its commissions had made their acts legitimate; it had furnished them with arms, and paid them for their prizes (only); the young officers had to find their own men, their boats and food. Burley and Maxwell had been two of the nine men with whom Captain Beall had begun his career. It was to the story of Beall's achievements and adventures after he and Maxwell had left him that Burley listened eagerly that September afternoon in the Toronto hotel.

Beall told of the cutting of the submarine telegraph cable under the Chesapeake; of the destruction of the lamps and machinery of lighthouses (notably that of Cape Charles); of the capture of ship after ship, all unarmed vessels, these, surprised, taken without the firing of a shot. One night they captured three small vessels; the next, a big schooner, the *Alliance*, loaded with sutler's supplies—the richest prize they ever took. They had had a bad time getting her. A terrible storm was raging—the equinoctial—a heavy sea running. . . . He had had eighteen men that night, in two little, open boats—the *Raven* and the *Swan*. . . . He thought every minute that they would be swamped. The *Swan* was in command of his lieutenant, Roy McDonald. . . . McDonald tried to board from the windward side; the *Swan* was dashed against the *Alliance,* the tiller broken, and McDonald was washed overboard, but the men got him back, and they rowed around to the *Raven,* and both boarded the *Alliance* from the lee side. It was such a storm that the *Alliance* had anchored; such a storm that attack seemed an impossibility; and her captain and mates were playing checkers in the cabin when he and his men burst in on them. . . . Next night they went out from the *Alliance* and took three sloops; they stripped them of what was aboard—not much; scuttled them, and set them to drift, sinking, out to sea. The prisoners they brought back to the *Alliance,* and the following night McDonald and his men started with all the prisoners, about twenty, overland for Richmond. He, Beall, and his men tried to sail the *Alliance* through the blockade and into the Plankatank River, from whence they could transport the cargo to Richmond. A Federal gunboat was anchored a mile below the river, and that had flustered their pilot, who had run them aground at the river's mouth. There was just time to get a small part of the cargo ashore before daylight. . . . The gunboat began to come up, firing as she came. He set fire to the *Alliance*—the richest prize they ever took!—and she burned to the water's edge. Even the little of her cargo that they saved brought them a tidy sum in Richmond.

From the Northern newspapers that regularly came through the lines they learned that they were making a great stir in the North; the papers were hysterical in their demands that "the pirates of the Chesapeake" be immediately captured. They found afterward that three regiments of infantry, a battalion of artillery, and ten gunboats had been sent to capture—eighteen men! But they did not know it then, and went gaily back to the old stand—Mathews County, Tangier Sound, and the coast of Accomac. They walked straight into an ambush. McDonald and two men were captured, and the rest of them had the narrowest of escapes.

After six weeks in Richmond, waiting for the peninsula to "cool," they stole back, and the very first night captured a schooner. It was their last prize. He had sent most of his men ashore to hide in a thicket until night; the waiting Federals quietly gobbled these, and that night came out in small boats and surprised him and the men on the schooner. The Northern newspapers of the next day called him the "notorious Captain Beall," and gleefully told of his capture "without the firing of a shot," and the whole press had clamored for his hanging.

He and his fourteen men had been sent in irons to Fort McHenry. Irons! They had had all the perquisites of pirates. But their guards had been kind; acting without orders, they had removed the irons for a time each day, that the prisoners might exercise. But when they had come to him to remove the irons, "Leave them alone," he had said, "until your *government* sees fit to remove them!" and he had worn his irons for forty-two days. They would all certainly have been hanged for pirates if the news of their plight had not reached Richmond. President Davis had nobly stood by them: "Privateers, Confederate officers and men—not pirates! Hang them, and that very day fourteen of your men and two officers shall swing in Richmond!" And so they had been treated as prisoners of war, and later exchanged, and he had fought in the trenches to help drive back Sheridan's cavalry, only six miles from Richmond. Then his old wound had begun to trouble him again greatly, and he had had to give up active service.

All that has been told thus far of John Beall had been brought about by one bullet. The wound never entirely healed; Destiny saw to that; Destiny had fired the bullet, which went on and on and marked out a broad, plain course that led straight to the first spy's-gallows to be erected in New York City since Nathan Hale's eighty-nine years before. But for that bullet received in his first fight (and only a skirmish at that!) John Beall might have gone on throughout the war as an infantryman of the Second Virginia Regiment.

From Richmond—he went on, to Burley—he had come to Canada. "Captain Carson" and Captain Cole had already gone far in the plan which *he* had submitted to President Davis the year before; the plan had not been deemed feasible then, and so he had gone to the Chesapeake. But now the plan was to be tried, and here he was in command of the fighting end of it, and here was Burley too, just in time to become second in command in this glorious opportunity! All that they had bagged for the Confederacy thus far had been but rabbits and reed-birds as compared with this—this was to be *big* game! Beall and Burley, Cole and "Captain Carson," would be on the next page of history! Thus they talked and planned, and thus in the Toronto hotel the September afternoon waned, and the time drew near to meet "Captain Carson."

The expected meeting took place that night. "Captain Carson" was none other than Jacob Thompson, formerly Secretary of the Interior under President Buchanan, now the Confederacy's chief secret agent in Canada.

Burley was told, or gathered from the talk, all that thus far had been done. He learned that Captain Charles H. Cole, formerly of General Forrest's command, supplied with thousands of dollars by the Confederate government, through Jacob Thompson, had been living for weeks at the West House in Sandusky, in the guise of a prodigal young Philadelphia millionaire. With his easy, affable manner and his apparently unlimited wealth Cole had had no difficulty in making acquaintances whom he had used as so many stepping-stones to cross over to Johnson's Island and the *Michigan,* which, watchdog-like, guarded it. He had entertained at lavish dinners and sumptuous banquets, and at each succeeding one more and more of the Federal officers, who, in turn, had entertained him on board the *Michigan* and on the island. He explored the *Michigan* from stem to stern. On the island he learned that the garrison, originally nine hundred strong, had, in the security of the *Michigan's* protection, been weakened by no fewer than five detachments for duties on the mainland. From the prisoners (to some of whom he had of course revealed his true character) he learned that there already existed an organization for an attempt at escape, which thus far had been thwarted only by the presence of the *Michigan.* The *Michigan,* then, above all else, was the stumbling-block. Then John Beall had come to Canada, and the plan had quickened into vigorous life.

At the meeting that night in the Toronto hotel the final details were arranged. Cole, in Sandusky, was to give at the West House his most elaborate entertainment—a wine party. Part of his guests were to be his secret agents, the rest every Federal officer who could be induced to attend. Those officers who could not be made sufficiently drunk were to be drugged; to be drugged likewise was the officer who remained in command of the *Michigan.* Of the crew of the *Michigan* more than one member was in Charles Cole's employ.

Beall and his men were to take passage on the *Philo Parsons,* a small steamer making daily trips between Detroit and Sandusky. Before they should reach Sandusky they were to capture the *Philo Parsons.* A signal, or message, from Cole in Sandusky, but two short miles away, would acquaint the prisoners on Johnson's Island, already warned, that all was ready; the prisoners then would show a signal to Beall. The approach of the familiar *Philo Parsons* would arouse no notice; she would be alongside before the *Michigan's* bewildered sailors, hesitating in the absence of their officers, would take action; in an instant Beall and his men would be aboard and at the sailors' throats. A cannon-shot would be fired through the officers' quarters on the island, and at this signal the twenty-five hundred waiting prisoners would rise against their surprised guards and by sheer weight of numbers overpower them.

At the signal-gun from the *Michigan* the Federal officers on shore would be made prisoners. Some of Cole's agents, scattered throughout the city, would cut every telegraph-wire; others were waiting to seize the arms of the National Guard. The location of every stable in the city had long since been ascertained, so that when the escaping prisoners landed they would find arms and horses with which to fight their way through the militia across the State to Wheeling and thence into Virginia. The treaty with Canada permitted the United States but one war-ship on the Lakes; thus the captured *Michigan,* manned by many of the freed Confederates, would steam out of Sandusky Bay, master of the Lakes, and with the Lakes' cities at its mercy. That was the plan to which Bennett Burley listened that September night; it seemed a plan that could not fail. The attempt, at this last meeting, was set for the night of Monday, September 19th.

On Monday morning the *Philo Parsons,* with Burley aboard, steamed down the Detroit River. At Sandwich, on the Canadian side, Beall and two of his men boarded the steamer, as passengers. At Amherstburg, Ontario, at the mouth of the river, sixteen men—farmers, mechanics, small tradesmen, or so they appeared—came aboard, paid their fares, and quietly mingled with the other passengers. The only piece of baggage in the whole party was one old, roped trunk, singularly heavy. The *Philo Parsons* steamed out into the lake and headed southeastward straight for Sandusky. At mid-afternoon the captain had been set ashore for the night at his home on Middle Bass Island; the monotonously pleasant trip began to draw toward its end; at four o'clock the last regular stop before Sandusky had been made at Kelleys Island, eight miles from the port of destination. When the *Philo Parsons* was well on the way once more, Beall and several of his men strolled into the pilot-house; the man at the wheel found himself looking into the muzzle of a revolver. At that same moment three men approached W. O. Ashley, ship's clerk, now the acting captain, and leveled revolvers at him. The few passengers present watched with staring eyes; not one of them moved or spoke; not a woman screamed; they seemed spellbound. There was a strange, uneasy pause, as though the actors had forgotten their parts. Burley hurried up. Behind him, in a small, unarmed mob, tramped his men. Burley stepped up to Ashley and tapped him on the breast with a long-barreled revolver: "Get into that cabin or you are a dead man! One—two—thr—" The clerk whisked into the cabin, and they shut him in. Through a small window he watched them bring out on deck the heavy trunk, unrope it, and distribute its contents—big revolvers, two apiece, and glittering new hatchets, terrible weapons in the hands of strong, fierce men. Then the Confederates, quietly, at revolvers' points, rounded up the dumfounded, terrified passengers—eighty of them, nearly half of whom were women—marched them into the cabin, and set a guard over them. It was all ridiculously easy. The *Philo Parsons* was captured!

The ship was put about and steamed in a great half-circle back to Middle Bass Island. As she drew into the wharf the *Island Queen,* Sandusky to Toledo, was seen approaching, and in a few minutes made fast alongside. The prisoners breathlessly watched from the cabin windows. Suddenly from the *Philo Parsons'* higher decks John Beall, heading his boarding-party, leaped down on the *Island Queen.* The *Queen* was crowded to her full capacity; twenty or twenty-five Federal infantrymen (unarmed), *en route* to Toledo to be mustered out, swelled the number of her passengers. There was an instant bedlam of shrieks and cries as Beall and his men, gleaming hatchets and revolvers in hand, charged into the crowd. There was a moment of half-incredulous resistance; shots were fired—the *Queen's* engineer wounded; then an almost instantaneous surrender. Within five minutes the *Island Queen's* trembling passengers were being herded into the cabin and into the hold of "the pirate ship." After fuel had been got aboard, the prisoners were set ashore.

Night had come, but with it a moon almost at the full. By its light the marooned passengers silently watched the *Philo Parsons* and the little *Island Queen,* lashed together, steam out across the moonlit lake farther and farther away; saw them separate; watched, till the *Island Queen,* helplessly drifting, slowly sinking, at last, before their eyes, went down. The *Philo Parsons,* her crew hot with their victories, steamed on alone to attack the *Michigan.*

It was still long until the hour for the attack. The *Philo Parsons,* her freight thrown overboard, her decks cleared for action, at half-speed slowly sailed nearer and nearer to Johnson's Island. The most trying hour had come, the dread inaction before battle, the hour of thinking. Beneath the faint glow in the sky were the unseen lights of Sandusky; somewhere among them would be the yet more brilliantly lighted windows from which would be coming the sound of revelry— Cole's wine party in full swing. Beall, alone in the extreme bow, could almost believe he heard the drunken laughter. Dead ahead hung the low clustered lights of the *Michigan* and Johnson's Island; one by one they began to wink out; faintly, over the waters, came from the *Michigan* "Eight bells"—midnight! Cole's signal was long overdue. Beall strained his eyes, watching, watching. Next moment it would surely come! The *Philo Parsons* crept, all but drifting, nearer.

There came the sound of some one running. Beall did not take his eyes off the island. "What is it?" he said.

"Captain Beall!" Burley cried, hoarsely. "John! The men have mutinied! Only two of them will go on."

"Watch here!" Beall answered. Almost staggering, he went into the cabin. His men awaited him, sheepishly, sullenly. The signal had failed, ergo, the plot was discovered; it would be madness to go on, they said. He raged at them, pleaded with them, cursed them; then, white with anger and disappointment, "Write out a memorial of your cowardice and treachery; sign it!" he thundered. They meekly gathered beneath the swinging lamp and wrote John Beall's vindication:

> On board the *Philo Parsons,*
> September 20, 1864.
> We, the undersigned, crew of the boat aforesaid, take pleasure in expressing our admiration of the gentlemanly bearing, skill, and courage of Captain Beall as a commanding officer and a gentleman, but, believing and being well convinced that the enemy is informed of our approach, and is so well prepared that we cannot possibly make it a success, and, having already captured two boats, we respectfully decline to prosecute it any further.

In the gray dawn the *Philo Parsons* steamed out once more from the Canadian shore; abandoned, she steered a wavering, crazy course; slower and slower as her fires died down, lower and lower as the water rose in her hold; and then, slowly settling, at last gave a plunge and was gone. The raid on Lake Erie was ended.

The signal from Johnson's Island had not been given because the plot had indeed failed, just as all such plots usually fail—through some one's treachery. On the morning of the 19th Captain Carter, who had returned to the *Michigan,* one day earlier than expected, received a telegram from the officials of Detroit which apprised him of the whole plot.

Between three and four o'clock that afternoon, almost at the very time the *Philo Parsons* was being captured, Captain Cole was made a prisoner in Sandusky. He had made an admirable spy, but he was a craven prisoner. Almost immediately he confessed, told all, voluntarily incriminated his Sandusky accomplices. In February, 1866, a Brooklyn, New York, judge quashed the charges against him and set him free.

Burley, believing himself safe in Canada, attempted no concealment. He was arrested and turned over to the Federal government. Like Cole, he was imprisoned, and, like Cole, eventually released.

But, what of John Beall? John Beall was hanged. He went mad—the madness of fanaticism, the madness of John Wilkes Booth, the madness of John Brown, and for that he hanged. What kinder palliation can be made for him? What else other than madness could have turned John Beall—wealthy, studious, retiring, he whose dream had been to enter the ministry—into a train-wrecker, an intending murderer of hundreds of men and women and little children whose only offense was that they were Northerners?

After the failure on Lake Erie some new campaign had to be devised. A train on the New York and Erie Railroad was to be derailed—wrecked, captured, between Dunkirk and Buffalo. As for the attempt to execute this plan, the story is quickly told. Nearly thirty men were to have taken part, but when the moment for the attempt arrived only four were at the rendezvous—Colonel Martin, in command, Lieutenant Headley, George S. Anderson (escaped prisoners—Raider Morgan's men), and John Beall. Once they failed, twice they failed, to tear up part of the track five or six miles west of Buffalo—bungling, futile attempts. On the afternoon of Friday, December 16th, the party (now five in number) tried for the third time.

Heavy snow had fallen. They drove in a sleigh to the selected spot and regained the tools which they had hidden there, a sledge-hammer and a cold-chisel—the same inadequate tools. Again the quarter-hours passed in ineffectual efforts to displace a rail. Dusk fell; the train was almost due. Then Colonel Martin discovered a spare rail close by, and laid it across the track. The whistle of the approaching train sounded; there was no time to make the obstruction secure; time only to hide in the thicket and watch. The engine screamed for "brakes"; sparks flew from the screeching wheels; the train slid up to the obstruction, struck it, and came in safety to a stop. Trainmen with lanterns leaped from the train. The conspirators fled to their sleigh, scrambled in, and set the horses galloping into the darkness. The trainmen threw the rail to one side, and the train went on. It seems almost necessary to apologize for having told such a story!

Perhaps the conspirators gave up the idea of any further attempt, perhaps only deferred it, but that night all five of them left Buffalo. At Niagara City, Colonel Martin, Lieutenant Headley, and the fifth wrecker, an unnamed soldier, walked across the Suspension Bridge to the comparative safety of the Canadian shore. Beall and seventeen-year-old George Anderson remained behind in the railroad station to await the arrival of the train from Toronto, which was to be boarded by the others at Clifton, across the river. There was a long wait. The boy, Anderson, fell asleep; near-by, Beall, too, was nodding. They posed as strangers to each other. The train arrived. Beall hurried aboard, but the boy did not follow, and he dashed back into the station. There Anderson still slept as soundly as a child. A few moments were still left before the train should start, and Beall sat down close to Anderson, planning to arouse him stealthily without disclosing to others that they two were friends. But two policemen observed the stealthy movement; they drew a hasty conclusion, and, accidentally, made an important arrest.

So swiftly and so unexpectedly did the police act that Anderson, still sleeping, was dragged from the bench, and Beall was seized before he could raise a hand.

The police accused them of being escaped Confederate prisoners from Point Lookout.

"I admit that." (Anderson gaped in astonishment.) "We *are* escaped Confederate prisoners from Point Lookout," Beall said. If only he might be sent to Point Lookout and there lose his identity among the prisoners of war! Perhaps he might have succeeded, but Anderson, the boy for whose sake John Beall had gone back from safety, turned State's evidence!

Only a young, frightened boy—so John Beall made excuses for him in one of the last letters which he ever wrote. He fully and freely forgave Anderson.

From the very first everything was against Beall. He asked that General Roger A. Pryor, a fellow-prisoner in Fort Lafayette, might act as his counsel. The request was denied. His lifelong friend and college room-mate, Daniel B. Lucas, a lawyer, hurried from Richmond to Toronto, and from thence wrote to General Dix, Commander of the Department of the East, begging that he be given a passport to New York so that he might conduct the defense of his friend. The letter remained unanswered.

Beall wrote to Richmond, asking for documents to prove that he had acted on the authority of the Confederate government; his letters were intercepted and became a part of the prosecution's evidence against him. A letter from Jacob Thompson in Canada, inclosing a statement by Colonel Martin, was not admitted in evidence by the commission; yet in this statement Colonel Martin asserted that the real purpose (known only to himself and Beall) of the attempted train-capture was to rescue from their guards certain Confederate prisoners *en route* from Johnson's Island to Fort Warren.

Five witnesses appeared for the prosecution; for the defense there was not one. Confronted by such witnesses as Anderson, Ashley of the *Philo Parsons,* and one of the *Philo Parsons'* passengers, Beall's position was desperate indeed.

For counsel, a prominent New York City lawyer, James T. Brady, generously came forward and undertook the defense—generously, since by law he was not permitted to receive any compensation for his services. The trial, before a military commission of six officers and the Judge-Advocate, was begun on February 1, 1865, in Fort Lafayette, New York Harbor; it dragged itself out through four weary days. No attempt was made to deny that the acts had been committed. The capture of the *Philo Parsons* and the *Island Queen* had been lawful military operations; as for the attempt to wreck the passenger-train, that—said the counsel for the defense—was for the purpose of robbing the express-car, a crime covered by the State's laws, hence no concern of a military commission. The Judge-Advocate seized the delicate logic of the counsel for the accused and tore it limb from limb.

On February 8th the commission met and reported their finding: John Y. Beall, charged with acting as a spy and in violation of the laws of war, was guilty on every specification in each charge. General Dix approved the sentence and decreed that "on February 18th John Y. Beall shall be hanged by the neck until he is dead."

Of all the strange inconsistencies in John Beall's story, perhaps the strangest is that of the untiring efforts of the Northerners who joined with Beall's friends in the attempt to save him from the gallows. Congressmen and Senators—fourteen from Ohio, seventeen from New York, among them James A. Garfield, Fernando Wood, and Samuel Cox, ninety-one in all, representatives of all but five of the Federal States—joined with such men as Ainsworth R. Spofford, Librarian of the Congressional Library; John W. Garrett, president of the Baltimore and Ohio Railroad; Thaddeus Stevens; Governor John Andrew of Massachusetts; ex-Postmaster-General Montgomery Blair, scores more, in the vain efforts to obtain from Abraham Lincoln the clemency of a commuted sentence for John Beall. There were midnight interviews, long, grave conferences, the appeals of women, personal friends of the President; every argument, every influence, every pressure, until at last the President closed his doors and sent out the knell of hope: "I will not interfere!"

Year after year a story has crept into print (may this be the last time!) of how the gallows-death of John Beall caused Abraham Lincoln's assassination. As Damon and Pythias, so John Wilkes Booth and John Yeats Beall—thus the lie begins; schoolmates, comrades in young manhood, "they rode, walked, dined, drank, and intrigued together." (They never met!) And then the war, and John Beall's death-sentence. On the night before the execution John Wilkes Booth, Washington McLean, John P. Hale (Senator from New Hampshire), and John F. Forney (on the tale's authority) drove at midnight to the White House. The President was awakened, and Booth, kneeling at Abraham Lincoln's feet and clasping his knees, implored him to spare Beall's life. At last Lincoln, with tears streaming down his face, took Booth by both hands and promised Beall's pardon. But Beall was hanged, for Seward had threatened to resign (so runs the merry story) if Lincoln meddled.

Booth's conspiracy long antedated Beall's sentence. Booth never was in the White House. John W. Forney asserted that he never met Booth, and publicly branded the story as an utter fabrication. And Booth himself unconsciously strikes off the head of the lie with the words of his diary (now in the possession of the War Department) under date of April 21st: "I knew no private wrong. I struck for my country, and that alone."

Two men became John Beall's biographers; the one, because he had seen John Beall live; the other, because he had seen him die. Daniel B. Lucas wrote of his college room-mate at the University of Virginia— his idolized friend. Isaac Markens, of New York City, as a young boy, received a permit to witness the execution; since then he has given months of effort to perpetuate the memory of John Beall. It is he who published for the first time the details of the efforts of the Northerners to save Beall. It is Isaac Markens who disproved, finally, the oft-published story of Booth's motive for assassinating Abraham Lincoln. It is from Isaac Markens's verbal narrative that many details have been drawn for this account of John Beall's last hour.

A respite was given Beall until February 24th while the commission reviewed the case to correct a technical error. His mother thus was given time to come from Virginia. Of their meeting he said: "I saw the moment she entered the cell that she could bear it, and that it made no difference in her whether I died upon the scaffold or upon the field." She could bear it, but must she?

"A pardon, my son—is there no hope?"

"No, mother," he answered, sadly, "they are thirsting for my blood. There will be no pardon." Thus they parted.

Beall was removed to Fort Columbus, Governor's Island, the appointed place of execution. The last night came. He passed it in mental calm, but in physical anguish from an old affliction—toothache. He wished for laudanum to still the pain, but would not ask for it, he said, for fear of being misunderstood. "If they but knew," he laughed, to one of his old friends who watched the night through with him, "I could have opened a vein at any time "(he tapped his left shoe as he spoke) "if I had wished to do so!" In the shoe were two tiny saws made of steel watch-springs. A rescue had long been carefully planned; it was thwarted only by the fields of floating ice that surrounded the island. The very elements seemed to work against him.

There was another way of escape; he could have bargained himself free. Instead, "Tell my friends in————," he said, "that every secret of which I am the depositary dies with me!"

Then at last came Friday, the 24th. The hour had been set for 2 P.M. It was a perfect winter's day, crisp, not cold, with a sky of glittering blue; over all was brilliant sunshine. Passes had been given with a prodigal hand; a great crowd was present—some hundreds—many of them women. A ferry-boat hovered close inshore, her decks—crowded as for an excursion—overlooking the parade-ground.

The great inner gates of Fort Columbus swung open, and a long procession marched slowly out: the Provost-Marshal, his aides, the prisoner, a minister, an escort of one hundred soldiers. A military band blared a funeral march. John Beall marched with the high-held head of a soldier, kept step to the music with the soldiers around him. A long military cape, thoughtfully thrown over his shoulders by a kindly officer, covered his pinioned arms to the tips of his gloved fingers. On his head already was the black cap, rolled up from his face, turban fashion; its long point and silken tassel, blown by the wind, tossed jauntily.

Full in the face of the gallows and the great crowd about it, the procession came to a sudden halt. The band stopped playing. For nine terrible minutes they stood in unexplained, apparently causeless delay. The crowd murmured loudly with pity and horror. Twice the prisoner spoke to the minister at his side: "How beautiful the sun is! I see it for the last time," and, "Tell my mother that you saw her son die without craven fear and without bravado."

The order at last, and the band struck up its march again; the procession moved slowly to the gallows; the officials and the prisoner mounted it. The prisoner respectfully rose from his chair as the adjutant began to read in a loud voice the charges and specifications and the sentence. The time had come! But no, the adjutant drew out another paper and again read loudly; it was the long, sermon-like manifesto of General Dix. At the first words of the manifesto, Beall coolly drew a chair forward with his foot and sat down again. His serenity in the face of death makes this bitter story beautiful. The crowd murmured again, and from beneath the gallows the executioner (a deserter, to be freed for the performance of this office) cried loudly, "The Captain wishes to be swung off quick; cut it short, cut it short!" "Brutal eagerness" the newspapers later called it; it was meant for kindness and mercy. The reading came at last to an end. Then John Beall stood up, and in a clear, firm voice spoke for the last time:

"I protest against the execution of this sentence. It is a murder. I have nothing more to say, except—I die in the service and defense of my country!"

From behind him came the sword-flash that was the signal.

Timothy Webster: Spy

Civilians fell in the great war. They fought in an army that was without flags or uniforms, without stirring music or flashing arms; an army ever in an enemy's country, surrounded and outnumbered. Theirs was an army of individuals; in little groups, in couples, or a alone, they fought against cities and communities, against whole armies, in one great, silent, unending conflict of wit and subterfuge and cunning. When they fell, their death was not a swift blotting out as in battle, but it was made a ceremony of horror and shame; for the men and women of this civilian army were spies—soldiers set apart from soldiers by the stern rules of war; sowers, whom we, the complacent reapers, "damn with faint praise"; patriots, sacrificing their innermost selves to a military necessity that is as old as war is old, that has been justified since the day when Moses "by commandment of the Lord" sent his twelve spies into the land of Canaan.

Several months before Sumter was fired on, the War had begun for Timothy Webster. At no time after the actual outbreak of war was he more liable to the fate of a spy than at Perrymansville,[1] Maryland, early in February, 1861, when he quietly took up his regular duties as detective of the private agency of Allan Pinkerton, of Chicago. At the outset his visit to Perrymansville was commonplace enough and quite within his routine—merely to expose the suspected plot of malcontents to

---

[1] Now Perryman

damage railroad property. And then of a sudden the situation became of national—more, of world-wide—importance, and for a time Allan Pinkerton and Timothy Webster held History in the making.

Had not the Maryland plot to assassinate Abraham Lincoln, while *en route* through Baltimore to his inauguration, been discovered and frustrated, what, to-day, would be the history of the American nation? And to Timothy Webster, Allan Pinkerton thus generously accredits the major portion of the achievement:

> He, amongst all the force who went with me, deserves the credit of saving the life of Mr. Lincoln, even more than I do.

Webster at this time was a man of forty; good-looking, tall, broad-shouldered, of great physical strength and endurance, skilled in all athletic sports, a good shot, strong-willed, and absolutely fearless. His face indicated a character of firmness and amiability, of innate force and gentle feeling, of frankness and resolution; a thoughtful, self-contained man of an appearance at once to attract attention. Such was Timothy Webster as Allan Pinkerton describes him.

As a boy of twelve he had emigrated with his parents from Sussex County, England, to Princeton, New Jersey; at thirty-two, some latent craving for excitement drew him from his trade of machinist to become a policeman at the World's Crystal Palace Exposition in New York City; there he was introduced to Allan Pinkerton, and with him went to Chicago.

Pinkerton's shrewd estimate of Webster's probable ability as a detective was more than correct; with experience he developed into a star agent of the force, so that when the call came from S. M. Felton, president of the Philadelphia, Wilmington, and Baltimore Railroad, asking protection for his railroad property, Webster was detailed to Perrymansville, which was believed by Allan Pinkerton to be one of the chief danger-points.

In 1861 President Felton's road was the only direct line connecting New York City and the New England States with Washington; that this railroad should be kept unbroken at this critical time was of the utmost importance. It was readily discovered that a plot existed among the Maryland secessionists to cut the line by burning the bridges; but the first hint of the real purpose of the conspirators came to Pinkerton in a letter from the master machinist of the railroad, Mr. William Stearns; he wrote:

I am informed that a son of a distinguished citizen of Maryland said that he had taken an oath with others to assassinate Mr. Lincoln before he gets to Washington.

This letter was received on February 10th—the day before Mr. Lincoln left his home in Springfield, Illinois, and started on his eastern tour *en route* for Washington.

Pinkerton sent for more of his men, and redoubled his efforts to learn something tangible of this or any other plot. Time passed rapidly. Such a conspiracy, well organized, did exist—he learned enough in Baltimore to convince him of that; also—through Stearns—that a branch of the organization was at Perrymansville in the guise of a cavalry company. Webster, who had been withdrawn from there, was hurried back, and within twenty-four hours had been enrolled as a member of the company.

Then, handicapped by the shortness of time, he made a supreme effort to gain the confidence of the inner circle of conspirators, who alone were in the principal plot. Few men could have succeeded as Webster did, few have such a personality as his. By nature he was of a quiet, reserved disposition, seldom speaking unless spoken to, and never betraying emotion or excitement under any pressure of circumstances; but, with the need, his reserve would vanish, and he would become a genial, jovial, convivial soul, with a wonderful faculty for making every one admire and like him. In a few cunningly worded sentences he would rouse the blood of his hearers until it fairly boiled with indignation against the Yankees and Abe Lincoln.

"Webster's talent for sustaining a rôle of this kind amounted to positive genius; in a lifetime of detective experience I have never met one who could more readily adapt himself to circumstances," Allan Pinkerton has written.

It was with such a weapon that Webster was making his great fight.

The tour of the President-elect was rapidly drawing to its end. Webster, consummate actor, was making haste slowly; grave, fiery, serious, boisterous—each at the golden time, he played with a masterful hand upon the excited, high-strung conspirators. From the first his efforts had been covertly directed against the cavalry company's officers: they were in the secret, or no one was. At last, one morning after drill, the captain with much secrecy asked him to call that night at his house, "and say nothing about it." How the time must have dragged till the appointed hour! But with the first step he made into a room whose windows were hung with heavy quilts and blankets he knew that success had come at last. Webster was introduced to three strangers in the group, members of the league from Baltimore; then took his place at the table with the rest and listened—joining in now and then with a word or two—as they discussed the plans for the assassination of Abraham Lincoln at the Calvert Street Depot in Baltimore, on February 23d. The plans were fully matured except for the selection of the person to fire the shot.

The story of how Allan Pinkerton placed his proofs of the conspiracy before Lincoln in the Continental Hotel in Philadelphia, on the night of February 21st; of the spiriting of Mr. Lincoln out of Harrisburg next evening back to Philadelphia in a private train—while Harrisburg, with telegraph-wires secretly grounded, lay cut off from all communication with the outside world; of the passage through Baltimore in the dead of night; and of the safe arrival of the President-elect, accompanied by Allan Pinkerton and Colonel Lamon, in Washington at six o'clock in the morning of the day he was expected in Baltimore, has been told again and again; but Timothy Webster's part is known to but few.

Just two months later Webster was back in Maryland; Sumter had been fired upon; the Sixth Massachusetts Regiment had been attacked in the streets of Baltimore; the war had begun. On April 21st several prominent men of Chicago intrusted the Pinkerton Agency with the delivery of some important communications to President Lincoln, and Pinkerton selected Timothy as his messenger. The papers were sewed into his coat collar and his vest lining, and he set out.

Washington was to all intents a beleaguered city; every railroad bridge about Baltimore had been burned by the order of the Baltimore authorities; tracks were torn up, telegraph wires cut, and the Potomac blockaded; even the wagon roads were picketed; the country-side swarmed with spies and zealots of the Southern cause; practically all communication with the North was destroyed, and no one might pass in the direction of Washington or Baltimore without a rigid examination.

At the Susquehanna the train could go no farther, and Webster, with the few passengers, was rowed across the river to Havre de Grace; from thence each man had to shift for himself. For fifty dollars the driver of a covered road-wagon agreed to take Webster and an Englishman, who said he was bearer of despatches to the British consul, as passengers to Baltimore. At Perrymansville they were halted by a cavalryman in the uniform of Webster's old company, but a stranger to him; before they could be questioned or searched a second cavalryman rode up, and to Webster's great relief recognized him, and hailed him genially, and, what was better, unhesitatingly gave a pass to Baltimore. So impressed was the Englishman that as they journeyed along he grew more and more friendly, until, at length, led on by Webster, he confided that he too was engaged in the cause of the South, and bore with him important papers to Southern sympathizers living in Washington.

Baltimore—and the two were boon companions; they spent the night there, and Webster, meeting many of the acquaintances of two months previous, had no difficulty, with their ready help, in procuring another wagon to carry them on to Washington. All morning they drove, and still the spy could find no opportunity to betray his companion. But as they ate their dinner at the Twelve-Mile House, with the end of their journey almost in sight, the chance came. Across the long table from them sat a man whom Webster recognized and whom he knew to be a Union man; fortunately the recognition was not mutual. The meal ended; the unsuspecting Englishman was got out of the way, and then Webster hurriedly told this acquaintance who he was and what he wished done. The man galloped away toward the city. Presently decoy and decoyed leisurely drove on again—toward a trap; at the outskirts of Washington they were halted.

"No one is permitted to enter the city without being examined," politely explained the lieutenant of the guard. The Englishman saw the indignant Webster locked into a cell; then, in spite of his protests, he too was led away and locked up. In a few minutes Webster was released, and he hurried into the city, direct to the White House. President

Lincoln with amused interest watched him take off his coat and vest, rip them open, and remove the letters. When, at the President's request, Webster returned the following morning, he received the thanks of the President, not alone for the letters he had brought, but for the arrest of the Englishman, whose despatches, President Lincoln said, were of the greatest importance, and revealed menacing disaffection in Washington itself. He then gave Webster several messages, and asked that they be telegraphed as soon as he should reach an office from which they could be sent in safety. One of these telegrams was to George B. McClellan, president of the Eastern Division of the Ohio and Mississippi Railroad, who had just been appointed major-general of volunteers in Ohio; the other message was a request that Allan Pinkerton come to Washington to confer with the President and the Secretary of War on the question of organizing a military Secret Service.

Fate from the very first seems to have marked this man, Timothy Webster, for a great war spy. At every turn his destiny flung down before him some new strand, which he unhesitatingly picked up and twisted into the rope of circumstance which one day was to hang him; the temporary laying aside of his trade to become a special policeman during the gaiety of the Exposition; the chance introduction there to Allan Pinkerton, the master who was to train him in his craft; the simple assignment to guard railroad property, by which he had been swiftly shifted into the heart of a great conspiracy and to the position of an all but military spy; then, while still in private employ—a mere carrier of letters—he had been forced by chance, in the case of the Englishman, again to turn informer and spy for his government; and now, by the order of the President of the United States, he bore the very telegram which was to result in the establishment of that service in which he was to perish.

Allan Pinkerton, under the *nom de guerre* "Major E. J. Allen," organized and commanded the first military Secret Service of the Federal army. Timothy Webster, without question, followed his chief and former employer into the new field; within a few days he had begun one of the most remarkable careers of which there is record in that remarkable service. Almost from the first he occupied that most dangerous position known in warfare, the double spy, the man who serves two masters, who carries water on both shoulders. He served the South with the knowledge of the North; he gave that he might in greater measure take; he betrayed, with permission, the Federal government in little things, in order that his opportunities in the Confederacy might be for a more complete betrayal. He was all things to all Southern men—an actor of a thousand rôles; unerringly he read character almost at a glance, shrewdly chose his rôle—his bait—as an angler selects his fly from the many in his fly-book, and cunningly made his cast of that personality which bid fair to entice his quarry into trustfulness; wherever he would he hooked his man.

In Alabama they would have made him colonel of a regiment; in Baltimore he was a member of the "Knights of Liberty"; Kentucky, Tennessee, Alabama, Mississippi, Virginia, Maryland—he was known to the foremost citizens of the principal cities, and to the commanding officers of camps and fortifications and armies, as an ardent Confederate who was doing important work for the Cause; until at last, as his position strengthened and as those persons who vouched for him were men of greater influence, he became a trusted emissary of the Confederate War Department in Richmond. There was no more dangerous Union spy within the Confederacy.

His connection with the Lincoln assassination conspirators was the chief, almost the sole, means of accomplishing this result.

For the most part the members of the plot were men of position and of wide acquaintance throughout the South; and Webster, who was believed to have fled to avoid arrest, as had many of the others, now went to those of his fellow-conspirators who had returned to Perrymansvile and Baltimore. He did not ask for their help—instead:

"I am going to attempt to get south," said he; "perhaps I can do you some favor there—at least carry letters to where they may be safely posted; perhaps bring others back to you."

And they gladly gave him letters to be posted, or to be delivered in person in those cities to which he was going—letters that in effect said, "Open sesame; this, our friend, is already proved." And the Confederates of Memphis and Bowling Green and Louisville, Mobile and Nashville, and later of Richmond itself, welcomed him, and he charmed them until he was introduced among their friends and loaded down with letters to be delivered when he should go north again. He was working within a circle, operating an endless chain; it seems very simple—credentials for any time or place! But all these letters, whether going south or coming north, stopped in transit at the headquarters of Allan Pinkerton, and were read, and their contents copied, before being resealed and allowed to continue on their journey. There was no limit to his capacity for gaining information for the Union. Yet each trip that he made was like a cumulative poison—only a question of repetition to result in certain death.

Timothy Webster served the Union for just twelve months; and the record of each month would in itself furnish ample material for an entire story.

In a Pennsylvania city—Pittsburgh—he was mistaken for a Confederate spy and nearly lynched by a hot-headed mob, from which he was saved only by the opportune arrival of Allan Pinkerton. Together, backed against the wall, with drawn revolvers, they held off the mob, until the chief of police rescued and identified them.

In Tennessee, on his very first trip into the Confederacy, he incurred the suspicion of a member of a committee of safety—of which each community was well supplied to investigate and question strangers. He was "shadowed" from city to city; all his skill could not enable him to shake off this man, a morose, sinister-looking fellow remarkably like a stage villain, but of a cunning equal to Webster's own.

The acquaintances which Webster formed, both civil and military, by aid of his letters of introduction, seemed only to augment the stranger's suspicion; it was one of those strange cases of intuition, of instinctive reading of character; Webster could not but admire, professionally, the man's ability, dangerous as he had become.

As long as Timothy continued to work his way south the man seemed content only to follow, but at last the time came for him to return to the North with all the information which he had set out to gain. He took a train for Chattanooga, though he did not wish to go there; he dared not start north until the man had been disposed of. It almost seemed as though his mind had been read; the man—he had entered the same car with Webster—was now for the first time in company with another. The train had gone but a few miles when a lady came and sat down beside Webster. Presently, without looking at him, she whispered: "I am no enemy to a Union man. I have overheard two men say that if you try to go north they will 'get' you; they believe you are a Yankee spy." He whispered his thanks, but she did not speak to him again. At a way-station he got off and walked up and down beside the train. The two men also got off, and he felt them stealthily watching.

"Conductor," he said, in a loud voice, "tell me a good hotel in Humboldt; I must stop there several days."

The train reached Humboldt in a deluge of rain. Webster and those passengers alighting there scurried for the shelter of the station; almost at the door there stood a heap of baggage, and Webster darted behind it; he saw his men—blinded by the dashing rain, and certain that he was ahead of them—run across the street and into the hotel. He had intended to take his old train the moment it should start; but when it was about to pull out, a north-bound train arrived, and when it left Humboldt for the north Timothy Webster was on board. He never saw the two men again.

Back in Baltimore once more, Webster, his position greatly strengthened by the results of his southern trip, assumed the part of a gentleman of wealth and leisure; he lived in the best suite of rooms at the best hotel, and drove a fine span of horses. There was a special purpose for assuming such a rôle.

Baltimore, though under martial law, and with several of her leading citizens confined in Fort McHenry—because of their too openly expressed Southern sentiments—was still dangerously active in secret aid to the Confederacy. Webster, as in the case of the Lincoln conspiracy, was expected to reach the leaders of whatever organizations might be there. He gave blockade-running as his ostensible business, and was thus enabled, while making Baltimore his headquarters, to travel about through lower Maryland, where he added many useful dupes to his staff of Confederate assistants, and gained much information for Pinkerton in Washington. Dangerous though it was, necessity compelled him to report frequently to Pinkerton and receive his instructions. At last there occurred the very thing that was most to be feared: he was observed going stealthily into the Secret Service headquarters; and next day, in Baltimore, as he stood in the center of a group of friends gathered about the bar, the door opened, and there entered a man known to all present as a brawler, a "rough"—Zigler by name—one of the leaders in the attack on the Massachusetts troops.

"Ha! Webster!" he cried. "I have been looking for you!" Then, turning to the group: "This man has fooled us in Baltimore long enough. He is a spy." There was a moment of absolute stillness, then half a dozen voices cried: "He's drunk! Put him out! We know Webster!"

"Ask him where he was last night," Zigler sneered, and there was silence again—a silence of involuntary suspicion.

"In Washington," Webster said, calmly. "These gentlemen all knew I had been there."

"I saw him"—Zigler pointed his finger dramatically—"go into the office of the chief of the Yankee detective force!"

Webster stared at him coldly. "You lie!" he said.

And then there occurred the most fortunate thing that could have happened; Zigler sprang furiously at Webster, who struck him a swift, clean-cut blow in the face which sent him rolling on the floor, and, as he leaped up with a knife in his hand, Webster drew a revolver and stopped the man before he could take a step.

"Go!" he said, in a tense, even voice; "go, or I will surely kill you!" Without a word Zigler turned and left the room. A dozen hands clapped Webster on the shoulder, his trusting friends cheered him enthusiastically.

"Gentlemen," he said, sorrowfully, "I cannot imagine what I have done to that man that he should try to injure me so."

But so far from injury, the affair greatly increased the respect and admiration in which he was held. In a short time he was invited to join the "Knights of Liberty."

This organization, together with the mummeries of a secret society, combined a deadly intent against the Union and some very effective work for the Confederacy. Webster was initiated with much ceremony.

Before the meeting was over he was astounded to learn the extent to which this organization had been advanced; the room in which he sat was the wooden horse within the walls of Troy; the men about him, the dragons' teeth sowed in Northern soil. The "Knights of Liberty" were in direct communication with the Confederate authorities in

Richmond; branch organizations of more or less strength were scattered throughout Maryland; in Baltimore were hidden six thousand stands of arms, which, at the signal, would be put in the hands of ten thousand men of Maryland, who would sweep down on Washington from the north as the Confederate army advanced upon it from the south; all that was needed was the landing of a Southern army on the Maryland shore. Such were the statements of the Knights, and such their plans. Webster attended the meetings for several weeks, and became known as an impassioned speaker who was eagerly listened to. He was able to work several of the Secret Service agents into the league by directing them to make the acquaintance of several of the members whom Webster had marked as being less shrewd than the others and more liable to vouch for new-comers; when his men had so established themselves in the society as to be accepted, in their regular turn, as doorkeepers of the outer door, Webster's plans were complete. On the night when these men were standing guard, Webster made an address; the room was crowded; the speech grew more and more flamboyant, until the peroration ended with the shouted words "—the smoking ruins of the city of Washington!" It was the cue; the room was instantly filled with Federal soldiers. There was no resistance—only a tumult of cries and a scurrying about in the trap. The "Knights of Liberty" as an organization was destroyed.

The months passed swiftly; the summer was gone and the autumn was midway to its close before Timothy Webster entered Richmond for the first time; he had left Baltimore for Richmond almost immediately after the betrayal of the "Knights of Liberty"; his friends—those who had not been imprisoned—in the belief that he was fleeing to escape Federal arrest, aided him to the utmost of their ability. When he ran the blockade of Union gunboats and patrols in the Potomac, he carried a heavy mail with him into Virginia—mail from which the fangs had been extracted in the office of the chief of the Secret Service. The results of this trip are embodied in a statement by Allan Pinkerton:

This first visit of Timothy Webster to Richmond was highly successful. Not only had he made many friends in that city, who would be of service to him on subsequent trips, but the information he derived was exceedingly valuable. He was able to report very correctly the number and strength around the rebel capital, to estimate the number of troops and their sources of supplies, and also the forts between that city and Manassas Junction, and his notes of the topography of the country were of the greatest value.

Four times he made the trip from Baltimore to Richmond. He never made use of the Federal aid which was at his command, but he risked death from Union guns as surely as did any Confederate blockaderunner. In Baltimore he was looked upon as a hero; in Richmond, as a valued employee of the Confederate War Department; for, after his second trip there, he was employed by Judah P. Benjamin, Secretary of War, to carry despatches and the "underground mail," and to obtain information in Washington and Baltimore; on one occasion he received the personal thanks of the "great Secretary of the Confederacy." The passes furnished to Webster by the Confederate War Department enabled him to go wherever he wished, and he made a long journey into Kentucky and Tennessee. There seemed to be no limit to his audacity, no measure to his success.

Once only—until at the very last—was he in imminent danger of arrest. In the fortifications of Richmond he met Zigler face to face—Zigler, whom he had struck and to whom he had given the lie and discredited in Baltimore; now, the spy met him, a Confederate lieutenant at his post. Both men stood looking at each other, their hands on their revolvers.

"What are you doing here, Webster?" Zigler slowly asked.

"I am here to deliver a letter from his father to your friend John Bowen; as you probably know, he is ill of fever at Manassas," Webster said, pleasantly.

"Let me see the letter."

As he returned the letter, Zigler held out his hand. "Webster," he said, "I once thought you were a spy: I was wrong."

Webster heartily grasped his hand; he used Zigler as he would use an information bureau, and laughed as he went away.

It was the same wherever he went, whatever he did—all things worked for his advantage; unsought information, invaluable to the Union, came to him at least-expected moments; he had only to stretch out his hand to take it. A surgeon deserting from the Union army became his companion in an effort to cross into Virginia. The landlord of the hotel at Leonardtown, Maryland, to whom Webster was well known, urged him to help the surgeon in every way, for—"He is carrying letters to our War Department!" The letters never got any nearer to Richmond; in fact, next day they went the other direction— to Washington. In Leonardtown there was stationed another member of the Secret Service, John Scobel—a negro. That evening as Webster chatted with the landlord—establishing a solid alibi—the doctor, strolling about in the dusk, was seized from behind and robbed; he staggered back to the hotel in terrible distress and excitement.

"But," said Webster, soothingly, "you can doubtless give a verbal summary of what was in your papers?"

"They were sealed," the surgeon groaned. "I know no more of the contents than you do." Thus, Secretary Benjamin forever missed some information which would have been extremely useful had it reached him. The surgeon and Webster, who still proffered consolation, proceeded arm in arm to Richmond.

In finding a trusty messenger to carry the stolen letters to Washington, Webster met with one of the strangest experiences of his career. At midnight he had slipped away from the hotel and had joined his negro spy, Scobel, who could not be spared from his own work in Leonardtown to deliver the papers. Together they passed out of the sleeping town and into the dark fields; at a ruinous house, with boarded windows and sagging roof, they stopped and knocked softly; Scobel's whispered password admitted them, and they entered. The staircase was gone, but a rope ladder was let down to them; the room to which they climbed covered the entire second story; the only light came from a lantern which stood on a barrel draped with an American flag. They carefully picked a way between huddled figures,— negroes.

Webster could see those seated close about the lantern—the rest merged into the gloomy shadows until only a rolling eyeball or a slight movement showed that the room was filled with men, silent, watchful men, seated row after row upon the floor. It was a meeting of one of the branches of the "Loyal League"—the secret organization of slaves banded together against the Confederacy. Reports were made by those who had had commissions assigned them or who had visited other lodges of the League; then Webster was called on for an address. Here at last he might be eloquent for, instead of against, the Flag, and his low-spoken, burning words roused the emotional negroes to an intense pitch of excitement; they gathered about him, each trying to catch his hand—some weeping, some calling on God to bless the work of this man who fought for them and for the Union. For two hours the meeting continued, then broke up in order that those who had come from miles away might steal back to their quarters before dawn. The president of the League took the stolen papers and carried them safely to Washington.

So perilous was Webster's position, even from the very beginning of his work, that, for his greater safety, he was known to but few of his fellow-operatives. Thus it happened that in Baltimore, after his return from his first Richmond trip, he was arrested as a spy—as a Confederate spy—by a Federal agent; Webster was in a cell for a day and a night before he could get word to Pinkerton to order his release; when the order came it was not for a release, but for an escape. To avoid suspicion Webster was permitted to make a sensational break from the wagon in which he was being driven ostensibly to Fort McHenry; there was a mock pursuit, and at midnight he crept to the home of one of his Confederate friends and begged shelter from the Yankees. To his friends he was as one returned from the dead; they feasted and fêted him in secret, and kept him hidden until he could make his "escape" to Richmond.

The accounts of his capture and escape as printed in the Baltimore *American* and the *Gazette* of November 22, 1861, must have given Timothy huge amusement.

Christmas morning Webster left Washington for his third journey to Richmond. He had climbed the hill of Success, had passed, unwitting, over the crest, and now commenced the journey down the side upon which rested the shadow.

At Leonardtown, Maryland, his old starting-point, he was met by bad news; his usual route across the Potomac had been discovered by the Federals, and was watched. But his stanch friend, landlord Moore, assured him that all was not yet lost—a new route had been developed; only in return for its being shown him he must escort to Richmond the families of two Confederate officers, that had been intrusted to the care of the worthy landlord of Leonardtown.

That night, after a hard ride, the little party—Webster, two ladies, three young children, and the boatman—put out from the swamps and thickets of Cobb Neck in an open boat in the attempt to cross the Potomac. The clear, frosty weather had come to an end; all afternoon the clouds had been banking over Virginia, and a gusty wind had moaned in the pines and scrub-oak thickets; the wind had risen with the coming of night, and now, as the little craft caught its full force, it rolled and pitched wildly. The women, mute with terror, clung to the wailing children and cowered in the bottom of the boat. Midway across, the boatman shouted that the storm was coming. Webster flung a tarpaulin over the women and children, and then gave aid to the managing of the sail; the rain and sleet cut and blinded like salt; the wind veered and rushed the boat to the land. All but helpless in such a wind, and bewildered by the lashing rain, the boatman lost his bearings and drove full upon a sand-bar within a hundred feet of shore. The boatman had all he could do to save his little craft from being swamped with all on board, and Webster caught two of the children in his arms, leaped overboard, and struggled ashore with them; the water was only waist-deep, but it was icy cold. Four times he made the trip from boat to shore; then, chilled through, and shivering so that he scarce could walk, he led his wretched party toward a distant light. For more than a mile they toiled through the underbrush and over the rough, soggy ground, and at last, utterly exhausted, reached an old negro's two-room cabin. They passed a miserable night—the women and children in the only bed; Webster, wrapped in a tattered blanket, on the floor before the fire. Half unconscious of what he did, he picked up a small packet wrapped in oiled silk; it had evidently been dropped by one of the ladies when she removed part of her wet clothing; he noted dully that it was addressed to Secretary Benjamin, and he thrust the packet into a slit in his coat lining.

At Fredericksburg, which they reached next day by steamer, Webster could go no farther; he was seized with inflammatory rheumatism, and was ill for days; the women heartlessly left him behind—the women whose lives he had saved, virtually at the cost of his own. It seems no more than just that he should have found their packet of papers—it was little enough reward, though it gave him the opportunity to strike a stout blow for the Union; for the packet contained complete maps of the country surrounding Washington, an accurate statement of the number and location of the Federal troops, and the probable plans of the spring campaign—indubitable evidence that some Federal officer had gone wrong. When Allan Pinkerton received the papers, he was able, by identifying the writing, to arrest the author—a clerk in the office of the Provost-Marshal of Washington—who narrowly escaped being hanged.

Webster at last proceeded to Richmond, and, though still suffering from rheumatism, indomitably continued from there his journey south.

By the middle of January he was back in Washington with a large mail, which included letters and despatches from Secretary Benjamin, General Winder, and others high in the Confederacy; also he brought reports of conditions, and military information, from as far south as Nashville.

He was still physically unfit for duty, but at once prepared to return to Richmond on what was to be his last journey. This time he did not go alone; he had need of Hattie Lewis, a young woman member of the Secret Service; she had already been in Richmond several times, and had been of help to Timothy on one of his previous visits. Webster, when he asked that Hattie Lewis might accompany him, received his chief's ready assent, and he and the girl crossed the Potomac together— that much "Major Allen" was able to trace weeks later; for, from the time they crossed the river, Timothy Webster and Hattie Lewis had disappeared completely.

The days passed into weeks, and still no tidings.

My anxiety [Mr. Pinkerton writes] was equally shared by General McClellan, with whom Webster was a great favorite, and who placed the utmost reliance on his reports. One evening, early in February, the General called on me, and advised the sending of one messenger, or two, for the sole purpose of hunting up Webster, or finding some trace of him.

Pryce Lewis and John Scully, old members of the Chicago force, were chosen; they knew Webster well, and they were experienced spies, men who had already proved their worth in the service. Yet in this case a worse choice could not have been made; for these men had been used in the early days of the war to search the houses of families suspected of disloyalty to the government; several of these families had been required by the authorities to leave Washington, and had been transported South; this was the flaw in the armor of Scully and Lewis. Their particular danger was appreciated by their chief, who questioned deserters, prisoners, and contrabands from Richmond regarding these expelled families; he learned that the Morton family of Florida had returned to that State, and the Phillipses had left Richmond for South Carolina. This cleared the way for Lewis and Scully; they safely crossed into Virginia; then they, too, disappeared. It was two months after Webster had left Washington before Allan Pinkerton heard of any of his agents again.

Lewis and Scully had little difficulty in reaching Richmond, and still less in finding Webster's whereabouts. Elated by the ease with which they had found him, the two, without waiting to communicate secretly with Webster, hurried to the Monumental Hotel, and were shown to his room. They found him in bed, the mere shadow of his former self, weak and emaciated, and still suffering intensely from rheumatism— still making payment for his rescue of helpless women and children. Let it be remembered that the presence of Scully and Lewis in Richmond had been brought about thereby.

Hattie Lewis, who posed as Webster's sister, and who had nursed him during his entire illness, sat sewing by the window, and at his bedside was one of his stanch Richmond friends, come to cheer the invalid. The two Secret Service men, in the presence of the unsuspecting Confederate, were greeted formally—as mere acquaintances; they gave Webster a letter written by Allan Pinkerton—a letter purporting to come from one of Webster's Baltimore friends, warning him to return by another route, as the Yankees were watching his old one to capture him. Webster read the letter and passed it to his friend Pierce. "I'm being well taken care of, you see," he said, lightly. But he was secretly dismayed at the coming of his fellow-spies, and they, intuitively feeling that they had in some way run counter to his plans, were ill at ease and constrained in manner; the call was short and cold, and they made the additional mistake of leaving before Pierce did, thus giving Webster no chance to warn them to keep away.

With rare fatuity they returned next morning, and again had the misfortune to find a Confederate visitor, no less than an officer from the provost-marshal's office, Captain McCubbin, a man whose friendship the politic Webster had diligently cultivated and entirely won. The interview was more pleasant than that of the previous day. McCubbin was a friendly soul and a good talker; it was not until he was leaving that he inquired pleasantly whether they had reported themselves to the office of the provost-marshal. They had not—they had been examined by Major Beale at the Potomac, and their passports having been approved, they had not thought it necessary, they said. It was most necessary, McCubbin told them—but any time within a day or two would do. McCubbin left, and Webster urged them to see the provost-marshal, obtain his permit, and at once leave Richmond.

They called next day at the office of General Winder, commander of the city of Richmond; his examination was a searching one, as was to be expected, but his manner pleasant and courteous; their story was thoroughly prepared, and they answered his questions readily; the General expressed himself entirely satisfied, shook hands with them, and wished them good day. Greatly pleased, they hastened to relieve Webster's anxiety by telling him of their success, and to bid him good-by. Hardly were they seated, when an officer—who had undoubtedly followed them from General Winder's office—called to question them regarding some trivial point in their examination. When the man had gone Webster struggled to a sitting posture. "Leave the city! Leave the city!" he cried. "The coming of that man means that you are certainly suspected!"

They tried to reassure him, dwelling on their interview with Winder; but while they spoke, the door opened and one of the provost's detectives entered, accompanied by Chase Morton, whose home in Washington had been searched by Lewis and Scully. They had dreamed of danger, they awoke—and found their feet on the trap of the gallows; in that instant three men and a woman felt the roper about their necks.

Scully completely lost his wits; without a word he rose and walked out of the open door; Lewis stolidly faced an introduction and joined in commonplaces of the talk, until presently he said good-by to Webster and left the room.

In the hall he was joined by Scully, who had in a measure recovered his composure; as they were about to descend the stairs the Confederate detective stepped out of Webster's room and quietly placed them under arrest; other detectives, by whom the house had been surrounded, closed about them and they were escorted to General Winder's office. There young Morton with positiveness identified them as Federal Secret Service agents, and they were sent immediately to Henrico Jail; for days they lay there, apparently forgotten; then Scully was taken away, and he did not return.

Lewis, half crazed by the uncertainty of Scully's fate, and his own ultimate fate, joined with his fellow-prisoners in a mad plan to break from the poorly guarded jail; most of them escaped into the country, where they wandered for several days, suffering horribly in the half-frozen swamps of the Chickahominy; in little groups they were recaptured—Lewis and three companions last of all—brought back to the city, placed in solitary confinement, and heavily ironed. Two days later Lewis was led to trial.

Webster, not daring to make inquiries, knew absolutely nothing of his two friends from the time that the detectives had followed Lewis and Scully out of the room, until, days afterward, he read in a newspaper that they had been arrested and were accused of being Federal spies; then came an order from the provost-marshal, demanding the letter which had been brought to him by the men. Scully was the first to be placed on trial, and Webster was called on to testify; but Webster was too ill to be moved, and the court adjourned to his bedside to take his evidence. He had known the men slightly since April, 1861, in Baltimore, he testified; there they were regarded as earnest secessionists; he knew nothing of their being connected with the United States government in any way, knew nothing further than that they had unexpectedly appeared in Richmond with the letter; that was all. When the members of the court had gone, Webster fainted.

The positive identification of the two prisoners by members of the Morton family convicted them; Webster, a few days later, read that his friends had been sentenced to be hanged within one week from the passing of sentence. His own position had been compromised, and some of his friends began to fall away; but no charge was made against him, and it seemed that he was to escape.

After sentence was passed, Lewis and Scully were confined in Castle Godwin, in separate cells; they had not seen each other since they had been parted in Henrico Jail; and Scully, feigning serious illness, pleaded to be allowed to see his comrade. Lewis was brought to him. The condemned men were left alone, and presently Scully, with some hesitation, said that he had sent for a priest, that, as a Catholic, he must confess and receive absolution before he died. Lewis took instant alarm. Would Webster's name have to be mentioned, he asked. Scully did not know; he grew sullen and was greatly disturbed.

Pryce Lewis pleaded with him. "Do not speak of Webster, John!" he begged.

"I tell you I do not know what I will have to say," Scully answered, irritably. And while they still argued, the priest came and Scully followed him away. Lewis was not taken back to his own cell for several hours. As at last he was being hurried through the halls Lewis passed detectives bringing in two prisoners—a man and a woman. In the dim light of the lanterns, with their shifting shadows, he could not be sure— could only be afraid; *was* it Webster and Hattie Lewis? What had Scully done?

Allan Pinkerton—"Major Allen"—with the Army of the Potomac, was before Yorktown on the Peninsula; in the midst of a hard campaign he scarcely for an hour forgot his missing men, but all his inquiries failed, until in a captured Richmond paper he read that the Yankee spies, Scully and Lewis, were sentenced to be hanged. Then, before he could make a move in their behalf, came the more bitter news that they were respited for having implicated the chief spy of them all—Timothy

Webster. Immediately Mr. Pinkerton, accompanied by Colonel Key of General McClellan's staff, hurried to Washington.

> Mr. Lincoln was readily seen, and he, too, filled with sympathy for the unfortunate man, promised to call a special session of the Cabinet to consider the case that evening. . . . In the evening the Cabinet was convened, and after a full discussion of the matter it was decided that the only thing that could be done was to authorize the Secretary of War to communicate with the rebel authorities on the subject. He was directed to authorize General Wool to send by flag-of-truce boat, or by telegraph, a message to Jefferson Davis, representing that the course pursued by the Federal government toward rebel spies had heretofore been lenient and forbearing; that in many cases such persons had been released after a short confinement, and that in no instance had any one so charged been tried for his life or sentenced to death. The message concluded with the decided intimation that if the Confederate government proceeded to carry their sentence of death into execution, the Federal government would initiate a system of retaliation which would amply revenge the death of the men now held.

> Secretary Stanton expressed in strong terms his willingness to assist Webster to the extent of the resources of the government, but he was but little disposed to assist the others, who had betrayed their companion to save their own lives.

Let this terrible story be brought swiftly to its more terrible end.

The trial of Timothy Webster, civilian spy, was immediately begun by a civil court; the man was still so sick that he could not be moved, and his trial was at first held in the prison. From the beginning there was no hope, and he had none; yet instead of sinking he struggled up, grew physically stronger, until able to take his place at the bar. His bearing made a wonderful impression upon all; he became magnificent in his calm dignity and his quiet, simple fearlessness. He was what he was, and had done that which he had done, for a mighty principle, and now he was given strength greater than his own to bear him up until the end.

So different from the swift, decisive—thereby more merciful—Court-Martial, this trial "by process of law" dragged its weary length for three weeks; witness after witness was examined; Lewis and Scully on the stand faced their comrade, and by their testimony—wrung from them and given in anguish—he was hanged. And, though he had able lawyers who fought an able fight for him, and though the Federal government convened a special session of its Cabinet and threatened bitter reprisals, and though the woman who loved him—Hattie Lewis—besought the wife of the President of the Confederacy to intercede for him, yet Timothy Webster, spy, was justly convicted and justly hanged.

On April 29th, 1862, surrounded by a great concourse of soldiers and citizens at Camp Lee—the old Fair Grounds of Richmond—the first spy of the Rebellion was hanged.

" . . . The knot came undone . . . and they carried him back upon the scaffold; as he stood swaying on the trap for the second time, he cried, from under the black hood, 'I suffer a double death!' "

Hattie Lewis was imprisoned for a year, Lewis and Scully for twenty-two months, and were then set free.

THE END